Reporting the Post-Communist Revolution

Media Studies Series

Reporting the Post-Communist Revolution

editors
Robert Giles
Robert W. Snyder
Lisa DeLisle

Routledge
Taylor & Francis Group
LONDON AND NEW YORK

Originally published in the *Media Studies Journal*, Fall 1999.

Published 2001 by Transaction Publishers

Published 2017 by Routledge
2 Park Square, Milton Park, Abingdon, Oxon, OX14 4RN
711 Third Avenue, New York, NY 10017, USA

Routledge is an imprint of the Taylor & Francis Group, an informa business

Library of Congress Catalog Number: 00-068277

Library of Congress Cataloging-in-Publication Data

Reporting the post-Communist revolution / Robert Giles, Robert W. Synder, Lisa DeLisle, editors.
    p. cm. — (Media studies series)
Originally published in Media studies journal, Fall 1999.
Includes bibliographical references and index.
ISBN 0-7658-0738-6 (pbk. : alk. paper)
    1. Mass media—Political aspects—Europe, Eastern. 2. Journalism—Political aspects—Europe, Eastern. 3. Post-communism—Europe, Eastern. 4. Europe, Eastern—Politics and government—1989- I. Giles, Robert H. 1933- II. Snyder, Robert W., 1955- III. DeLisle, Lisa. IV. Series

P95.82.E852 R47 2001
070.4'499470854—dc21

00-068277

ISBN 13: 978-0-7658-0738-0 (pbk)

We gratefully acknowledge the advice of Elżbieta Matynia,
Jeremy Druker, Jerzy Halbersztadt and Jamey Gambrell in
preparing this volume. We are grateful to Roza Vajda also, who
brought to this volume her intellect, ingenuity, and
living memory of 1989.

Contents

Part 1: Reflections

One of the creators of a Polish émigré quarterly evokes the changes in Polish immigrant journalism since the days when the best she could hope for was "to tear the veil of anonymity that covered our friends in Poland and made them vulnerable to persecution."

"Communism fell because it gave a mendacious account of the world both to itself and its citizens," writes the former managing director of the BBC World Service. "The foreign broadcasts played their part in freeing the ordinary listener from relying on official media."

"After 10 years, it is easy to see how unprepared and naive the Czechoslovak dissidents and journalists were," argues a Czech dissident and journalist. "Lacking know-how and contacts in the real world of media, they failed to analyze the changes of 1989 and prepare for them."

An author with a special interest in Berlin reconstructs the press conference where the East German government prematurely announced the opening of the Berlin Wall. "Sooner or later," she concludes, "you find that the last straw that breaks a regime's back is sheer human error."

A Moscow journalist recalls her work at Ogonyok, the magazine that was at the center of perestroika: "For all of us, 1989 was a taste of freedom, a conscious choice of freedom, which would define our lives henceforth. And contemporary journalism owes its existence (with all its pluses and minuses) to the rush and enthusiasm of 1989, which destroyed the invisible Berlin Wall in people's souls."

A journalist who thrived in Solidarity's "carnival of dissent" remembers how a year taught her "that everything is possible if we just want to put our imagination to it."

Part 2: Media Systems

"What we see in many postcommunist countries generally are not 'emerging,' but at best latent, markets and democracies," argues a Polish policy-maker and media analyst. "We know now that there is nothing preordained about the direction, pace or ultimate result of change in postcommunist countries and their media, and that Western-style capitalism or media systems cannot be simply transplanted to Eastern Europe."

"In the 10 years since 1989, as the countries of Eastern and Central Europe emerge from communist rule, the evolution of print and electronic media has been central to the larger process of political and cultural restructuring," writes the assistant editor of Media Studies Journal. "The journalism of Central and Eastern Europe has left behind the old days of communism, but the contours of its future have yet to be fully defined."

"An investor surveying Central and Eastern Europe in the early '90s would have thought the Czech Republic the last place where a television channel featuring naked bodies and severed heads would boom," writes an editor in Prague. "Today, 10 years after the Velvet Revolution, the image has changed considerably. The turning point was February 4, 1994, the day TV Nova went on the air."

"We are glad that Poland's happiest decade in the last 300 years also happens to be the best 10 years of our lives," writes the editor in chief of Poland's highly successful daily newspaper. "The joy of this decade was created not only by *Gazeta Wyborcza*, but by all of democratic and independent Poland."

A Hungarian lawyer who sat in his country's parliament while it debated postcommunist broadcasting laws considers the lessons of his experiences: "It is difficult to transform a political dictatorship with a state-controlled economy into a liberal democracy with a market economy. The creation of new institutions is not enough. The culture, the mind-set, the imperatives of the people who give them life must also develop, particularly for the media."

"Journalists were among the first to call for foreign aid," writes a dean with experience in international aid programs. "As the ones who know and care most about a free press, they should make the propagation of independent media their special mission. The task is too important to be left to anyone else."

The fall of the Berlin Wall transformed the environment of the German media, East and West, notes a media analyst in Berlin: "The consequences of these changes for journalism, politics and culture in a unified Germany are at once momentous and subtle—and likely to be visible for years to come."

Part 3: New Stories

"Civil society is an open sphere," writes a professor who sees lessons for American journalism in the events and ideas of 1989. "Governments rise and fall against its backdrop. Politics flows into it and feeds off it. Journalism finds its audience there, and much of its purpose."

"Decades of neglect and mismanagement by past Communist authorities in Central and Eastern Europe have left behind a bitter legacy of polluting power plants, coal mines and chemical factories, badly designed hydroelectric projects, depleted forests, dying lakes and a host of other environmental catastrophes," writes an environmental reporter. "But paradoxically, the fall of hard-line regimes and the ushering in of a new era of experimentation in free-market economics and popular sovereignty may have led to a decline of interest in the environment."

"I am a witch and I have proof in writing," writes a journalist from Croatia. "In the press, that is. How is that possible? In many postcommunist countries like Croatia, bizarre things are possible—among other things to be proclaimed a witch."

"In times of instability—yesterday the world wars, today the transition out of communism—images associated with Gypsiness appear in the Hungarian media: the dark-haired criminal paraded in handcuffs, the swarming family of 10 living in squalor, the passionate musician," a Hungarian journalist argues. "These images have dangerous consequences for the Roma—stifling exotic stereotypes, inferior citizenship and, at worst, physical violence."

"Especially in the countries where the transition to the market economy has progressed more smoothly and rapidly, publishers are trying to come up with their versions of The Economist, The Wall Street Journal and—right down to the pink paper—the Financial Times," a trainer of economics journalists in developing countries reports. "And perhaps most important of all, the economics and business story has migrated from specialized publications into many of the region's larger-circulation newspapers and magazines."

"The new Jewish media in postcommunist Europe reflect both the general changes since the fall of communism and the specific concerns of Jewish communities and individuals," writes an author and columnist. "Jews in Central and Eastern Europe are trying to construct—or reconstruct—identities and ensure a Jewish future in a region where, until a decade ago, such a future was virtually unimaginable."

"The fight for a strong independent press in Central and Eastern Europe, despite stubborn dictatorial opposition, has reached significant milestones and generated important lessons for global media assistance elsewhere," writes a professor who has led media assistance programs in the region.

"Ten years after 1989, at the end of the Kosovo war, Serbia found itself stuck where it was a decade ago, with no functioning independent media outlets," writes the founder of OpenNet, Radio B92's Internet service provider. "But the experiences of B92 and OpenNet provide critical lessons to help rebuild Serbian media and, indeed, to support independent media in many other harsh political environments."

"For viewers of the network news each night, coverage of the Cold War did not end in the fall of 1989," argues a media analyst. "The unraveling of the post-World War II European order over the past 10 years has not been miraculously peaceful. And the networks have not turned their backs on the murderous conflicts that ensued."

REVIEW ESSAY

In books from and about Central and Eastern Europe, a journalist and historian discerns the corrosive effects of communist lies, the power of the people and the "re-Europeanization story in East Central Europe."

Preface

After the Fall

IN BERLIN, A WALL THAT DIVIDED A city and a continent fell before men and women who surged through its gates, climbed on top of it, hammered it and finally tore it down with their bare hands.

In Prague, in a great square where secret police once lurked, exultant crowds defied a regime and reclaimed their government.

In Warsaw, workers and intellectuals who remembered beatings and prison cells stepped from the shadows to negotiate the end of their oppression.

The shocks reverberated across Central and Eastern Europe. Even as the miracles unfolded, there was no doubt that they were the kind of news that makes history. With words and pictures, journalists strained to capture a year when the story of a lifetime seemed to appear every week.

The events of 1989 were the stuff of great reporting. They also revealed the power of journalism. Long before people in Central and Eastern Europe liberated themselves, they had discovered a democratic freedom in putting to print their own ideas and chronicling their time. Indeed, long before they had democracies in law, they had invoked them on paper.

In the Solidarity network that produced books and leaflets and news bulletins, in the essays of Václav Havel, in the samizdat publishing house in Budapest that used a portable printing machine, Eastern Europeans demonstrated the organic link between journalism and self-government. They showed how journalism can nurture the imagination, dialogue and honesty that are basic to democratic life.

If history had really ended in 1989, there would be cause for easy optimism. The changes that swept Central and Eastern Europe passed with relatively little bloodshed. But in the agonies of the former Yugoslavia, the convulsions of the former Soviet Union, and the enduring battles with censors and would-be censors that bedevil emerging democracies, new questions appear. Not only is there much for journalists to cover in Central and Eastern Europe, in some places there the fate of journalism is still an open question. For all these reasons, our *Reporting the Post-Communist Revolution* explores not just the epic events of 1989, but the new stories that have emerged in Central and Eastern Europe over the past decade.

As THE EVENTS OF 1989 BECOME A part of history, it is appropriate to gauge the relationship between past and present. In "Recollections," Irena Grudzińska Gross evokes from New York the changes and continuities in the émigré journalism that she found as an immigrant from Poland in the 1970s. John Tusa weighs the role of the BBC World Service in bringing down communism. Jan Urban considers the legacy of Czechoslovak dissent for postcommunist journalism. Ann Tusa illuminates a bungled press conference that led to the opening of the Berlin Wall. From Russia, Nadezhda Azhgikhina recalls the journalism of perestroika. Anna Husarska remembers the pathways of her reporting to and from 1989.

The communist order that collapsed in Central and Eastern Europe was in part a regime for the centralized control of communication. The media systems that have emerged over the past decade, therefore, have been fundamental to defining post-communist politics and culture. In "Media Systems," Karol Jakubowicz offers ways to measure the media's transitions. Joel Rubin presents a nation-by-nation summary of media developments and freedom of expression in nations of the Warsaw Pact. Jeremy Druker evaluates the impact of TV Nova on Czech television. Gazeta Wyborcza Editor in Chief Adam Michnik celebrates the newspaper that has grown up with Polish democracy. From Budapest, Péter Molnár chronicles how both the Hungarian left and right fail to embrace fully independent broadcasting. John Maxwell Hamilton enumerates lessons from the history of foreign aid that can improve media aid. Stephan Russ-Mohl explores German unification and German journalism.

In "New Stories," we look beyond the media to explore new questions for journalists. Jay Rosen looks at how the concept of civil society, so important to Eastern dissidents, can help American journalism. Václav Havel weighs the impact of television on democracy. Reshma Prakash explores environmental reporting. Slavenka Drakulic illuminates a poisonous strain of sexism and nationalism in Croatian journalism. From Hungary, György Kerényi identifies media stereotypes of the Roma. Mark M. Nelson chronicles the emergence of business reporting in Eastern Europe. Ruth Ellen Gruber portrays a renaissance of Jewish media. Jerome Aumente surveys struggles for independent journalism. Dražen Pantić presents the stories of B92 and OpenNet, two forces for independent journalism in Serbia. Andrew Tyndall outlines trends in American network coverage of Central and Eastern Europe. Owen V. Johnson closes *Reporting the Post-Communist Revolution* with a review essay exploring books from and about Central and Eastern Europe and its media.

Ten years after the fall of the Berlin Wall, in the world of the news media, two things are easy: cynicism at the shortcomings of journalism in new democracies and despair at the propagandists who whitewash Balkan slaughters. For journalism and for democracy it is more difficult, and more important, to recall the hardheaded idealism of the underground essayists, samizdat publishers and adventurous readers who turned the world upside down in 1989. Freedom is a constant struggle.

—THE EDITORS

Part 1

REFLECTIONS

The spirit of 1989 should be remembered and recalled in order to make other miracles possible. —ANNA HUSARSKA

1

Stars in the Gutenberg Galaxy

1989 and the Polish émigré press

Irena Grudzińska Gross

I CAME TO THE UNITED STATES of America for Christmas of 1972. Since I am still here, it was the most permanent of my temporary decisions.

New York had at that time just one Polish language daily: *Nowy Dziennik (The New Daily)*. Founded in 1971, it has stubbornly survived all these years and is still here today while other dailies appeared and folded. In the 1970s, it was a rather modest newspaper, financially strapped and looking it, paying very low wages to its few journalists. It was unable to afford correspondents, and few journalists from communist Poland were reckless enough to risk their freedom and regularly contribute to its pages.

Nowy Dziennik fished out wire service news about Poland, reported on life in Polish émigré communities around the United States and extensively celebrated each and every Polish historical anniversary and religious holiday. In what the exiled Croatian writer Dubravka *Ugrešić* once called "the Gutenberg galaxy," the star of Nowy Dziennik was not very bright. Reading *Nowy Dziennik* was not one of my priorities.

It is hard to remember now how different the information landscape looked then, just a couple of decades ago. Getting reliable news from Poland and the rest of Eastern Europe was a slow and difficult task.

3

Indeed, the very beginning of the opposition movement, its very principle, was an effort to collect and spread true, real information. Already in Stalinist times the belief that factual truth would bring freedom was part of the work of such people as the Russian poet Anna Akhmatova or the author Aleksandr Solzhenitsyn. But it was also of utmost importance for human rights ideology that lay at the basis of the East European opposition.

To MONITOR ABUSES, TO DOCUMENT and convey information were the function of the Workers Defense Committee (KOR), founded in 1976 in Poland. The first such oppositional institution in the Soviet bloc countries, KOR collected and published reliable information about the political and social situation in Poland. It was KOR's bulletins and information sheets that inspired other groups to publish. They were the backbone of my information universe.

Nowy Dziennik, especially in the '70s, did not reprint these bulletins. The divide between Poland and the emigration, and between various waves of emigrants, was great. We, then the latest emigration wave, were not yet assimilated into its older layers. We were all members of the defeated group of what would now be called "pro-democracy students." Most of us were "lucky" enough to be of Jewish origin and therefore able to emigrate: the Polish government hoped that Poland would have a better future without our "foreign element." We left behind friends and relatives to whom we wanted to be of use.

Along with others from the 1968 generation of immigrants, I became involved in the creation of a Polish-language quarterly. We wanted to add to what we had left behind in Poland, so the name of this quarterly, which eventually was edited in France and printed in England, was *Aneks* (*Annex*).

We were convinced that everything that was important was happening in Poland. It was there that people risked their freedom, coped with political changes and provoked them. We in exile were listening attentively, trying to understand, to help if we could. The best we were able to do was to tear the veil of anonymity that covered our friends in Poland and made them vulnerable to persecution. This was a difficult task, especially in the '70s. The term "dissident" did not yet exist, and President Carter had not yet enshrined human rights as a principle of American foreign policy.

Our other important task was to provide our friends with ammunition for their fight: books, articles, translations of important documents and, later, printing equipment and money to survive. We were a distant star in the Gutenberg galaxy, there to beam our feeble light back on our friends.

THE MODESTY THAT CHARACTERIZED our efforts was caused by another important element: the existence of an émigré monthly, *Kultura*. Founded in the West right after the Second World War by a group of demobilized Polish Allied officers, *Kultura* was a highly literate, politically innovative monthly, which counted among its authors the future Nobel Prize laureate Czesław Miłosz and writers of such excellence as Witold Gombrowicz and Gustaw Herling-Grudziński. Its political line, established by its editor Jerzy Giedroyc, was open, intelligent, flexible and not governed by historical traumas—a rare thing among émigré publications. *Kultura* also had a line of books that had an overwhelming influence on my generation. We read them avidly not only because of their content but also because they were difficult to come by and dangerous to possess. *The Gulag Archipelago, The Captive Mind* and *Doctor Zhivago* are the most indicative titles.

In the '70s we were too young and too inexperienced (most of us were college students at the time of emigration) to compete with this towering achievement to which we were profoundly indebted and with which we often collaborated. *Aneks*, an acknowledgment of that consciousness, became a relative success. Its editors, Aleksander Smolar and Irena Grosfeld, were interested in politics and economy, so the quarterly had a somber social-scientific character. The accompanying book series, published by Eugeniusz and Nina Smolar in England, had a similar character. Both books and quarterly were devoted to the accumulation of knowledge, but not in a hasty, impatient mood. Nobody expected a rapid breakdown of the system and its information world.

At the end of the '70s, however, bulletins and underground publications in Poland became more numerous. The technique of printing (silk screen) was simple, although time-consuming. As the Solidarity trade union was created, in 1980, a group of dissidents established a press agency, AS (Agencja Solidarność), that published a regular bulletin of outstanding journalistic quality. The people who organized the AS were real information age heroes (or rather heroines, since the majority of them were women).

When Solidarity was crushed and martial law introduced, the AS people funded an underground newspaper, *Tygodnik Mazowsze* (*Weekly of Mazowia*), an almost-regular weekly that occasionally reached 80,000 copies per issue. A four- or six-page, small-print, tightly packed, not-so-easy-to-decipher sheet, *Tygodnik Mazowsze* would come to my house in New Haven, Connecticut, via air mail with better regularity than other publications. My brother, who was one of its many underground distributors, would fold every new issue, put it in an envelope and send it to my address—always inserting a different last name (he fished for them in American movies and English novels, sometimes addressing me as Jane Mansfield or Charlotte Brontë). We believed, probably rightly, that it was my name that was "arrested," and not my address. In the second half of the '80s, I became very dependent on that "subscription," as were the readers who shared the copy that I received.

Struggling with a lack of space, *Tygodnik Mazowsze* always put all the news in a most succinct form. (People used to joke that a telephone pole is a tree cut down and edited by *Tygodnik Mazowsze*.) You can see today the same sparse style on the front page of the biggest Polish newspaper, *Gazeta Wyborcza*. *Gazeta* was founded in 1989 by the crew that published *Tygodnik Mazowsze* (and who previously founded Agencja Solidarność). Recently, the London stock market appraised *Gazeta Wyborcza* at a value of U.S. $800 million.

A YEAR AFTER THE *ANNUS MIRABILIS* 1989, the quarterly *Aneks* folded—obsolete or, to put it more positively, its mission accomplished. *Kultura* is still going strong; Giedroyc, now in his late 80s, plans to keep it in operation till his death. It now sells most of its copies in Poland proper and has an air of normalcy about it that I, still a devoted subscriber, always find surprising.

Gazeta Wyborcza can be bought not only in Poland but also in the kiosks of Greenpoint, the Polish neighborhood of New York. Other Polish dailies also can be bought there. Yet *Nowy Dziennik* is still, for Polish New Yorkers, the Polish daily of choice. And there are good reasons for this. New Yorkers want to read about the United States and their city, and *Nowy Dziennik* is a good source of local news in Polish for every new wave of immigration. It offers an enlarged TV section, a number of correspondents who now have no reason not to write from Poland, and a distinguished cultural weekly that caters to the interests of the Polish-American intelligentsia. Also, its information is based on the complete service of Polska Agencja Prasowa (Polish Press Agency): the removal of the ideological divide between Poland and the West made the work of this state agency perfectly suitable for export. *Nowy Dziennik* now reports extensively on political and cultural events in Poland, and has substantial editorial comments on world and Polish politics. It is quite similar to all the other Polish newspapers everywhere, with an American regional flavor added.

But it is the competition that keeps *Nowy Dziennik* on its toes. When, in the morning, I take the No. 6 local subway to my job in midtown Manhattan, I see many people coming from Brooklyn (where Greenpoint is) and reading that day's issue of *Nowy Dziennik*. But in the evening when I come back downtown on the same No. 6 local, I occasionally see some people coming back from their offices reading that day's *Gazeta Wyborcza* printed from the Internet. In color. Feeling very fresh. A far cry from the faded bulletins of the '70s. A bright star among many other stars.

Irena Grudzińska Gross is author of The Scar of Revolution *and editor of* Letters from Freedom: Post-Cold War Realities and Perspectives *by Adam Michnik.*

2

Radio and the Fall of Communism

Did BBC broadcasts make a difference?

John Tusa

IT WAS ALWAYS SOMETHING WE puzzled over as international broadcast-ers. What effect did our radio broadcasts, mainly on shortwave fre-quencies, have on our listeners in Eastern and Central Europe and in the Soviet Union? After all, broadcasts to Poland and the Soviet Union were often jammed. We could not conduct audience surveys anywhere in the communist bloc. Listeners' letters were few and far between, listeners' phone calls virtually nonexistent. We were metaphorically broadcasting in the dark, and many of our listeners were actually listening in the dark.

Could we ever establish any idea of the impact that our broadcasts had? Did they change the way people thought; did they influence the way they behaved or resisted? And did the open flow of information have a direct effect on the way states were governed?

In 1990, writing about the interaction between communication and politics in an essay ambitiously entitled "Truth Saves Lives," I looked at the contrasting cases of India and China. There was compelling evidence from a recent book that India had fewer famines than China because its public information media were free whereas China's were controlled. The case of China's famine between 1958–61 was glaring. Because Chinese leaders were convinced by their own statistics of

9

food abundance—which were never challenged by an independent press—they reduced food imports to zero. Worse still, they actually increased the volume of grain for export. As a result, 16 to 30 million Chinese died.

THIS WAS A FUNDAMENTAL EXPERIENCE in our own learning process about how providing free information could help listeners in practical ways. For many years, as the communist bloc remained closed, we knew the questions we had to ask; but as we were denied the chance of conducting an independent inquiry, the answers were beyond our reach. But as circumstances changed during the 1980s, from Mikhail Gorbachev's policy of *glasnost* onwards, we began to piece together a picture of how BBC foreign broadcasts influenced listeners' ears and minds. By the end of the decade, we were learning that even the Soviet leadership had begun to understand that a closed, Party-led information system, featuring a servile press and media, had been a major contributor to the terminal policy error that was the Soviet invasion and occupation of Afghanistan. This was the way the evidence pointed when I wrote in 1990.

In February 1989, Valentin Falin, then head of the Soviet Central Committee's international department, was reported on Moscow Radio's World Service as making this comment on the lessons to be learned from the decision to enter Afghanistan: "Our tragedy in the past" he said, "was that many decisions were taken either by individuals or by groups of people behind closed doors. Often both the Party and the government were excluded from decision-making. Many decisions were prompted by caprices of some leaders." In other words, the entire communist system, even in its policy over Afghanistan, was deteriorating into mere leadership by whim. But their media allowed it to happen.

The rot was more profound still. In September 1990, a leading Soviet thinker on international affairs, Oleg Bogomolov, wrote a devastatingly candid article in the outspoken magazine *Ogonyok* (*Small Fires*) called "I Cannot Absolve Myself from Guilt." He had strongly advised the Brezhnev leadership against sending Soviet troops to Afghanistan. "The invasion of Afghanistan might have never happened if those who in 1968 objected inwardly to the crushing of the Prague Spring had spoken out and acted openly." But inward objections were not enough; they must be spoken, expressed, reported. We should have, wrote Bogomolov, "protested openly against the deceit, the lies, and the violence." Once again, the Brezhnev leadership successfully kept the truth from the people. But apart from killing 100,000 Soviet troops needlessly, and deepening the tensions and miseries of the Cold War, they led their country into a diplomatically disastrous dead end. In May 1989, the leading official Soviet literary magazine, *Literaturnaya Gazeta* (*Literary Gazette*), carried an article on the stagnation of public debate within the Soviet Union. The academic author wrote: "You will not find even a single mention of the slightest mistake or error in books or articles about our foreign policy. No matter what was done, everything is depicted as infallible. Of course Soviet foreign policy enjoys high esteem. But was everything done correctly?"

That evidence—most of it internal from the regimes that were most devoted to controlling information flow—strongly suggests that the realization that the denial of free information that cost the regimes themselves dear came late but strong. They fooled their people but they fooled themselves as well. But, did they really fool their citizens? The Communist populations may have been victims, but were they also ignorant of what was going on?

OVER TIME IT BECAME CLEAR THAT they were not ignorant—in large part because they were informed by broadcasters such as the BBC World Service. But our broadcasts would be heard and trusted only if we addressed our listeners effectively. It was much more than a problem of speaking to them in their native language. In 1988, I surveyed some of the key internal BBC statements about the right tone to adopt in talking to listeners behind the Iron Curtain. As long ago as 1971, a mere three years after the crushing of the Prague Spring of 1968, Alexander Lieven, then head of the East European Service, had put pen to paper on the question of "Broadcasting to Communist Audiences." He warned of the ingrained skepticism of an audience that had learned from harsh experience that all sources of information were to be distrusted. They did not need to be told that communism was discredited; their daily lives were evidence of that. Lieven concluded:

> All this imposes on us a particular need not only to be, but also to appear to be well informed, authoritative, balanced and fair in our output on Communist affairs. We should not adopt an automatically hostile attitude, avoid the "black and white" approach and, at all costs abstain from pettiness, pinpricks, rubbing salt into the wounds, sarcasm, polemics or superior "holier than thou" or "you are always wrong" attitudes. A cool, detached, almost clinical approach is called for.

In 1971 too, the greatest of BBC commentators on Soviet affairs, Anatol Goldberg, also set out his thoughts on his work. He told a graphic tale of how not to broadcast to the captive audience on the other side of Europe:

> To ensure credibility, presentation is just as important as content. At the time of the "Spring in Czechoslovakia"—when every word we broadcast to Russia about events in that country was dynamite from the Soviet point of view—a not very experienced colleague was about to introduce a talk on this subject with the remark: "And now we are going to tell you about events which your press prefers to pass over in silence." This kind of pinprick would have ruined the talk, since it would have been tantamount to saying that we were giving the information to Soviet listeners only because we knew that it would annoy their Government. Soviet listeners are very sensitive to this sort of thing.

This cool, clinical, even dispassionate style had its critics both inside and outside the Soviet Union. Russian novelist Andrei Amalrik complained when he visited the BBC that its output showed what he called "a certain wishy-washiness: on the one hand, on the other, I suppose that is how the British are."

In 1986 a group of former Czechoslovak journalists wrote to us setting out their comments on foreign broadcasters. What was revealing was the hostility of their response to the Voice of America practice of broadcasting a daily commentary "which expresses the view of the U.S. government." The Czech former journalists commented:

> When VOA first announced a commentary "expressing the view of the U.S. government," listeners in Czechoslovakia were flabbergasted. Why, oh why, has VOA taken to putting out outdated and naive propaganda? The first of these commentaries sounded just like Prague Radio in reverse, with their primitive and often shameless arguments. The program reminded us of circulars and news-sheets put out by the party's propaganda department. "When Radio Prague launches such a stupid propaganda tirade, I switch off. So why should I listen to something similar from VOA?"

By 1990, THE HEARSAY EVIDENCE WAS accumulating that the BBC approach set out above had had an impact. In November 1990, I reviewed it in an essay called "Voices in the Dark." I noted that in the communist bloc, as in the New Testament, truth was most vividly contained in stories. The American journalist, Nicholas S. Daniloff, provided the definitive Russian joke about thought control:

> INTERROGATOR: Ivan Ivanovich, what do you think of Soviet-American affairs?
> IVAN IVANOVICH: Well, I think what Pravda writes about it. What Pravda says is what I believe.

INTERROGATOR: Ivan Ivanovich, what do you think about relations with China?
IVAN IVANOVICH: Well, what Izvestia says about relations with China totally reflects what I believe.
INTERROGATOR: And what do you think about President Reagan?
IVAN IVANOVICH: Well, what Tass put out on its wire yesterday is exactly what I think about President Reagan.
INTERROGATOR: Ivan Ivanovich, don't you have any ideas of your own?
IVAN IVANOVICH: I do, but I don't agree with them.

Into such a wholly closed system the foreign radios, among whom BBC World Service was a major player, provided an unwelcome intrusion. For what did they do? They reminded the listener that there was another way of looking at events than the official way; they suggested that there were others besides the listener who could challenge the official line with alternative facts and clinical interpretation. Daniloff wrote about the compelling reason for listening:

> Many people used to say to me in Russia that listening to the BBC had developed into something of a habit or an instinct. The need for truthful information was felt almost like a physical need such as hunger or thirst. Time was thought of as either when the BBC was on the air or off. This special sense of time persisted even at moments of great stress, emotional shock or illness. Even when he was being searched or about to be arrested such a person would look at his watch: time to switch on.

This is corroborated by an extraordinary incident recorded for us in August 1985:

> On August 19, 1968, a group of Moscow intellectuals gathered at the flat of one of the dissidents to compile and sign a letter supporting the reforms in Czechoslovakia. The KGB got wind of the gathering and decided to prevent this act of "ideological diversion." Four plainclothesmen and three uniformed militia burst into the flat with a search warrant. At 5:45 p.m. sharp, while the search was still going on, the dissident looked at his watch, turned to his friends and said loudly: "Gentlemen, time for the news, let us listen to the BBC." Nobody tried to stop him turning on his radio.

The depth of penetration of foreign broadcasts into all areas of Soviet society was graphically confirmed on the occasion when Aleksandr Solzhenitsyn visited Bush House, the BBC's headquarters in London, soon after his release from the Soviet Union into exile. An eyewitness to that meeting had made a note of Solzhenitsyn's observations.

He opened his remarks by saying that we should not mislead ourselves into thinking that our broadcasts to the Soviet Union were only heard by a small number of malcontents, dissidents and intellectuals. The whole of our broadcasts were monitored and transcribed for the Politburo in full. A substantial digest was distributed to the Central Committee throughout the country. So what we were saying had considerable influence on the way they reacted to sensitivities. The Soviet authorities were so impressed by the broadcasts that they felt they ought to know what was being said "so they could answer in their propaganda" and to find out what was being heard by their own population.

A DECADE LATER, A CELEBRATED Western spy, Oleg Gordievsky, spoke out about aspects of life under communism, and it gave me the opportunity to put questions of my own to him about how people thought and stayed independent under the withering daily blast of state propaganda. Gordievsky told me that the four key foreign broadcasters, BBC World Service, Radio Liberty, VOA and Deutsche Welle, were known collectively as the "Voices." He had personal experience of their influence. In March 1953, as a young, well-ideologically schooled schoolboy brought up on the Soviet foundation myths of Stalin as all-wise, all-knowing and all-powerful, he stumbled across one of the "Voices" on his radio and was shattered by hearing a full account of the crimes Stalin ordered, the assassinations, the camps, the autocracy.

"I was in a feverish state for weeks afterwards," Gordievsky told me, and as a result, when he went on to further Party education, was far readier to look critically at the official line than most of his colleagues.

Gordievsky confirmed to me the impact that listening to the BBC World Service in English had on the KGB. For a start they liked the English accent, and the journalistic approach. KGB students at the main training institutes had to listen regularly; thereafter, officers in the first and second directorates of the KGB listened as a matter of professional duty.

As for how the BBC could have had an impact on the higher political reaches of the Party, since Politburo members are not known for much knowledge of English, Gordievsky replied:

A senior figure like that got his information from four sources; first, from official reports from Ministries; second, from the digest made by his assistant of the daily Tass summaries of foreign broadcasts and newspapers; third, from papers submitted by research and academic institutes; and last from his family, for his children listened to the "Voices." And perhaps in the evening, he would himself tune into the "Voices" at his bedside.

By the early 1980s, Gordievsky told me, Soviet citizens no longer bothered to conceal that they listened to the foreign radios. On a return to Moscow in 1983, Gordievsky recalled walking by a huge block of Moscow flats, the kind with several staircase entrances. There was a group of people clustered at each staircase. Every group was listening to a radio. But each staircase had adopted, he noticed, its own radio station—one was listening to the BBC, the next to Radio Liberty and the next to VOA. Each staircase had become a fan club of a different foreign station.

Gordievsky then added these two thoughts:

> At 5:45 in the evening, the average Russian would start drinking; the person with the shortwave radio would tune to a radio station. It was a Happy Hour for intellectuals. They would go to extraordinary lengths to listen in. Some worked out that jamming was less effective in rural areas and would take their holidays there in order to get brief access to a good signal, even rowing a boat out into a small lake to be able to listen in peace.

What the BBC taught its listeners was to judge critically, to apply critical questioning to problems. In the end that example had its own impact on people reared on ideological certainties. Gordievsky's conclusion is almost embarrassingly fulsome. "It is impossible to overestimate the importance of the BBC in the Soviet Union. You were like a university to us."

INCREASINGLY, THE EVIDENCE GREW that the totalitarian societies and their people learned the hard way that covering up the facts cost them dear. Take the case of the nuclear disaster at Chernobyl.

After Chernobyl, Radio Liberty research in Munich carried out a brief survey of Soviet visitors to the West, to pull together clues about how Soviet listeners gathered their knowledge of that dreadful event. Of the 214 respondents, 38 percent cited Western radio stations as their first source, compared with 31 percent who heard of it first on Soviet television. Once they had heard the news on their own media, 53 percent of the sample said they turned to Western radio for additional information. Selected comments from respondents were harsh: "When Soviet TV started to broadcast about Chernobyl, we didn't believe what was said. Since they'd been silent it meant they were hiding something and if they were hiding something they must have been lying." Or, more critically, this from a Lithuanian agricultural worker: "If the Western radio reports exaggerated a bit, it's the fault of the Soviet authorities who are used to hiding information of serious significance from the whole world. I think Western radios were right to warn the world about the accident's dangerous consequences."

Well before the end of communism, the shortcomings of the Soviet Union's own information media were no longer a matter of dispute between East and West, they had become an in-joke between those in the know.

On the night of the U.S. bombing of Tripoli, Libya, in 1986, I was preparing for a discussion in Moscow with the Brooklyn-accented Radio Moscow's answer to Norman Mailer, roly-poly Joe Adamov. He was up to the minute in his knowledge of the turbulent events of that day. Like a stooge feeding the lead comic his line, I asked: "How do you know all this?" "Why, from your World Service, of course." One of my predecessors was sparring gently with a Soviet ambassador at an international conference on the subject of information and disinformation. "I suppose you would regard the BBC World Service as disinformation?" inquired my friend. "Of course," replied the Russian with a straight face. "I disinform myself every morning."

Communism fell because it gave a mendacious account of the world both to itself and its citizens. The foreign broadcasts played their part in freeing the ordinary listener from relying on official media. It confirmed that there was a huge discrepancy between what individuals saw as the facts of life and what their government and party told them was reality. Did all this bring the Wall down? It certainly undermined the foundations.

John Tusa was managing director of the BBC World Service from 1986 to 1992.

3

Until Old Cats Learn How to Bark

*Czechoslovak dissidents fought communism without learning
good lessons for journalism.*

Jan Urban

TEN YEARS AGO THE CZECHOSLOVAK dissidents were just about to take power. They did not know that until they had to do it. They were absolutely unprepared for the task. They had no plans and no expectations. Being on the defensive for too long, they did not really see that the other side's defensive line was crumbling until it ran off the playing field.

In the middle of the 1980s when Solidarity in Poland had, despite the losses suffered during martial law, a perfectly functioning network of underground printing machines spewing 10,000 copies of the most diverse opposition literature, including weeklies, the Czechoslovak dissident journalistic culture still lived in the world of "one plus 10." One original and 10 copies of any text typed on a typewriter were the legal maximum that one was allowed to have at home without being accused of one of the many criminal acts that the Communist justice system used to silence the opposition. To have at home several packs of typing or carbon paper was suspicious. Typewriters were registered.

Not until 1987 were the first few Xerox machines smuggled into Czechoslovakia. The first fax machine and first laptop came in 1989. When Czechoslovak dissidents needed to print something in a larger volume, the manuscript was smuggled across the mountains into Poland, and the entire run, at most a few hundred copies, was then carried back across the mountains in the knapsacks of brave young couriers.

ANY RESEARCH OR ATTEMPT AT AN analysis of the opposition journalism of that period necessarily reflects the context of that time. The greatest and most significant action of the journalistic opposition, in a Czechoslovakia of 15 million people, was the revival of the *Lidové noviny* (*People's News*) newspaper in 1987. It had been banned by the Communists for 40 years. Even in the famed times of 1988–1989, *Lidové noviny* was just a monthly in the A4 format (roughly 8H by 11 inches), photocopied on regular office paper in runs of 500 copies at most. Its paste-up was done with scissors and glue. Nevertheless, the demand was enormous. According to the secret police, *Lidové noviny* was later mass copied at the state-run offices and factories, and every month it reached, in some form or other, maybe up to 40,000 to 50,000 readers.

Decades of concentrating on bare survival, and the inability to build their own organization and amass technical support, inevitably affected the style and form of Czechoslovak dissidents' reporting. Feeling perpetual danger for decades, every writer, after a while, had the tendency to write as if the thing he was writing at that moment represented his last message to humanity. The most accessible, and at home the most influential, media that the Czechoslovak human rights defenders could use were foreign broadcasts, such as Radio Free Europe/Radio Liberty, Voice of America or the BBC. There was no room for full-bodied Czechoslovak journalism—only for the simplest, facts-presenting news service, which the opposition used to inform the public about cases of human rights violations, together with popular short and ironic observations, and a flood of moralizing and philosophizing commentaries and essays that tried to look like high-class literature. Full-bodied journalism— that gave background to a story, disclosed sources, used and confronted public records or quoted differing reactions—opened up very slowly.

Additionally, and most importantly, the majority of opposition writers had no continuity on which to build. Only the most elderly remembered the fireworks of independent periodicals and the multicultural climate of the prewar First Republic. The Nazi occupation and the fast rise of the Communist dictatorship after the war interrupted for decades not only the development of journalism, but also the normal, natural evolution of language and education.

The short thaw in the '60s that culminated in the famed Prague Spring in 1968, was not strong and free enough to ground anything firmly. Fireworks are not to educate and stabilize. Fireworks can only inspire. During this time, a new and very successful generation of Czech artists and writers appeared, led by young rebels such as Milan Kundera, Miloš Forman, Ludvík Vaculík and Václav Havel. Despite their indubitable bravery and the quality of their writings, it is necessary to recognize that their style was not openness and factual work, but some sort of "between-the-lines writing," avoiding confrontation with the communist power and testing the limits of what was possible. The dictatorship may have been loosening its grip, but that didn't mean that freedom had arrived, or that trafficking in truthful information would cease to be a crime.

Symbolism, double, even triple meanings of expression, striving for universal values—all these are good building blocks of higher culture. In the craft of journalism, however, these just represent clutter that obscures the view and a sense of facts. Between-the-lines writing became a drug. Facts were still inaccessible or too dangerous. Or there was no space left for them. With the exception of those few months in 1968, when censorship in communist Czechoslovakia was abolished, there was nothing that would resemble a journalistic obligation to provide readers with the story's background information or its further development. And so the style of the '60s brought to Czechoslovak journalism, besides the feeling of freedom, mostly yet another flood of highbrow philosophizing commentaries.

THE SOVIET OCCUPATION OF Czechoslovakia in August 1968 not only halted the normal development of the society for the next 20 years but pushed it back. A well-thought-out system of periodic purges, tough "prior censorship," and absolute communist control of every individual's life made the Czechoslovakia of the '70s and early '80s a dead zone. During this time the dictatorship defeated society, breaking it into the smallest atoms incapable of independent life. Only individual people expressed any opposition—and that mostly in words alone. It is sad and ironic that any word that was written without prior approval by the appropriate authorities was considered heroic at that time. Indeed, the regime considered anything written without its approval a subversive act and prosecuted it as such. Due to the paranoia of the Communist police regime, everything, even the smallest human gesture, had political significance—the person one met on the street, books in one's library, paintings on one's walls, records lying next to one's record player. People who listened to foreign broadcasts in the evenings always remembered to redial to the official Czechoslovak station before turning off the radio—that way, an unexpected visitor wouldn't find out that they sought information from anywhere other than official sources.

From today's impartial viewpoint, the courage to write independently of the regime also had a negative side. In times when a writer could be persecuted for anything, all writings, even the ones of lesser quality, acquired an aura of being exceptional, mysterious and romantic. Consequently, the feeling of moral and professional uniqueness became—unintentionally—one of the main traits of dissident journalism and literature. Confined in the isolation of the miniature dissident ghetto for many years, we lived under the impression that due to our suffering, persecution and resistance we reached some deeper truth and higher professional quality. Since one could be imprisoned, or at least harassed and interrogated, for a tiny essay or commentary, everybody who had the courage to read anything of this kind found it a bit difficult to criticize the quality of the text. Similarly, as in all primitive arts, a critical perspective virtually didn't exist. On the contrary, it was widely believed that if we ever lived to see the end of the communist regime, volumes of fabulous works by their persecuted authors, written only "for their desk drawer," would emerge into the light. When communist power in Czechoslovakia collapsed within one week in November 1989, it became clear that this expectation was a fiction. Not one substantial piece of writing was published, and the surprise was necessarily followed by depression.

Until the very end of the regime the system of apartment classes or underground universities tried to connect Czechoslovak dissidents with knowledge and debates of the world outside the communist bloc. Sometimes dozens of people gathered in an apartment to hear a lecture and discuss at length philosophy, literature, economics or ecology. During the two years prior to November 1989, similar informal gatherings were even organized by the less timid members of the official establishment. To my knowledge, never, not once, did such a "class" in Czechoslovakia address the subject of journalism or media. Journalism and media weren't perceived as something that needed to be studied or learned about from developments outside the borders of communist countries. It was automatically expected that bringing down the communist dictatorship was enough, and that freedom and democracy would somehow naturally and without any further effort change everything else. For Czechoslovak dissidents, the issues of media ownership, organization and development didn't really exist. Therefore, there were also no expectations.

AT THIS POINT, IT IS necessary to mention two important factors. First is the exceptionally low number of activists of the opposition movement in communist Czechoslovakia. Contrary to Poland, where the anti-communist trade union Solidarity had tens of millions of members, and where a number of dissident groups had actively worked as early as the end of the '60s, the dissident community in Czechoslovakia, despite all efforts, consisted of a couple of hundred individuals at the most. In January 1989, the state police prepared for the Politburo of the Communist Party an analysis of the "anti-socialist forces." This cruelly precise report, based on the work of tens of *Státní bezpečnost* (state security) secret police officers and on information supplied by many agents that infiltrated the dissident groups, estimated the size of the "hard core" of these "forces" at 50 or 60 people who, of the entire 15 million in Czechoslovakia, had the support of only 500 activists at most. In contrast to Hungary, where many people within the Communist Party itself worked toward the changes, the Czechoslovak Communist Party didn't show a hint of any effort toward reform. Until the very end, the leaders of the Czechoslovak Communists viewed Gorbachev's *perestroika*, and most of all *glasnost*, as unacceptable heresy.

The second limiting factor was technology. Even though a small, isolated group of Czechoslovak dissidents increasingly made contacts with the young generation, they were not strong enough to persuade the older generation, brought up in the mind-set of one plus 10, that they needed to start using computers. A few privately owned computers were used only as better typewriters. The first, now legendary, dissident Toshiba 1000 laptop computer was brought to Prague in June 1989—thanks to the kindness of our friends at the New School for Social Research in New York—and immediately became a reason for a house search by the police. Fortunately, the secret police were too eager and arrived before the operating system and the Czech fonts could be loaded onto the computer. Not even the most maniacal interrogator could prove that the computer had been used in some antigovernment activities and therefore must be confiscated. The owner received an official warning from the prosecutor's office stating that his actions were endangering the state's interests abroad, and that if he didn't stop with such activities, he was risking up to 10 years in jail.

Thus independent journalism was developing somehow incidentally, through the work of a few people who never thought of a deeper analysis of their profession, except that they scrupulously tried to verify their facts about human rights violation cases before their publication. Ironically, the first significant inaccuracy that led to an immediate imprisonment of one of the bravest journalists and dissidents, Petr Uhl, didn't occur until the November revolution. Uhl, despite all his caution and efforts to verify his information, published a report that the police had beaten to death a student, Martin Smíd, during a November 17 demonstration in Prague. This news flashed around the world and electrified the entire country, sparking sit-ins and strikes at universities and theaters that later grew into a general strike and led to the collapse of the regime. Today, we know that nobody was killed during the demonstrations. Most probably, this information was partly police provocation aimed at securing a criminal charge of incitement and spreading false-alarmist information against Uhl and his colleagues. The November 1989 events developed so fast that after a few days of detention, Uhl, together with other political prisoners, was released.

ANOTHER HANDICAP WAS LACK OF information about developments outside Czechoslovakia's borders. Numerous proclamations and documents of the dissident groups, especially Charter 77, got considerable publicity—thanks to foreign broadcast stations and the Western policy of supporting human rights movements in communist countries. Individual dissident writers such as Havel, Vaculík and Jiří Dienstbier even had their own Western publishers. But the power and influence of these individual voices obscured the fact that independent journalistic and literary production in Czechoslovakia represented the work of just 30 people at most. And most of them worked simultaneously with several *samizdat* magazines.

The only international organization that linked dissident journalists from several communist countries in the two years before the changes was the East European Information Agency. Using the telephone, it acquired and exchanged information about human rights violations in Poland, Czechoslovakia, the Soviet Union, East Germany and sometimes also in Hungary and Yugoslavia. In Czechoslovakia, the euphemistically named "agency" was actually just the occasional work of three people. In the official media of that time, there was no room for free, independent journalism. Tough "prior censorship" existed until the very last moment. The first meeting of three editors of the illegal *Lidové noviny* with several young editors of the official Prague dailies didn't take place until the fall of 1989. There was no time left to develop any cooperation. The Czechoslovak dissidents weren't even aware of their handicaps. Their inability to compare their situation with the outside world, their inability to abandon their pre-computer age mentality and their self-image of being unique and morally superior as the persecuted victims of the regime were a guaranteed recipe for a quick defeat in the moment of change.

One of the most fascinating illustrations of how self-absorbed and isolated Czechoslovak dissent was at that time is the fact that not one of the tens of interviewed former dissidents could remember one instance when they would have discussed, at some meeting, the possibility of the end of communism or the steps that the opposition should take to bring such an end. No one raised such topics, except the economists who worked on theoretical models of never-realized economic reform. To talk about expectations in such a situation was impossible. There were none. Despite the apparently growing discontent, the communist regime still relied on the silent cooperation of the intimidated society and the loyal police. The majority of active dissidents were willingly risking more and more open confrontations with the regime, but inside they expected to end up in jail sooner or later.

THE CONTRAST WITH THE SITUATION in Poland is very difficult to explain. When in the spring of 1989 Solidarity won every possible seat in the Polish elections, the dissidents and enemies of the state became senators, ministers and deputies. Four of the most respected dissidents—Adam Michnik, Zbigniew Bujak, Zbigniew Janas and Jan Lityński—arrived in Prague for a hurriedly organized visit. Czechoslovak and Polish dissidents, who until now were always meeting clandestinely on the border in the mountains, were to meet in public for the first time. Nothing could have been a bigger provocation than the brand new diplomatic passports in the hands of the former Polish "contra-revolutionaries." And the silently furious Czechoslovak Communist secret police couldn't do a thing. Granted, the customs officers held them on some pretense for several hours at the border, but at 2 a.m., some 20 people were still waiting for them in Petr Uhl's apartment.

Michnik, who was in Prague for the very first time, immediately wanted to see the nearby Wenceslas Square, the heart of Prague. The gently sloping square was then, as today, lined with dozens of lamp-posts. At every one of them, a neon red star was glowing. On many buildings, communist slogans about eternal friendship with the Soviet Union, or the proletariat of the world, shone into the night.

Standing in the empty square, Michnik looked around and in his typical halting voice said: "In one year, in 12 months, there will not be one red star here." The Czech dissidents present were perhaps a bit nervous about the constant presence of several known police faces who were, at this late hour, standing nearby as if by coincidence. The Czechs started to explain to their Polish friends that the Czechoslovak situation was different, that the Polish experience couldn't automatically be applied. "Listen. Don't you understand it?" interrupted Adam Michnik. "It is over. Within one year, there will not be one red star here." None of the dissidents present could imagine it yet. Four months later, they were forming the government of noncommunist Czechoslovakia.

AND NOW, WE ARE GETTING TO THE biggest mistake of the Czechoslovak dissent and its journalist members. Already in the summer of 1989, some dissidents began to feel that the current forms of presentations and acts of opposition against the regime were not sufficient. A small group, in deep conspiracy, attempted unsuccessfully several times to jam the broadcast of the official TV with its own sound signal using small transmitters smuggled in from Poland. New *samizdat* titles appeared. It was clear that Prague's students were getting mobilized. More than 20,000 people signed a petition, "Několik vět" ("A Few Sentences"), which demanded that the government and the Communist Party open a dialogue.

But they failed to understand that important changes in the world outside, even all domestic changes, were happening so fast that none of the Czechoslovak dissidents managed to react and reflect on them—never mind change tactics. During a few short months, the anti-communist opposition took over Poland. Hungary opened its borders and renounced its allegiance to Moscow. The Berlin Wall fell. And on November 17, even Czechoslovakia found itself in a belated direct confrontation with the Communist authorities.

All Czechoslovak dissidents, with some exceptions, ended up, at least temporarily, in high political posts and were lost from any development of independent media and journalism. The absolute majority of the new postcommunist media were thus managed by people who acquired their professional skills while being subordinates of the communist regime. Similarly, the majority of journalists, who learned their craft under tough prior censorship, remained at their positions. People who were conditioned by the official policy that facts and objective reporting to the public must never play an important role, were now supposed to become overnight independent and nonideological professionals in the public service. Of course, none of it happened.

Knowing the old saying that "you cannot teach an old dog new tricks," the postrevolutionary Czechs and Slovaks accepted the belief that you can teach old cats to bark. And the results were adequate. The malady of the communist perception, that all events were political, continued. The media started to do politics instead of reporting information. Turning everything into ideology and offering only preformed opinions, instead of an objective presentation of facts and context, became absolutely the predominant way the old-new media worked for many years. Hopes invested in *Lidové noviny*, which came out of illegality and for several months became the highest selling daily in the country, brought only disappointment. The incompetent management was as damaging as the petty politics, ideological games and silencing of unpopular opinions. Several remaining dissident journalists, who didn't become politicians, met at *Lidové noviny*. But even they got addicted to the belief that until the war against the communist danger is over their newspaper also has to "do politics." This resulted in its rapid decline, which couldn't be prevented even by its hasty sale to the Swiss publisher, Ringier.

The Polish *Gazeta Wyborcza*, a one-time exclusively dissident paper, is today the best and largest daily in Poland. It owns radio and television stations. It is a commercial success, and all leading European intellectuals are its contributors. Michnik has been its only editor in chief since 1989. *Lidové noviny*, on the other hand, continuing with boring ideological practices of preselecting facts or engaging in political preaching and moralizing, has for several years been on the verge of bankruptcy; it has already replaced seven editors in chief.

After 10 years, it is easy to see how unprepared and naive the Czechoslovak dissidents and journalists were. Lacking know-how and contacts in the real world of media, they failed to analyze the changes of 1989 and prepare for them. They just helped to open a door through which someone else entered.

Since then, a new generation of young journalists has grown up; it insists more and more often on independence and quality. The changing of democratically elected governments also helps to dispel too-close relationships between some journalists and politicians. Excellent editors and war correspondents such as Karel Hvížď'ala, Petra Procházková and Jaromír Štětina have appeared. The path that a few inexperienced dissident journalists helped build 10 years ago is now open. No longer need we try to teach old cats to bark. The future belongs to the young dogs.

Jan Urban, former dissident activist and journalist with the Civic Forum in Czechoslovakia, is a writer and war correspondent. Translated by Suzanna Halsey.

4

A Fatal Error

The press conference that opened the Berlin Wall

Ann Tusa

AT ABOUT 7 O'CLOCK ON THE EVENING of November 9, 1989, some 300 journalists from all over the world are crammed into a room in East Berlin for a routine press conference. For months past they have been covering a great story. For the first time since the foundation of a separate Communist East German state in 1946, the German Democratic Republic, there have been massive demonstrations against the regime. There is an organized, though illegal, opposition—New Forum—demanding freer travel and speech and change within a socialist framework. Other clusters of dissidents are calling for more radical reforms. The Communist Party's only response so far has been to shuffle the men at the top (the longtime East German leader Erich Honecker resigned in October; his replacement, Willi Stoph, went on November 7 with all his cabinet). But new faces have not meant new minds. The state is still run by intransigent old ideologues.

So East Germans, who have not known a free election since 1933, have been voting with their feet. From January to October 1989, some 200,000 people had left their country. By early November the figure was up to 250,000—and that was out of a total population of 16.7 million. At first, many East Germans went out on "holiday visas" to Iron Curtain countries, then claimed asylum in West German embas-

27

sies in Warsaw, Budapest or Prague. The thousands more have driven or walked round the East German frontiers looking for an undefended crossing or a guard with a blind eye, wriggled across, then headed for Austria and a refugee camp. When the Hungarians (encouraged by a fat fee from Bonn) opened their frontiers to visa-less passage on September 11 and the Czechs followed suit on November 3, the steady stream of refugees grew to a flood—22,000 East Germans fled their country in the three days after the Hungarian borders opened.

Over the first weekend in November an almost unimaginable 1 million East Germans, half of them in Berlin, were illegally demonstrating on the streets while tens of thousands were on the move to the nearest available neighboring country. And, most ominously, in those two days the 380,000 Soviet troops stationed in the GDR stayed in their barracks while the Kremlin spokesman, Gennadi I. Gerasimov, gave "off-the-record" briefings to the international media that they would not get involved in suppressing internal unrest.

The East German regime is clinging desperately to control of its border with West Germany and especially to the section that slashes through Berlin—the Wall. Those concrete slabs, rolls of barbed wire, watchtowers and gun emplacements, the raked-sand death strip set with mines, were set up in August 1961 to staunch a previous hemorrhage of East German citizens. The Berlin Wall is the international symbol of ruthless communist repression; for the East German regime it is the expression of its authority and the guarantor of the GDR's separate existence.

The November 9 press conference is handled by Günter Schabowski. He was once editor of *Neues Deutschland* (*New Germany*), a government newspaper famous for printing more photographs of Honecker than any other journal. He has also been the Party's Central Committee secretary for the (control of the) media and a member of the Politburo. But unlike most of his old colleagues he has learned fast in recent months. He is now a smooth, genial operator, with the reputation, rare among East Berlin officials, of being honest and open.

This evening he feeds the press a startling hint that there might soon be free elections. Good story. Everyone wants to go out and file it. But then Schabowski turns up a sheet from the bottom of the pile of papers on his table. "This will be interesting for you." And in a style that suggests it is all news to him, slowly reads aloud: "Today the decision was taken to make it possible for all citizens to leave the country through the official border crossing points. All citizens of the GDR can now be issued with visas for the purposes of travel or visiting relatives in the West. This order is to take effect at once."

Journalists bellow questions, rush to the table. "When does this order come into force?" "Soon or now this minute?" Schabowski, tired and confused, pauses, then comes to the obvious conclusion. "It just means straightaway." The journalists charge out, to the phone or the studio. This story is sensational. Free travel means freedom of information and of choice. It means the end of the Berlin Wall and everything it was built to protect.

The news is broadcast on an East German television bulletin at 7:30 p.m. The station's switchboard is immediately jammed with callers. "Is it true? I can't believe it." They always believed West German television, though, and it is soon flashing the announcement. A few East and West Berliners go to the Wall to see what is happening. Nothing at first: the crossing points are still barred, the East German guards are still patrolling. Finally, a young couple find a guard who seems to be listening to the radio. He raises the barrier but warns that, like Cinderella, they must return before midnight. They take one step, then another and hesitantly, fearfully walk out of the GDR into another world.

Others begin to trickle across, still unable to believe it is possible. Then at 10:30 a discussion program on Sender Freies Berlin, the West Berlin television station, is interrupted by a live broadcast from the Wall. No preamble, just shots of a small crowd milling round a checkpoint, then a man runs toward the camera: "They've opened the crossing at Bornholmer Strasse." After that the news spreads like wildfire, by radio, television, telephone, shouts in the street. The trickle across the Wall swells to a flood. That weekend 2 million East Germans are reckoned to have stood in West Berlin. One reaction is common to them all: "We've seen the West on TV, of course. But this is real."

EAST GERMANS HAD NEVER BEEN fully able to grasp the reality of life outside their rigid, dour, isolated state. Travel was rare except for Soviet bloc visits by groups of Party members, trade unionists or approved businessmen. The newspapers were state controlled. So was official radio. The illegal alternatives from outside were often jammed, and if you were caught listening to them your radio set was confiscated; persistent offenders were liable to 15 months' imprisonment.

Those in or near Berlin tuned to RIAS—Radio in the American Sector—which was less likely to be jammed and, because it catered to an audience on either side of the Wall, gave a sense of contact, of community.

The impact of television came late to the East. For a long time TV sets were in short supply and were always expensive. State controlled programs gave news of government pronouncements or visits to and from Soviet bloc worthies, occasionally interrupted by some jolly folk dancing or an aged musical with chorus girls of the same vintage. As technology improved, however, East Germans could get programs from West Germany or Austria. By the late 1980s, 85 percent of East Germans tuned in to them at some time or another on a regular basis—not necessarily for uncensored news or lessons in democracy, but for pop music, visions of laden supermarket shelves and scenes of faraway places. Every evening at 8 o'clock, the entire viewing audience "emigrated": switched to the regular main West German news bulletin. The regime gave up trying to stop them. Indeed given complaints in the Dresden region, known as the Valley of the Clueless because few television signals reached it, the authorities finally decided to put it on cable. Television, however, was not a new Opium of the People. In 1989, Dresden was one of the main centers of opposition to the government.

BACK TO THAT PRESS CONFERENCE ON November 9, 1989. Günter Schabowski's statement had been dynamite. It brought down the Berlin Wall and everything it stood for. How tempting to assume that the GDR regime had been sapped by foreign media presentation of the delights of the Golden West, that its announcement was one of surrender.

But the following year, a distinguished BBC journalist, John Simpson, who had always been puzzled by the timing and presentation of the announcement, went to see Schabowski and finally hit the truth. The fatal piece of paper had been hurriedly swept up as he left for the press conference. It had never been intended for publication. It was a draft based on a recent Politburo decision: unable to control the tide of refugees, thrashing around for ways to quiet the demonstrators on the streets, they had decided that in their own good time they would ease travel restrictions, having first made arrangements for a limited issue of visas under carefully controlled circumstances.

No wonder then that when an official who was working on the new travel scheme turned on his television that evening and saw the film of Schabowski and the live coverage of East Germans surging westward, he exclaimed, "What a cock up!" It was. In fact, you can look at any major revolution in history and enumerate political, social, economic or religious causes to explain it. Sooner or later you find that the last straw that breaks a regime's back is sheer human error.

Ann Tusa has written widely on Berlin, Germany, and the Cold War. With John Tusa, she is the co-author of The Berlin Airlift.

5

A Taste of Freedom in Russia

Journalism between the past and the future

Nadezhda Azhgikhina

IN 1989, I DEFENDED MY DOCTORAL dissertation at Moscow State University and went to work at *Ogonyok* (*Small Fires*), a magazine that addressed issues once spoken about only in a whisper. For this reason, it became for millions of people a symbol of *perestroika* and the hope for the renewal of journalism and of our country.

I immediately felt like a member of the team. The word "team" was common then: that's what friends called themselves when they gathered late at night to read a banned book in the kitchen; that's what like-minded people who wanted to change the status quo called themselves. That's how *Ogonyok* editor in chief Vitaly Korotich talked about his editorial staff. Later, in interviews with Western colleagues, he would tirelessly repeat that he assembled his magazine staff the way the commander of a partisan detachment assembles a group that must blow up a bridge. We all faced the task of blowing up something bigger than a transport structure—the whole Soviet ideological system, the reinforced concrete edifice of Party journalism, and in the end, the Soviet state apparatus itself—then euphemistically called "the administrative-command system" (or simply the System).

A symbolic year in the development of Russian journalism, 1989 was marked by two sessions of the Congress of People's Deputies (the

33

first freely elected Soviet parliament), the destruction of the Berlin Wall and the exit of Soviet forces from Afghanistan. It was a wonderful time, full of hope, joy, potential, infinite romanticism, reality indivisible from illusion and inexhaustible enthusiasm. The country was discovering the truth about the past and the present, beginning to breathe more freely and acknowledging the vast world that was leaping out from under the rising Iron Curtain. When I meet now with former colleagues from the magazine, we all agree that we have never experienced similar feelings anywhere and are unlikely to experience them again.

Of course, being involved in the democratization of society was not always exhilarating. There were moments when we all understood clearly that freedom really did not yet exist, that censorship and the ideological wing of the Party Central Committee still did, and that the situation in the country could change dramatically. In 1989, we regularly joked about whom they might arrest first in the event of an ideological retreat. Every week the nominees changed, depending on the explosiveness of the week's editorial content, but everyone understood that candidate number one was Vitaly Korotich.

IN MANY WAYS, *Ogonyok*'s history represents trends throughout Soviet and post-Soviet journalism. The magazine dates to 1899, when it was an illustrated entertainment periodical focusing on society news, handy advice and art criticism. In the Soviet period, it was transformed into an organ of propaganda for the new authorities. During the Second World War, the magazine's popularity soared as it published descriptions of the front by Soviet writers such as Konstantin Simonov and Ilya Ehrenburg, and work by top photojournalists like Yevgeny Khaldei and Dmitry Baltermants. After a short fascination with liberal ideas during Khrushchev's "thaw," the magazine retreated rather quickly to a conservative position. During the Brezhnev period, *Ogonyok* was a synonym for Soviet idiocy.

Touched by a stroke of genius, Alexander Yakovlev, a member of the Central Committee and the head ideologue of *perestroika*, brought to the magazine his friend Vitaly Korotich, a popular Ukrainian poet. Korotich came from Kiev in the spring of 1986, several days before the tragedy at Chernobyl. This marked a new stage in the life of the magazine—and in the development of journalism.

Weeklies, not daily newspapers, played the most important role in shaping ideas during *perestroika*. *Ogonyok* was probably the most cutting edge in political and literary content, which was determined by its position as a photo magazine and its unaffiliated political status. During the Soviet period, every publication had formal guidance—a sponsor in the guise of a Soviet body or organization. The newspaper *Pravda* (*Truth*) was the periodical of the Central Committee; the newspaper *Izvestiya* (*News*), of the Supreme Soviet; *Literaturnaya Gazeta* (*Literary Gazette*), of the Writers Union. *Ogonyok*, with its offices in Moscow, belonged to the Pravda publishing house, which put out dozens of diverse magazines and newspapers, including *Pravda*. However, for reasons that have been forgotten, the magazine was not itself the organ of any Soviet organization. This lack of formal ties to a specific Soviet institution eventually helped *Ogonyok* become one of the country's first independent magazines.

Before *perestroika*, however, this structural feature did not mean much—Soviet ideologues filled leadership positions at the magazine anyway. After Korotich's arrival, when censorship was less strict but still present, *Ogonyok*'s status helped editors to publish a lot of controversial material. Still, its subordination to the publishing house required that all expenses and revenue, its printing schedule and so forth be under Pravda's control. In practice, this meant that all revenue that the magazine brought in under Korotich—when its popularity was growing month by month—was redistributed within the publishing house to the newspaper *Pravda* and the magazine *Kommunist* (which held positions contrary to *Ogonyok*) and for their staff salaries, which were significantly higher than at Korotich's magazine. This conflict peaked in 1989 and became grounds for the magazine's fight for independence, which it attained in that year.

WHILE *OGONYOK* WAS MATURING IN 1989, Soviet journalism was marked by a shift in both the types of articles journalists were writing and the very principles of the profession; it was a change from publishing according to the Soviet model to new forms.

Journalism in the late Soviet period can be understood through the framework set forth in the popular *perestroika*-era writings of the philosopher Mikhail Kapustin, who wrote that Soviet culture was divisible into three main parts. The first, "machine-gunner culture," served state ideology directly and unconditionally; the second, dissident culture, focused on criticizing the regime; and the third, which balanced between the first two, worked within censorship but subtly alluded to imperfections in the machine. *Pravda* belonged unconditionally to the "machine-gunner culture"; *samizdat* magazines, like the *Chronicle of Current Events*, that were distributed illegally belonged to dissident culture. A significant number of publications, such as the popular *Literaturnaya Gazeta*, fit into the "intermediate" culture and published interesting material about problems of morality, education and art. The intermediate publications encouraged a high literary style, exact details and vivid images. Writers employed "Aesopian language," which was extremely developed in Russian journalism as a whole beginning in the 19th century: a writer would not name an event or the accused directly, but layered his text in such a way that the reader could think and recognize what was really going on. Under Korotich, *Ogonyok* fell somewhere between the intermediate and dissident publications.

In the Soviet period, newspapers and magazines were the main sources of information. Television was rather boring and full of monotonous ideological chatter, but the market for print media was quite evolved: newspapers were cheap and every Soviet family subscribed annually to five or six newspapers and magazines. Many publications had huge circulations—sometimes more than 10 million copies. The government subsidized the publication of newspapers, considering it an important ideological venture, and one way or another reconciled itself with press content, which in any event was almost always blurred by censorship.

The most popular format in the culture, teetering between the official and the legal yet liberally oriented journalism, was the analytical article, particularly the essay. This kind of journalism, which appeared was still only marginal during the first years of *perestroika*, became less reliant on Aesopian language and more accustomed to calling things as it saw them.

TALK IN THE LATE '80s REVOLVED not only around the discovery of the "blank spots" in Soviet history and criticism of the country's existing economic and political condition, but also affirmations of "renewed socialism" and "socialism with a human face." The letter Nikolai Bukharin wrote before his death, criticizing Stalin and affirming a socialism cleansed of totalitarianism, received wide attention after its publication in *Ogonyok*. Thousands of letters from people sharing Bukharin's views were delivered to our offices.

Ogonyok moved faster than its competitors. "*Perestroika* is teaching us to see more clearly," wrote Korotich in the editor's forward to one of the first issues of 1989. "This obvious truth buttresses the openness of today's emerging criticism. It is important that each of our positions becomes less ambiguous: are we talking about a revolutionary ideal, about economic theory and practice in *perestroika*, about the nature of spirituality, about the fight for reason and our national soul?" These words might serve as an epigraph for the whole year and the magazine's overall content. *Perestroika* was understood to be the reformation of socialism: the USSR still existed, and no one truly believed that the empire would collapse. New economic ideas were progressing only timidly, yet several authors outpaced the majority and foresaw changes that many could not have guessed at.

The idea of a genuinely popular magazine that would address people's vital interests without prohibitions was Korotich's basic philosophy. Most of *Ogonyok*'s content was dedicated to the problems and changes in domestic affairs. Shortages of goods and foodstuffs remained an issue throughout 1989. Ten years ago shelves in Russian stores were a far cry from today's abundance—long lines formed for sausage, meat, cheese and other products consumed daily. There were not enough manufactured goods. The war against alcoholism undertaken at the start of perestroika forced people to cope with unpopular measures limiting the sale of alcohol. All this was reflected in the pages of *Ogonyok*.

The first steps toward civil society were taken in 1989 as new nongovernmental organizations and philanthropic movements formed. *Ogonyok* informed readers about the creation of the first philanthropic and social organizations—the most important of these was "Memorial," which was assembled to tell the truth about Stalin's repression, about the new Committees for Soldiers' Mothers. In 1989, the foundation "Ogonyok–anti-AIDS" began its work to help prevent AIDS in the USSR.

Letters to the editor occupied a special place in the magazine. In 1988, *Ogonyok* received 13,000 letters, a figure that grew by 50 percent in 1989. Every issue devoted two pages to letters. Workers and collective farm laborers, victims of Stalin's repression, cultural figures, leaders of political movements, émigrés and Western readers all contributed. Letters to the editor of newspapers and magazines had become a tradition in the Brezhnev era. People did not believe the authorities, and they frequently turned to editorial staffs as a last resort for help and as a forum in which they could participate. Pressing social issues were often conveyed in letters more sharply than in articles.

THE ANALYTICAL ARTICLE AND THE essay dominated the magazine's style in 1989. The articles were mostly dedicated to Russian history and problems of building a modern state, or paths to democracy in Russia. Some articles about current problems were printed in installments over several issues, like future Yeltsin press-secretary Vyacheslav Kostikov's "The Splendor and Poverty of the Nomenklatura," which was the first article in the Russian press to give a principled criticism of Soviet leadership right before *perestroika,* or like Dmitry Likhanov's "Coma," dedicated to corruption in the higher echelons of Soviet power during the Brezhnev period. Particularly worthy of note was a series by Artyom Borovik about the war in Afghanistan. His description of the Afghan escapade as the "sex act of an impotent" remained a popular saying for many years.

Nina Chugunova and the young journalist and writer Alexander Terekhov, who wrote a series of essays about life in the Russian provinces and Russian nationalism, founded a tradition original to *Ogonyok*—an intermingling of artful prose with sharp analysis that soon became a synonym for journalism in the era of *perestroika.* This story type, having blossomed between 1989–91, slowly started to recede in the years that followed, giving way to controversial exposés and investigative reports on current events. In this sense, *Ogonyok* in 1989 really served as a frontier in the growth of Soviet journalism— from the cryptic writing of the past to the sharpness and directness of the future.

The active participation of specialists on editorial staffs—economists and political scientists, historians and cultural figures—became a norm of journalism in 1989. At *Ogonyok,* just as at other weeklies, public figures served as regular writers. Long, serious articles about the fate of the national economy and culture became commonplace. Discussion of Stalin occupied a central place in the magazine and in journalism of the period in general. Victims of the Terror as well as its participants wrote testimonies about events of the 1930s.

Throughout these discussions, the Communist Party's leadership role was still not subject to debate. *Ogonyok* regularly published reports of plenary sessions of the Central Committee and interviews with party leaders. Even the decision to grant *Ogonyok* independence from the party-affiliated Pravda publishing house was rubber-stamped by the party collective.

Ogonyok published interviews with Western leaders like Margaret Thatcher and Shimon Peres. Several Western experts, like Strobe Talbott, wrote for the magazine. Soviet foreign policy became a topic of muted discussion.

The first free elections to a Soviet parliament and the proceedings of the first Congress of People's Deputies occupied a special place in the press. *Ogonyok* reported broadly on the campaign and the positions of the candidates (among whom were many democratically leaning intellectuals, including Korotich). Special attention was given to the position of deputies personifying the struggle for human rights, including Andrei Sakharov.

A NEW TREND TOOK SHAPE IN THE magazine—investigative journalism, which had pivotal meaning for the profession in subsequent years. *Ogonyok* printed material on corruption and abuse of power in the leadership of the republics, including the famous "Uzbek affair." Once the story about corruption in Uzbekistan was published, talk picked up at the Congress of People's Deputies, and President Mikhail Gorbachev angrily asked Korotich about the article. The editor of *Ogonyok* dramatically presented him with several folders filled with documents about Uzbekistan. The exchange appeared on television in prime time as the entire country watched, glued to their television screens.

The event was without precedent: journalists had demonstrated to the authorities their competence and right to have a say in the country's future. Everything that year was unprecedented. For the first time in Soviet history, all meetings of the Supreme Soviet were broadcast— there were televised debates. People carried transistor radios on subways and buses, listened to the radio at work and discussed the latest speech of one or another candidate. The names of members of "Democratic Russia," intellectuals speaking out for the renewal of the state and the economy, became symbols of the new Russia. The birth of Russian democracy was accompanied by feverish debate. If *Ogonyok* and other democratic weeklies articulated a bold democratic position, then many other publications covered the opposing one. Leningrad Communist Nina Andreeva's letter (actually an article the size of a newspaper page) in *Sovetskaya Rossiya* (*Soviet Russia*), "I cannot forsake my principles," became a hot topic, as she subjected the ideology of *perestroika* to harsh criticism.

Discussion flared over aesthetics, as it used to in the Soviet period, rather than politics. Critics defined 1989 as a "civil war in literature." Democratic publications, such as *Ogonyok* and *Literaturnaya Gazeta* stood against conservative publications such as Literaturnaya Rossiya (*Literary Russia*) and *Moskva* (*Moscow*). *Ogonyok*, which traditionally dedicated a significant part of its space to literature, was at the epicenter of the battle. Debate essentially centered on stylistics, ideological content in contemporary literature and the history of aesthetic thought. Two groups locked horns: the innovators, fighting for art free from ideological onlookers, and adherents to the Soviet aesthetic model. The polemics somewhat recalled the magazine debates during Khrushchev's thaw, when criticism was reminiscent of the 19th-century debate between the Westerners and Slavophiles—itself a thinly veiled discussion of the country's future course.

Ogonyok had almost 5 million subscribers in 1990—a huge circulation even for a country as big as Russia. The year ended accompanied by discussions of the magazine's independence from the Pravda publishing house. It was an event for journalism, a first attempt to seek real independence. Everyone believed in it. No one supposed that later, with the revocation of censorship and the beginning of market reforms, discussions about the dependent status of the press would start up again—only this time about its dependence on the money of its owners. Nevertheless, the introduction of market economics lead to impractically high prices for printing. Consequently, newspapers and magazines became hostages of either the government or powerful private capital.

IN 1989, A RATHER ENERGETIC PERIOD of rethinking old values and structures came to an end, and a new era began—the post-Cold War era, with all its pluses and minuses. Journalism ceased to be an art and became more of an information service. Analysis gravitated toward irony, which was unknown to *perestroika*'s romantic enthusiasm. The artistic essay gave way to investigative and cutting-edge reporting. More blood flowed through the articles, more shots rang out and more bribe money exchanged hands. Television acquired greater significance and became the main source of information, crowding out print media, creating a new subculture and forging its own relationship with the viewer.

Many of the high points of 1989 are almost forgotten today. It's a pity—for the perfection of the essays in *Ogonyok*, for the romantic tone in reporting, which all writers believed in and were nourished by. It was a first taste of freedom, a first enchantment with an independent press—or at least a dash for independence. We believed in a common cause, in the right of the talented, in the right of the citizen. Today, when journalists write *zakazukha*, or "commissioned articles" paid for under the table by politicians or oligarchs, these values are somewhat lost.

In the wake of liberating weeklies such as *Ogonyok*, the contemporary Russian press is like a freed serf. It is less fettered, and becoming harsher and more ironic by the day. One can even condescendingly speak now about the costs and problems of democracy in Russia. Of course, investigative journalism is evolving (and very successfully). A new generation of reporters and analysts has grown up—but the best writers, strange as it may seem, worked in their youth at the weeklies of the *perestroika* era.

Today's readers look at the Russian press with a more discriminating and critical eye. Censorship has disappeared, and newspapers and magazines (beginning with *Ogonyok*) that received the right to be self-directed have begun to live independent lives for the first time. There were an incredible number of them in 1991—dozens, perhaps hundreds of new publications appeared, and the weeklies did not play as serious a role. The central discussion in journalism shifted to the daily newspapers. The weeklies' analysis gave way to the reporting and cutting-edge investigative material of the newspapers. The artistic essay (or the "*Ogonyok* essay"), as it was called, receded into journalistic history and was replaced by the sensationalized article. Newspapers and magazines in general were read less—television swiftly began to gather strength and weight.

The quality of newspaper and magazine content in the '90s also changed significantly: journalism almost ceased to be a literary endeavor as the style became more telegraphic. Not only youth but also criminal slang became routine. Articles about culture receded into the background, with primary attention being given to uncovering contemporary life. It is telling that after 1990 many publications ceased to actively discuss Stalinism and concentrated much more on current events. New names appeared in journalism—and new boundaries for harsh criticism. Advertising appeared, and as a result of an underdeveloped market, so did *zakazukha* articles—a form of hidden advertising.

The mass media, having lost their dependence on ideology, almost immediately became dependent on prominent capital and began to talk about it. Journalists, who formerly had comprised a rather homogeneous group, were divisible into rich and poor, depending on their place of work. Privately operated entertainment publications appeared. Large-scale victimization of journalists began, especially authors of investigative articles; the first journalists died in the course of raging ethnopolitical conflicts in the ruins of the Soviet empire. Journalism began to develop in newly independent states. Journalists became cynical, and not a trace remained of the romantic expectation of a new Russian heaven. Readers no longer wrote hundreds of thousands of letters to editors and almost stopped responding to articles and asking for help in general. Institutions of civil society became active, although they did not always function effectively.

THE FATE OF OUR "TEAM" IS interesting. Very different people worked at *Ogonyok* in 1989—graduates of Party publications and independent men of letters, *samizdat* authors and journalists from *Komsomol* (Communist Youth League) newspapers. Some were already 50 years old and some had not yet reached 30. I would particularly like to talk about my peers, who were approaching 30 at that time. We began our professional work in the Soviet period, we grew up during "stagnation" in an atmosphere of total hypocrisy and, upon entering *perestroika*, acquired our first life experience without becoming disillusioned. This was very important. It's no accident that many of us, one way or another, found our niche in the profession, having tasted that vivifying air of freedom (although not everyone did). Nina Chugunova left serious journalism, and today works for a fashion magazine. Terekhov, who published several books of prose, works in the publishing house Sovershenno sekretno (Top Secret), which Artyom Borovik heads. Likhanov started the magazine *Nyanya* (*Nanny*), about bringing up children. Alexander Golovkov went into business, like many other colleagues from the magazine. Still another bright writer from 1989, Vladimir Vigilyansky, became an Orthodox priest at the Cathedral of St. Tatyana, not far from Moscow State University. Valentin Yumashev wrote two books with Boris Yeltsin, became head of the Administration of the President of the Russian Federation and presently serves as a presidential advisor. In his work for the acclaimed television show "Kukly," Viktor Shenderovich treats Russian political life with irony. Vitaly Korotich taught in the United States for several years (after 1991) and currently lives in Russia and in Ukraine. He publishes a new Ukrainian popular magazine, *Bulvar* (*Boulevard*), which features sensations, social news and lots of pretty girls in bathing suits—all in the spirit of contemporary journalism after the great enthusiasm of 1989.

Today, 10 years later, leafing through the old collections of once celebrated weeklies, it's difficult not to be surprised by the swiftness of *perestroika*'s changes. After being a servant to the Soviet system, journalism's victories were great—becoming a real Fourth Estate and creating a new ideology for democratic development. It is striking how quickly the consciousness of such a huge country changed. How a new generation of journalists grew, inspired by their first taste of freedom. How people's souls were liberated, after growing up in a country without freedom. A golden time of enthusiasm and hopes, 1989 played a great role in the fate of the professionals of my generation, the generation that grew up in the Soviet period and at the very beginning of the journalist's track and ended up in the thick of discussions of *perestroika*, when they could utter their first free words.

For all of us 1989 was a taste of freedom, a conscious choice of freedom, which would define our lives henceforth. And contemporary journalism owes its existence to the rush and enthusiasm of 1989, which destroyed the invisible Berlin Wall in people's souls.

Ten years later, one can see that several of the principles of that period are returning to the profession: a new interest in the essay is appearing; many publications have rejected their proclivity for slang and begun once again to write in a pure literary language; interest in the analytical article has awoken again, addressing problems of history, economics and culture. The last decade has shown that there is still more to learn and to evaluate, and that time is needed to see without anger or bias the ground we have traversed.

Nadezhda Azhgikhina, an analyst at Nezavisimaya Gazeta (The Independent Gazette), *teaches creative journalism at Moscow State University. From 1989 to 1995 she worked at* Ogonyok. *Translated by Eric Ros*ton.

6

From Hellholes with Love

Insurgent journalism from Poland to Priština

Interview with Anna Husarska

MSJ: *you grew up in communist Poland wanting to be a journalist or a film director. Back then what did you think it meant to be a journalist?*

Anna Husarska: As a kid I imagined that being a journalist would be like writing letters to my mommy and publishing them. And I am still trying to do that.

MSJ: *Instead, you started by working as a translator.*

Husarska: I thought that it was a less compromising profession. I became a journalist by becoming a foreign journalist. This was one way to avoid being a propagandist for Communists and still be a reporter. Not that I didn't step into a different mine field, mind you. I made my debut in the *Buenos Aires Herald*, an Argentine English-language paper. Before and during the Falklands War, it was often targeted by the military regime. I guess it is my destiny to be in such predicaments. And to think I went to Buenos Aires to become a housewife. What a failed project this was!

MSJ: *Then in the late '80s you worked for Solidarity in Paris and New York—how did that shape your journalism?*

Husarska: I happened to be in Paris when martial law was declared in Poland, and automatically I drifted towards the Solidarity activists from Poland who were stranded in Paris. I soon started in the Paris bureau of Solidarity, known as the "information bureau abroad." All the underground press from Poland was sent to us—and a great lot managed to be sent considering the conditions of operating under martial law. Our task was to make a selection of texts from different sources and put together a bulletin, something that would be both interesting and informative.

At that point I had lived for five years in the West; I spoke fluent French and I knew the local political scene in France, and this was knowledge very much needed for our Solidarity bureau. I did translations and acted as a bridge between Solidarity—which needed to inform and generally operate in a new Western environment—and the people in the West who wanted to learn about Solidarity and support it but lacked the necessary data. I was a journalistic matchmaker, if you want.

MSJ: *What sort of things did you put in the Solidarity bulletin? Was it public relations or straight news?*

Husarska: A little bit of both. We tried to be informative and engaging but not pompous or boring—you see, many national liberation movements tend to be boring to tears. For instance, one thing would be to say "please, please, please contribute some money to support Solidarity—here is the account number." Another was running a little paragraph about one of the workers fired from his job for union activities and put in jail. And then we would say, "By the way we are in contact with his wife, and they have two boys, ages 7 and 9. And if anyone in France has boys a little older why don't you send some hand-me-downs to the Polish boys. And if you want to write a letter, we will translate it and then deliver it and will try to get you an answer."

We got a great response because people react better to concrete things, to individual faces that you give to the suffering. People may not react to the thousands of miseries of humanity, but then they will react emotionally to the concrete misery of one human being.

MSJ: *Have you brought that idea to your reporting today?*

Husarska: I guess so. I try to be concrete and am mostly interested in introducing to my readers the unrich and unfamous, because they are the majority.

MSJ: *What was it about the role of journalism and writing in Solidarity that was distinct in creating civil society in Poland?*

Husarska: Oh, everything. The media and especially the print media were Solidarity, in my opinion. All right, Solidarity was a trade union and the workers had demands and the intellectuals supported the workers, but the civil society in Poland was built through the underground press.

Almost everybody was involved in either the writing or the printing or the distributing or the transporting or even the producing of the ink—whatever. Every single profession was potentially useful. Everyone felt involved.

We had several hundred different publications, from thick literary magazines to leaflets about miners struggling for healthy working conditions in the mine shafts. And sometimes, you know, those local bulletins were not saying much new. They were mostly repeating what the central clandestine media said, but they felt that they had a voice and this was incredibly important to them, to be a subject and not the object of politics, to be empowered. "Paper munitions" we called those underground publications.

MSJ: *In '89 you worked for* Gazeta Wyborcza, *and you reported from Poland and Czechoslovakia, Romania, the USSR and other places. What were your best hopes and your worst fears for Eastern Europe that year when you saw everything changing around you?*

Husarska: My best hope was that everything was going to go as smoothly as it went in Poland. Solidarity was an extremely media-friendly and very manual-like case of a buildup of civil society. In fact the whole Solidarity movement, that marvelous carnival of dissent, was exemplary. It was a great opportunity to learn how to do it the right way. But on the other hand, it raises the stakes for someone who lived through Solidarity—nothing else is ever going to be good enough. It is almost a problem to have lived your first big revolution on the high note because everything that comes afterward is less wonderful; the people are less engaging. You see, the Polish revolution in '89 brought the best out of people because it was the atmosphere of ultimate confrontation. I saw the same repeat itself among the Sarajevans when Sarajevo was under siege. But extreme conditions like these do not last forever.

MSJ: *Did this carnival of dissent convince you to return to Poland?*

Husarska: And how! At the time I was in the States, working at the once-Menshevik magazine *The New Leader*, and I was quite happily starting to write for some major U.S. media.

I went to Poland in April '89, and I stayed through the elections—
the first almost free elections since the Communists grabbed power.
Then I went back to the States, but I could not stay there—what was
happening in Poland was just too exciting to miss.

I waited for just a little bit because I had a long essay about the
underground press coming out in *The New York Times Book Review* in
October. Afterward, taking advantage of this one week of name recognition, I approached *The New Republic*. I was lucky: the literary editor, Leon Wieseltier, had read my essay and liked it. He and the editor,
Rick Hertzberg, took me to lunch before I went back to Poland, and
this is how I made my first step towards an assignment. Leon agreed
to take collect calls from me if I happened to be in some shithole that
was journalistically hot. Do not forget, this was 1989, and everyplace
in Eastern Europe was hot! I was soon making collect calls from
Bucharest and Timişoara.

MSJ: *You travel very light and you travel very fast and you report
from the bottom up. Did you develop this style around '89?*

Husarska: Of course. *The New Republic* was not picking up any
expenses, and *Gazeta* didn't have the money to pay for my trips beyond the very basic, or else they would be very short and rare foreign
assignments. So it was a survival technique of sorts. Either I travel
light and cheap or I do not travel. I never stay at fancy hotels unless I
have to; I avoid those media beehives. I broke this rule twice, both
under pressure from the local state security: In Baghdad I stayed at Al
Rasheed, and in Algeria two plainclothes with machine guns simply
drove me to Hôtel El Djazair. The third place where I did it was
Sarajevo. But I was doing a story for *The New Yorker* on the Holiday
Inn and the media coverage of Bosnia so I had to stay at the Holiday
Inn. Otherwise I always try to stay with the local people and live their
lives and their problems with them as much as possible. From every
shithole that I report on I come with a load of newfound friends. It's
from them that I get my local knowledge.

MSJ: *Do you worry that by doing it you lose a sense of detachment or
distance?*

Husarska: I don't believe in detachment. Why should I have detachment? I am trying to reduce the distance. I am not Christopher
Isherwood, "a camera ... passive, recording not thinking."

MSJ: *Your reporting is crammed with facts, crammed with firsthand
impressions. Are you suspicious about generalizations and theories?*

Husarska: Yes.

MSJ: *Is that part of growing up under communism?*

Husarska: Now that is a daring conclusion, isn't it? But I guess you are right. I also think that it is better to make the reader come to the conclusion on his own. Generalizations don't go down as well with the reader. When people come to the conclusion by themselves they adopt it. They think it is their idea.

All I ask the reader is to connect the dots, but because he connected the dots he thinks he did the drawing.

MSJ: *You go to all sorts of trouble spots—what do you hope that your reporting is going to accomplish?*

Husarska: Just get the story that nobody else is getting. This is probably the dream of every journalist, but most journalists want a scoop. I simply want to cover what others do not. And the fact that I travel light and cheap turns out to be a blessing of sorts.

Take for instance 1989: I went to Romania in December that year with, as sole preparation, a letter of introduction to the commercial representative in Romania of the Polish locomotive exporter, Kolmex. They had their branch in Bucharest, and I thought this would get me somewhere. Perhaps not the most obvious contact to have as the Romanians were about to execute their dictator, but better locomotives than nothing at all, right?

So while almost all the foreign journalists were housed at the Intercontinental Hotel in Bucharest, I went to stay in an unheated room of this commercial locomotive factory office in Bucharest. Plus I had an additional problem: everything that I had was stolen from me on the day that Ceaușescu was killed. I had to use the subway instead of taxis. But thanks to this I got to know the students' movement—much of it was physically operating in the subway.

There was a whole lot of literally underground life happening there, but you would never suspect it if you operated on the surface. My unheated apartment provided me with an insight to the basic survival problems of Romanian society—not the problems of the rulers or of the leaders of the opposition but of the man on the street. I had very little money on me the day my luggage was stolen so there was no question of paying a translator; all I could do was try to learn the language. I watched a lot of television in the evenings: they were showing a series, a Polish love story called "Days and Nights," and it was like a private video tutoring for me: I would listen to the Polish and read the Romanian subtitles. Soon I was ready for romantic encounters with Romanian speakers!

In two months I learned quite reasonable Romanian. I was buying a Romanian newspaper every day and listening to the BBC, so I would then compare what I heard to what the Romanian newspapers were printing. I would thus supplement the romantic vocabulary from the series with the political vocabulary from the newspapers and the BBC. This very limited knowledge of Romanian often got me a few checkpoints further than my colleagues.

Later in Croatia and Bosnia, I rather shamelessly traded my knowledge of Serbo-Croatian for a seat in an armored car or access to a satellite phone. I am now learning Albanian, which is so difficult and rare that I could probably trade it for an entire armored train!

MSJ: *What is the scariest situation you have been in?*

Husarska: I can't really think of anything very scary. I often get detained by the state police, be it uniformed or plainclothes, in the rogue countries that I tend to visit. I was detained several times by the Bosnian Serbs for instance. I got expelled from a few countries, most recently Burma, and I once spent a week in detention in the Ministry of Interior of a country that I prefer not to name. And after one op-ed I wrote, I got a letter inviting me to the U.S. National Security Council. Now, having been raised in a country where the word "security" never promises anything pleasant, I did not feel very encouraged, but it went all right.

All the rest of my contacts with "security" other than U.S. were rather unpleasant, but none of it was really scary. Afghanistan and Kashmir were dodgy, especially because women reporters were uncommon there and I do not speak the local languages. But the odds of getting hit by a Scud missile in Israel during the Gulf War were so small that it never really concerned me.

I am more afraid of the unknown. Flying into Mogadishu in November 1992 without knowing what I would find there was very unsettling. But once on the ground, pulling my carry-on bag across the tarmac, I felt rather excited. In El Salvador, Nicaragua and Guatemala there were a lot of people with Kalashnikovs around, but I am fluent in Spanish so I knew (well, I hoped) that I would have a chance to talk myself out of trouble.

I guess the most scary time was my first night in Sarajevo under siege. There was a thunderstorm, a really very, very heavy thunderstorm. And I was very inexperienced with heavy artillery, even with lighter stuff. I could not tell the incoming from the outgoing mortars. I thought that all those thunderclaps were incoming artillery. As far as I was concerned, this was going to be the end of the world. Or of me. Later I learned that this was all just a thunderstorm, that it had nothing to do with enemy fire. Again, it was ignorance of what was happening.

MSJ: *You write in five languages. Are you a different writer in each?*

Husarska: Yes, I think so.

MSJ: *How so?*

Husarska: Each language imposes its discipline. I feel most comfortable writing in English, translating into Spanish (I translated several books and theater plays) and speaking Polish and English, but also French because I did my university studies in Paris.

MSJ: *What is it about writing in English that works for you?*

Husarska: I think that there is something very attractive in its compactness. And then there is the semicolon; gosh, I love the semicolon.

MSJ: You translated into Polish the collected essays of George Orwell. Has his writing had an impact on the way you write?

Husarska: Hell it has! Translating him was like being in a literary boot camp with him. It was like dissecting his prose, and I enjoyed every bit of it—his political essays, his straightforwardness whether he was writing about Shakespeare, the Soviet Union, the common toad, about his time at a British public school or about politics and the English language.

I especially admire and try to apply his philosophy, that you do not need to like the people in whose defense you stand. His column, "As I Please," in the *London Tribune*, was a wonderful example of how much a writer can achieve by using simple common sense and plain language. I try to imitate him, and before turning in any piece I have written, I give it an "Orwell read" and eliminate all the pretentious or boring words. Plus I check my pieces for political decency, if you see what I mean.

MSJ: *You have written strongly against all sorts of dictators and despots, but I am curious, is there any kind of set of principles that you are for, that you try to affirm in your work? George Orwell said that he wrote for "democratic socialism." Is there any set of guidelines like that for you?*

Husarska: I don't know because those labels are losing much of their sense. Let us just agree that I am writing with an agenda, and this agenda is that through my writing I want to call attention to certain problems and to perhaps spur or shame some people in positions of power to do something to stop abuses and atrocities.

But it becomes more and more difficult to write about subjects that have no drama and no glitz. There is only so much that the readers want to hear about the unrich and unfamous. Yes, on one conflict— that season's conflict—there would be plenty, but an in-depth analysis of an "other" conflict with a lot of foreign names is almost impossible to sell anywhere.

There are still some excellent and at the same time privileged spaces that accept outside contributions such as the op-ed pages of the *International Herald Tribune* and the *Los Angeles Times*, the "Outlook" section of *The Washington Post* or my own *New Republic*. But as you know, the coverage of foreign news is generally shrinking in the United States, and the coverage of unpleasant foreign stories is shrinking even more.

If I had someone who wanted to send me, I would be in Teheran today probably, or in East Timor. Or in Kashmir. But I want even more eagerly to go to Belarus or Libya or Cuba—in fact I am trying to secure assignments for all three places.

MSJ: *Tell me why you went to work for the International Crisis Group.*
Husarska: Well, there you go. I was having problems getting assignments for stories that were not yet the Stories with capital S. Plus I thought that I wasn't having much impact by simply writing op-eds. I was getting very, very good exposure with reports that were printed in *The New Republic* and with the op-eds that I was writing. But apart from perhaps spoiling the breakfast of President Clinton every now and then, I was a lonely squeak in the wilderness.

I knew about ICG ever since its foundation in 1995. It was inspired by former ambassador Mort Abramowitz and the late Fred Cuny, the maverick humanitarian worker who disappeared in Chechnya in 1995. It is, as its charter says, a multinational nongovernmental organization aimed at heading off crises before they develop into full-blown disasters. We, the political analysts at ICG, write reports that help focus the attention of governments, international organizations on humanmade crises. Think of those reports as super extra long op-eds.

We made a great difference in Bosnia, although it was already saturated by NGOs, because our presence brought this added value of speaking plainly and expertly and giving practical and concrete recommendations.

I lived for three years in Bosnia, but then I drifted towards Kosovo. In 1997, I was mostly working in Kosovo and on Kosovo. When the first clashes between the Serb Army and the Kosovo Liberation Army erupted, I had already written a 150-page report called *Kosovo Spring* that was a kind of "everything you never expected to know about the political situation in a forgotten land." I know it has been extensively used by journalists, governments and all those who were working in and on Kosovo.

MSJ: *In Kosovo, how good a job does the U.S. press do of putting these policy options before the American people?*

Husarska: The media did the best that they could, but Clinton was not reacting. Yes, in the end, the United States intervened both in Bosnia and in Kosovo, but a lot of people in both places were killed while Clinton was ducking the responsibility. He had himself recently acknowledged that he oversimplified his vision of the Balkans. Unless a story hits page one, he can duck it, and he tends to do exactly that. And it hits page one only when there is plenty of blood and plenty of footage of that blood. A little blood or blood that was not filmed won't do.

MSJ: *I was reading a review that you wrote about two books of photographs from the time of the Holocaust. You said that they were compelling because of their understatement. Is one of the problems of international news today that it is all visual and it is all overstatement and people get burned out?*

Husarska: Yes. And the other big problem that I see is in American television. The same pool images get used so very differently on the two sides on the Atlantic. I often watched what British TV and American TV would do with the same footage. American editors would crop the piece very tightly. Anything that was not bloody or dramatic was often cut out—clip, clip, clip—so only the bloody body, the skull and the charred ribs would be left.

The same footage in British TV would let the camera linger on, just showing you a little bit of something else. The result was not diminishing but increasing the drama. After being knocked in your face with the skull and the blood and the charred ribs, the British viewer has the time to think "Bloody hell, this could have been *my* mother," or "Oh my, my little sister wore a red dress like that on holidays."

You need this extra time to digest the atrocity, so that it gets into your system. If the images are cropped so tightly that only the most atrocious parts remain, the editors are effectively raising the barrier of bloodiness. The result is that terrible things never get into the media because they aren't visually bloody enough.

MSJ: *But the struggles of Solidarity weren't bloody, and they were covered in the American media.*

Husarska: Precisely. That was then, years ago. Nowadays things like civil society activities or other nonviolent forms of dissidence have little chance to make it to the TV screens or newspaper headlines. This is partly what happened over the last 10 years with opposition in Kosovo—it never managed to really get the international media on its side. But don't get me on this subject; it is for a thick book.

If I may go back to your previous question: I have seen what impact the incredibly media-friendly approach of Polish dissidents had on the attitudes and behaviors of politicians around the world. It made me believe that if a movement or a people know how to gain the media's support they may more easily achieve their goals.

MSJ: *Is this also the legacy of 1989 for you?*

Husarska: Yes, certainly. I started believing in miracles because I reported or lived through Czechoslovakia, Poland, Romania and the Baltic States. For the same reason, I was one of the few journalists in Managua, Nicaragua, to predict the electoral defeat of the Sandinistas in February 1990. I knew something about the Sandinistas, but in political miracles I was an expert.

MSJ: *Ten years have passed since the events in 1989. When you look at Serbia and the democratic opposition there, do you see any possibility of a kind of repeat of what you saw in 1989 in Poland?*

Husarska: Yes, some things could be done. The *anciens combattants* from Eastern Europe are so accomplished and so eager to teach others that it is contagious. It is important to see what tactics can be revived from Poland and the events of 1989, what we can expect to repeat and what has to be done from scratch. You remember how French families contributed clothing for the children of Solidarity activists who were in jail? Today Polish families are helping children of Belarus dissidents spend summer holidays away from an oppressive state, and are thus helping the dissidents.

The spirit of 1989 should be remembered and recalled in order to make other miracles possible.

MSJ: *What was the spirit of 1989?*

Husarska: The fact that everything is possible if we just want to put our imagination to it. The Wall can fall, Ceauşescu can be gone. In 1989, everything was possible. *Annus mirabilis.*

Anna Husarska, a 1998–99 Media Studies Center fellow, is a special correspondent for The New Republic. *Robert W. Snyder interviewed her for* Media Studies Journal.

Part 2

MEDIA SYSTEMS

What we see in many postcommunist countries generally are not "emerging," but at best latent, markets and democracies.
—*KAROL JAKUBOWICZ*

7

The Genie Is Out of the Bottle

Measuring media change in Central and Eastern Europe

Karol Jakubowicz

IT WAS ONCE ASSUMED THAT THE transition to democracy and a market economy would happen in Central and Eastern European countries quite naturally, and that this would be accompanied by the "Westification," as some have called it, or "Europeanization" of their media systems. By the time Central European countries are serious candidates for the European Union, Owen Johnson, an American media scholar, predicted in the early 1990s, "their media systems will be virtually indistinguishable from those of today's Western Europe." And when Marius Lukosiunas of Vilnius University in Lithuania recently considered "Is the Transition Over?" his answer was affirmative: in the Baltic countries the media are capable of applying Western journalistic practices and of integrating seamlessly with Western media. The downside, adds Lukosiunas, is such phenomena as yellow journalism, deteriorating ethical standards, and the impact of big money on reporting.

However, the media transition is far from over in Russia. There, according to Sergey Kovalev, the prominent human rights activist, the media are "free but not independent." In part, this is because most of them serve the interests of the "oligarchs"—people like Boris Berezovsky, Vladimir Gusinsky and Vladimir Potanin—who have added considerable media assets to their powerful financial-industrial groups. When they do not, their situation is like that of the Crimean newspaper whose editor once asked me: "We want to be independent, so we take no money either from the government, or from any political party, business or the Mafia. How can we make a profit?" Since the paper is not even sold for a fixed price (on the cover, it says "Price: negotiable"), I had no answer to his question.

The optimistic view hardly applies to Azerbaijan either. The 1998 U.S. State Department Report on Human Rights Practices notes that though military censorship has been lifted in that country, censorship of political topics continues. The Ministry of Information can legally close a newspaper for one month for violating censorship rules. And of course, the "transition" is very far from over in some post-Yugoslav countries, where nationalism and chauvinism have made a mockery of media freedom and impartiality.

What we see in many postcommunist countries generally are not "emerging," but at best latent, markets and democracies. We know now that there is nothing preordained about the direction, pace or ultimate result of change in postcommunist countries and their media, and that Western-style capitalism or media systems cannot be simply transplanted to Eastern Europe. Indeed, some are pointing to the emergence of "an indigenous Russian (Eurasian?) media system" with many features quite unlike those of Western ones.

Still, it is far too early to pass final judgment on the success or failure of any aspect of postcommunist transformation. Zbigniew Brzezinski, the Polish-American political scientist and former national security adviser for President Jimmy Carter, has warned that the transition out of communism might last as long as the communist regime itself did. In Central Europe that was nearly 50 years; in the countries of the former Soviet Union, up to 80—and we are now only into the 11th year of transition.

GIVEN THE LONG-TERM NATURE OF the process, it is important to develop criteria by which to judge change in the media of particular Central and Eastern European countries. For example, the current situation is often measured against the plans of the 1980s dissidents whose goal was the far-reaching democratization of social communication. Their objectives amounted to the communicative empowerment of civil society, a guarantee of justice and equality in communication for all.

Everyone would have access to the media and participate in running the media. Since these goals are far from realized, the transition is pronounced a failure—even though the objectives were hardly realistic from the start.

Another set of criteria can be developed by checking whether the media systems of postcommunist countries, long frozen into the centralized command structure, are now replicating the same processes that meanwhile have been unfolding in developed Western countries. On the one hand, these involve media decentralization and specialization; demonopolization and deregulation of the broadcast media. On the other, there has been commercialization of private, and partly also public broadcast media, by subjecting the latter to market mechanisms and the increasing role of advertising in financing them; concentration of ownership at the national and international levels; and internationalization of content (especially in television and film) and in many cases of ownership, as well as of the scale of operation. Of course, technological change has also been a major factor in reshaping the media scene in Western Europe.

These processes can be aligned to produce very different media systems. As we look for evidence of these changes, we could especially note the progress of those that are indispensable for the development of media systems qualitatively different from those of communist times.

For this to happen, media monopoly must be eliminated, and the media must be liberalized and gain autonomy. Development of public service broadcasting and decentralization of the media system are indispensable aspects of this process, as is at least a degree of democratization. What also needs to happen is the professionalization of journalists, the redefinition of their professional identity from disseminators of propaganda to providers of competently collected and written information and non-partisan, impartial and neutral interpreters of social reality.

Given the long-term nature of this process, we should perhaps in some cases apply the criterion of last resort: can the process of change—however slow and halting—be reversed? Can totalitarianism be reintroduced in postcommunist countries?

No medium is an island. At a time of fast change, the media can ride the crest of great transformations, serving as a battering ram to accelerate the demise of a system as it collapses or is overthrown. At other times, however, the prospects of the media depend largely on the social, political and economic context within which they operate. Democracy, it is argued, cannot take root in conditions of economic decline. As we will see, media independence, too, is difficult to achieve in such circumstances. But even given a favorable political and economic context (and this is rare enough), we must remember that change in Central and Eastern Europe is also "cultural." Without the emergence of the political culture of democracy and civil society (including acceptance of the rule of laws and procedures of democracy and market economy) and a different value system (individual freedom instead of collectivism, human rights and civil liberties instead of respect for authority, citizenship instead of submission to authoritarianism), change elsewhere will be incomplete. And it is this cultural change, a change of social consciousness, that takes a particularly long time.

IN ALL SOCIETIES, "POLITICAL CULTURE" emerges only when the political system has achieved long-term stability, democracy has become consolidated, a degree of social consensus on major issues has been achieved—and when, by trial and error, all other alternatives to political culture have been tried and found ultimately unproductive. It is this trial-and-error period that postcommunist countries are going through today. A lot of time is also needed for public opinion and the electorate to gain enough confidence to insist that politicians and officials observe those norms and rules, including respect for media independence and impartiality, and to punish them at the ballot box when they do not.

Table 1			
Processes of media change as determined by change in key areas of social life			
Depending on political factors, the media can:	Politics, economy determine whether the media can:	Economy, market mechanism favor or hinder:	"Cultural change" is required for:
Be liberalized	Gain autonomy	Abolition of media monopoly	Depoliticization of media
Become pluralistic and open	Decentralize	Commercialization	Rule of law
Be deregulated	Diversify in content	Concentration	Ability to define and serve the public interest
Promote professionalization of journalists	Address minority groups	Globalization	Role for public opinion
	Internationalization		The media to serve as impartial watchdogs

A Council of Europe expert has told me of meeting the same Albanian politician on three successive trips to that country over a number of years to advise on the development of a broadcasting act. First the politician was in government, then in the opposition and then again in the government. On the third occasion, he said: "This time, I will try to write a law that will serve me well when I am out of power once again." At the societal level, many more experiences of this nature must be amassed and thought through over a considerable period of time for the political culture of democracy to take root.

Table 1 shows the main elements of change in the media, as affected by the complex and intertwined process of change in general. It is a way to develop criteria to apply in analyzing the situation in Central and Eastern European countries.

In the October 29, 1994, *Polityka*, Brzezinski distinguished three major stages of postcommunist transformation. In Table 2, they are shown in the left column—I would add to them only, in the breakthrough phase, the economic goal of stabilizing an economy in crisis. The right column presents some of the main processes of media transformation, identified by the present author, roughly corresponding to the particular stage of transition. Naturally, this presents a simplified and schematic view of the succession of processes and events, which need not have happened in each country in the same way or order.

The record on processes of change needed to produce a qualitatively new media system is decidedly mixed. While lip service may be paid to media liberalization everywhere, the growth of genuine autonomy for the media (their disentanglement from state and political structures, combined with financial viability as an underpinning of independence) often runs into difficulties. In Belarus and Ukraine, for example, state agencies and politicians are prominent among the owners of the print and private broadcast media. Public service broadcasting, where it has been nominally created, is usually "parliamentary broadcasting": the role of parliament in appointing broadcasting regulatory and supervisory bodies is so strong that "public" broadcasters do not really represent the public, but the parliamentary majority. In Hungary, ruling and opposition parties are directly represented in the governing bodies of public radio and television organizations, making them a pawn in their political battles. In any case, public service broadcasting can hardly develop fully where civil society is weak, politicians are pre-eminent in public life and any notion of the public interest and public service is overshadowed by political interests.

Table 2
Media change at different stations of postcommunist transformation

Stage 1 (1-5 years):
The Breakthrough

Society in General	The Media
Political Goal: Transformation—Introduction of the basics of democracy, a free press, an end to the one-party system, development of an early coalition oriented to promoting change;	1. Dismantling of some of the main controls characteristic of the old media system;
	2. Demonopolization of the printed press; early signs of commercialization;
Economic Goal: Stabilization of an economy in crisis. Elimination of price controls and of subsidies; end of collectivization; early, haphazard privatization;	3. Beginning of decentralization and specialization (especially of the print media);
Legal Regulation: Elimination of arbitrary state control over all areas of life.	4. Rapid internationalization of content (especially film and commercial television).

Stage 2 (3-10 years):
Change Takes Hold

Political Goal: From transformation to stabilization—new constitution and electoral law, elections, decentralized local government, stable democratic coalition, new political elite;	1. Adoption of the first laws creating the legal framework of press freedom, including some basic elements of democratization;
	2. Continued commercialization;
Economic Goal: From stabilization to transformation—banking system, small- and medium-scale privatization, demonopolization, emergence of a new business class;	3. Continued decentralization and specialization (extending also into the electronic media, as private stations begin to look for market niches);
	4. Early signs of journalist professionalization in a few successful independent private media;
Legal Regulation: Legal regulation of ownership and business.	5. Elements of globalization as foreign capital moves into the printed press and broadcast media;
	6. First signs of media concentration.

Stage 3 (3-15 or more years):
Emergence of a Stable Democratic Order

Political Goal: Consolidation—emergence of stable political parties; a democratic political culture takes root;	1. Continued development of the legal framework in order to create legal and institutional guarantees of media autonomy and regulate the economic aspects of the media market; and to accommodate the requirements of international organizations such as the European Union;
Economic Goal: Steady economic growth—mass privatization, emergence of a capitalist lobby and of a culture of private enterprise;	2. Momentum for media autonomy and professionalization of journalists;
Legal Regulation: Emergence of an independent judiciary and legal culture.	3. Media concentration and globalization threaten to subvert gains achieved in media emancipation;
	4. Technological changes (such as digital TV and convergence) begin to reshape the media market.

Also, market conditions may bolster or undercut media independence. Poland's daily *Gazeta Wyborcza*—the centerpiece of a budding
media empire, encompassing radio stations and television interests—is
hugely successful in both journalistic and business terms. When it
recently rewarded its founders and several dozen of its senior person-
nel with stock options, it suddenly created a crop of millionaires (in
U.S. dollars). Where there are only "latent" markets that generate little
advertising, as in the entire former Soviet Union, the breakup of mo-
nopolistic media systems is impeded. This is especially true for broadcasting. In such conditions, the media are subsidized by the state. The
journalists receive, in addition to their salaries, kickbacks from whoever is willing to pay for their services. As Andrei Zolotov Jr. noted in
Moscow Times in March 1999, "Patronage is still seen by many media
firms as being of much more importance than advertising or circulation as the basis for a viable operation...." In 1997, prices for *zakazukha*
(newspaper stories written to order) ranged from $2,500 for two type-
written pages in *Izvestiya* (*News*) to $300 per one page in *Vechernaya
Moskva* (*Moscow Evening*). During the 1998 election to the St. Petersburg Legislative Assembly, a newspaper article cost a candidate from
$30 to $100, depending on the journalist's stature.

This speaks volumes on the prospects—at least in the short term—
for genuine journalistic independence and professionalization in Russia. Disentanglement from political structures is difficult where journalists' corruption, or sincerely intended political involvement, makes
a mockery of any existing legal and institutional safeguards of media
independence and impartiality. In Poland, it has been pointed out by
Jacek.
Żakowski, himself a noted commentator, that the "civic attitude" of
journalists—who believe that as individuals and as a professional group
they have a personal responsibility for the country's future—has resulted in a situation where "the Polish press market has become dominated by politically affiliated journalism masquerading as objective."
In Romania, as Mikhail Coman, a media researcher has put it, "combative, militant journalism concentrated on ideological issues and a
discursive discussion of opinions that combined news with comment
and paid scant regard to objectivity. Consequently, the younger journalists became very much like their older colleagues and dedicated
their services to propaganda."

EVERYWHERE, THE VIEW OF JOURNALISM as politics conducted by other means dies hard. Hence the comment of Yuri Vdovin, vice chair of Citizens' Watch in St. Petersburg, on Russian journalists: "Being involved for decades in propaganda and agitation, in brain-washing and forming public opinion on orders from rulers of totalitarian states, they cannot get rid of their Messianism even when free of communist dictate. . . . Messianic feelings brought on by 70 years of experience of Soviet journalism have today resulted in overstating the significance of the rights of a journalist to present his own judgement at the expense of accurate facts."

Poland's *Gazeta Wyborcza* has been known to topple a cabinet minister or two when they were guilty of corruption or other offenses. Public radio and television in Poland enjoys almost watertight legal protection against outside interference from the government, parliament, president or anyone else. On the other hand, Central Asian countries theoretically allow free media—but make it very difficult for them to practice their trade. For example, they deal with television stations that do not conform to the authorities' wishes by imposing punitive taxes on their nonexistent advertising revenue. While the stations typically retransmit somebody else's programming and do not get a penny for the advertising included in that programming, they are still taxed as if they did.

Libel law is greatly in vogue everywhere as a means of bringing pressure to bear on journalists who do not show enough respect for politicians. The independence of the judiciary can be a barrier to abuse of this method, but of course that in itself can only be possible in a democracy.

IN VIEW OF THIS STATE OF AFFAIRS, what are the prospects for the future? In 1994, Brzezinski believed that only five of the 27 postcommunist countries could have any realistic degree of certainty that they would become politically and economically successful liberal democracies.

In 1996, Charles Gati, an American author, divided postcommunist countries into three groups:

1. The seven "leaders": the Czech Republic, Poland, Hungary, Slovenia, Estonia, Latvia and Lithuania;
2. The 12 "laggards": the semiauthoritarian regimes of Slovakia, Albania, Bulgaria, Romania, Croatia, Serbia, Bosnia and Herzegovina, Macedonia, Russia, Ukraine, Moldova and Belarus, where leaders reluctantly pur-

sue modest market reforms, tolerate a press that is partly free and legitimate their rule in seemingly fair but manipulated elections;
3. The eight "losers": the authoritarian, though no longer totalitarian dictatorships of Central Asia (Uzbekistan, Kyrgystan, Kazakhstan, Tadjikistan) and the Transcaucasus (Armenia, Azerbaijan, etc.), an area that is essentially unreformed and oppressive.

Gati concluded that in all but the seven "leader" countries, transition to democracy had been unsuccessful. His tone was gloomy, but he was already being more optimistic than Brzezinski. At this writing in July 1999, we might add Romania, Slovakia and Bulgaria to the list of hopefuls. That's 10 out of 27, double Brzezinski's original forecast— and counting. If NATO's victory in Kosovo produces the results for the whole Balkans that it should, then there is a glimmer of hope that in addition to Slovenia other post-Yugoslav countries may be launched on the long and painful process of recovery and a birth of democracy.

And what of Russia and the other countries of the former Soviet Union, where the "Eurasian" media model is said to be coming into being? Russia is "faking it," Vdovin has commented—it is going through the motions of democracy but in fact it is reproducing the old form of hegemony, a kind of oligarchic capitalism. As Grigory Yavlinsky, leader of the Yabloko liberal, reform-oriented party, has explained: "Transferring ownership from the state to private persons will not, in itself, guarantee the emergence of a market economy. ... The new 'owners' do not seek to maximize their profit in competition with other firms, but rather to maximize their immediate personal wealth and to gain additional subsidies from the state."

Here, we need to apply our criterion of last resort: is it conceivable that media change in Russia, however limited it has been so far, can be stopped, or even reversed? While it is difficult to predict the future, we already have evidence from the past: Gorbachev's attempt to promote limited media change in the form of *glasnost* was rejected.

In Azerbaijan, government censorship and control of the media is stricter than in Russia, yet, as the State Department report notes, the independent and opposition press continues to play an active, influential role in politics. Articles critical of government policy and high government figures—(with the exception of President Heydar Aliyev)— appear routinely in the opposition and independent print media. Newspapers have begun to discuss censorship itself. Newspapers are able to publish articles opposing government views in sensitive areas such as

Azerbaijan's relations with Russia and Iran and Nagorno-Karabakh peace negotiations. Newspapers also expose government shortcomings in economic reform, corruption in high government offices, and conflicts within the presidential administration and the president's political party. Of course, independent and opposition media—mostly newspapers—exist on the margins of the media system, but (barring major reversals) their importance can only grow over time.

ONE PHRASE COMES TO MIND AS a way of summing up the media situation in Central and Eastern Europe and that is "business as usual." The choice of this phrase may seem surprising. However, it reflects a number of realities quite accurately. Where change in the region has been slow, it is business as usual in the sense that—as in the old days—politicians treat the media as their fiefdom. Elsewhere, it is business as usual in the sense that the media are shaped by the market, and it is increasingly the media that control the politicians, rather than the other way round.

And everywhere in Central and Eastern Europe, it is business as usual, because so far the region has not really been able to develop any new, original patterns of media operation that go beyond what we know from elsewhere.

However, as in all other aspects of transition, it is early days yet. Let us hope the great historic change in the region will not merely lead to copying other people's ideas and that Central and Eastern Europe will be able to contribute more than just imitations of the way things are done elsewhere.

How realistic is this hope? Well, they said communism could not be abolished, didn't they?

Karol Jakubowicz, lecturer at the Institute of Journalism, University of Warsaw, and head of Strategic Planning, Polish Television, has published extensively on media transformation in Central and Eastern Europe.

8

Transitions—A Regional Summary

*A country-by-country review of the media and press freedom
in former Warsaw Pact nations since 1989*

Joel Rubin

IN THE 10 YEARS SINCE 1989 and the end of the communist era in
Central and Eastern Europe, the evolution of print and electronic media has been central to the larger process of political and cultural
restructuring. Struggles for independent journalism are at once both
symbolic of democratic aspirations and central to the building of the
postcommunist governments.

Enough time has passed since the fall of the Berlin Wall to reveal
common and distinct characteristics in development of Central and
Eastern European media. What changes have the media undergone?
Where do they stand today in relation to the ideal of a free and independent press? Where will their momentum take them in the next
century?

Each country's experience has been unique, but common threads
and patterns are evident throughout the region. In the first years after
communist rule, all countries (with the partial exception of East Germany) struggled with the absence of legal and administrative codes
concerning the media, journalists habituated to censorship and vulnerable economies. While governments scrambled to establish precedents
and infrastructure (and contending political parties used control of the
media as leverage in their battles), foreign capital from Western Eu-

rope and the United States flowed over borders and laid claim to this new media landscape. In this uncharted and highly polarized environment, hundreds of new publications sprang up overnight. Markets were saturated.

As the people of Central and Eastern Europe situate themselves in new global contexts, they confront the uneven remains of a break from an authoritarian past that was dramatic but far from clean. Throughout the region, criminal libel laws continue to be used to make it dangerous for journalists to criticize their governments. The second half of this decade has been one of correction and painful reality checks. Governments institute new media policies on licensing and regulation, publications face economic crisis, and journalists wrestle with the purpose and definition of their craft. The Internet has begun to set down roots, with several major newspapers on-line, but it is yet to be a major media force and information concerning usage is scarce. The journalism of Central and Eastern Europe has left behind the old days of communism, but the contours of its future have yet to be fully defined.

Bulgaria

FOR THE PAST DECADE BULGARIAN media have been marked by a dominant state television and radio and by a government reluctant to clear the path for privatization and broad freedom of the press. Print media, with some exceptions, has developed in a manner similar to that of other nations in the region—with an initial influx of new titles followed by corrective measures in the face of an unstable economic and political situation.

More than in most other Eastern bloc countries, Bulgaria experienced an explosion of new publications after communism's demise. Perhaps more so than in neighboring countries, the idea that one could read anything he or she wished was embraced by the Bulgarian population in the first years of transition. In 1993, there were 928 newspapers and 777 magazines for a population of 8.5 million. By mid-1994, the number of magazines had risen to more than 1,000, and many large towns had five to 10 newspapers, with the capital Sofia boasting at least 60. Many titles were far from professional ventures, and by 1996 many had disappeared while new titles appeared much less frequently. The most prominent independent Bulgarian daily is the tabloid *24 Chasa* (*24 Hours*), which, along with a sister weekly, *168 Chasa* (*168 Hours*), presents a mix of sensationalism and in-depth reporting. In a media market with severely limited advertising, the two publications—run by former Communists—are financially profitable.

While foreign investment is a major theme in Central and Eastern European media, Bulgaria's print media have been slow to attract international capital. It was not until late summer 1996 that Westdeutsche Allgemeine Zeitung, a German press group, acquired 70 percent of Bulgaria's largest publishing company, owner of *24 Chasa* and *168 Chasa*.

State-run television and radio are the only significant bodies in Bulgaria's electronic media. Bulgarsko Radio operates on four national stations while Bulgarska Televiziya transmits over two national channels in a country that had approximately 4 million radio and 2.4 million TV receivers in 1996. The Committee for Television and Radio regulates broadcasting and, in theory, is responsible for licensing commercial projects. Reality, however, has shown the government to be reluctant to license private competitors. Beyond Rodopi, a regional station, and Nova Televizia, available only in urban centers, there is little independent TV programming. The government has yet to deliver on its promise to privatize one of the state channels. Most Bulgarians, then, must rely on official programming with little credibility for information. While there is more diversification in the radio sector—with 46 independent, licensed stations active in 1995—all are regional with weak frequencies. Many more stations broadcast clandestinely without proper licensing but are subject to the government's closing them. None of the independent radio stations compete with the nationalized networks in terms of listeners.

The Bulgarian parliament has debated various media laws since early 1996. With parliamentary lines drawn along strong political and economic interests, no legislation has been passed. In 1998, parliament passed a media law that would have given state broadcasting exclusive domain over news and public affairs while private radio and television would have been entitled to only music and entertainment. President Petar Stoyanov vetoed the bill, and it is expected to be rewritten in 1999. Until legislation is passed, Bulgarian reporters will continue to be prosecuted under criminal libel laws, and the government will maintain direct control over broadcast media.

Czech Republic

THE CZECH REPUBLIC (which remained officially united with Slovakia until the close of 1992) was among the first countries in the region to establish policy concerning commercial broadcasting. By March 1991, the government, dedicated to a model of free-market media, had passed legislation concerning licensing, and regional television and radio broadcasting had commenced. Premiera was the first television station on the air, broadcasting to Prague and parts of southern Bohemia. By 1994, in this country of 10.5 million people, there were 3.3 million television receivers and 2.9 million radio receivers.

In February 1992, legislation created an administrative board to license private media groups that was accountable to parliament. Immediately questions arose concerning the board's ability to remain impartial to political influence, an issue that has continued to plague Czech media throughout the decade. TV Nova, the first station to receive a national broadcast license in January 1993, is a prime example. With the station quickly assuming a 66 percent audience share by 1995, two of Nova's senior directors were closely tied to liberal political parties that had been in control of parliament at the time the station received its license. As debate raged concerning the station, with its American financing and programming style, politicians cried foul and accused the board of being politically motivated. Controversy over control of the station and content continues to surround Nova today.

Political influence still colors the Czech media. The country's leading daily, *Lidové noviny* (*People's News*), proclaims itself independent but until recently has widely been thought to be closely aligned to President Václav Havel's voice.

As *Lidové noviny's* circulation declined from 450,000 to 125,000, the Swiss company Ringier purchased the paper in 1993—adding it to 16 other acquired Czech titles. Another major Czech daily, *Mladá fronta dnes* (*Youth Front Today*), is also largely controlled by foreign interests. Such control is significant in a country of 10.5 million in which more than a million newspapers are sold each day. By mid-1994, 50 percent of the Czech print media was in foreign hands.

In October 1995, Prime Minister Václav Klaus' cabinet passed a new press bill that addressed many pressing issues but failed to guarantee media access to the government and to protect a reporter's confidentiality of sources. Furthermore, the press law left the country's defamation law unchanged, which allows for criminal prosecution of a reporter for defaming government officials.

Germany

Prior to the fall of the Berlin wall in November 1989, the media landscape of the German Democratic Republic consisted only of print and electronic media controlled by the Communist Party and state. What has been unusual, however, is the GDR's transition to democracy after communist rule. As postrevolution reality settled, other Warsaw Pact countries faced the difficulties of restructuring all aspects of government, economy and culture—including media. But within a year of the Wall's tumble, the GDR had officially unified with the Federal Republic of Germany —a process that largely exempted the GDR from the problems typical of this postcommunist decade. Certainly, the unification process was marked by the social and economic difficulties of merging two disparate countries speaking the same language. But the strength of the FRG and its media allowed them to absorb the eastern region.

Early in 1990, even as momentum moved Germany towards reunification, Communist leaders were reluctant to relinquish their control of the GDR's media systems—it was crucial to any hopes for Party influence over the approaching and formative months. Only when pressured by opposition groups in formal negotiations did Party leaders begin in earnest to change the media of the GDR. Top-level directors of both print and broadcast media were removed and replaced by noncommunists. State television and radio were divided into separate public service entities regulated by politically independent supervisory boards. And in February 1990, the 24-member Media Control Commission was established to create media legislation based on the principals of a free and independent media. Such legislation is far from insignificant in a country of 81.3 million people that in 1993 had 72 million radio receivers and 45.2 million television receivers.

Today, the former GDR has a media infrastructure that closely mirrors that of the western half of the Federal Republic of Germany. Each of the five eastern *Laender*, or states, has semiautonomous media systems with both public and private broadcasting and privatized print media. While frequent amendments and rewritings of the country's media laws dictate the media organization of the eastern and western

Laender, the process is not without complications. There is a widely held belief among eastern Germans that their views are poorly represented by a media heavily dominated and owned by western German groups.

Ironically, as eastern Germans adjust to their new freedoms and their new identity as Germans in a unified state, they live within a nation that has led in the West's aggressive acquisition of publications and stations throughout Central and Eastern Europe. Once, East Germans—or at least their leaders—viewed Warsaw Pact nations as allies in the struggle against capitalism. Today, they live in a country whose investors buy up the media of their former comrades.

Hungary

PROLIFERATION AND PRIVATIZATION of media had early and considerable momentum in Hungary. In 1988, the government greatly relaxed its censorship of the press, and 85 new publications started up. In 1989, as communist rule came to a nonviolent, gradual end, the number of titles rose to 250. In early 1990, with the country wavering in the limbo of transition, the media continued rapidly towards privatization: *Népszabadság* (*Freedom of the People*), the Communist Party's daily and the nation's largest circulating paper, broke from the Party and sold a 40 percent share to the German-based Bertelsmann AG. *Magyar Hírlap* (*Hungarian Journal*), a major government daily, followed suit in breaking from government control and selling a 40 percent share to the Mirror Holding Company. In April, with the country in the midst of elections, seven papers declared themselves private and transferred full ownership to Axel Springer, the German media magnate. Before the center-right coalition led by the Hungarian Democratic Forum (MDF) had even solidified control of the government, the Hungarian press was both the most privatized in Eastern Europe and the one with the most foreign investment. Nearly 80 percent of newspapers were owned by foreign money.

After four years in office, during which the MDF accused the media of "declaring war" against the government and failed to pass any significant media law, a socialist-liberal coalition was elected in May 1994 and made promises to end the media impasse. At the close of 1995, legislation established a board to grant licenses to private TV and radio stations. The legislation also reorganized state television and radio into public service organizations, but left them open to political control. The government resisted the privatization of electronic media, however, and made the licensing process a difficult one. By the end of 1996, while more than 20 local television and 30 radio stations had been licensed, no national television station had yet been approved. And with a population of 10.1 million people, the country had 6.3 million radio and 4.4 million TV receivers. It was not until July 1997 that the state monopoly of national broadcasting was broken. Two Western-led consortia—in which Bertelsmann AG and Disney have interests—received broadcast permission and were on the air by October. Looking to the future, cable companies have been taking advantage of the slow evolution of broadcast media in their development of networks that make possible a digital, Internet-integrated system.

Poland

THROUGHOUT COMMUNIST RULE, a dissenting and uncensored press had existed in Poland, most notably in the Solidarity publications established after 1980. Fortified in part by this tradition, Poland has emerged from the past decade with one of the region's more stable media foundations.

On May 8, 1989, a month before a Solidarity victory in parliamentary elections that would mark the end of the communist era, the daily *Gazeta Wyborcza* published its first issue in Warsaw with a run of 500,000 copies. Throughout the decade the paper has remained by far the most widely read—even when more than 200 Party-controlled newspapers and magazines were privatized in late 1990 (of which many folded or merged soon after when they could not meet production costs). In May 1992, the number of national dailies stood at 19.

In March 1993, the Polish parliament introduced legislation that restructured the operating rules for both public and commercial radio and television. Effectively ending the state monopoly on electronic media, the new laws established the National Radio and Television Council to work with the Ministry of Communication in the granting of broadcast licenses to private media groups. By late 1994, seven commercial television stations and many radio stations were broadcasting regionally; in October 1997 two commercial TV stations were broadcasting nationally. The 1993 legislation also broke up Polskie Radio I Telewizja—the state-run radio and television—into separate

entities. Public radio would operate on five national stations and several regionals while public television would broadcast on two national
channels and many local stations.

By the end of 1996, this country of 39.75 million people had 17.1
million radio receivers and 11.6 million TV receivers. Today, Poland
has established itself as a regional media leader with continued market
growth and an extraordinary plan to license two digital television stations. With the private media sector poised for such progress, pressure
is inevitably placed on the state broadcasting systems to evolve and
advance as well.

Political parties, the Roman Catholic Church and international investors all have a hand in shaping the Polish media. In the first part of
the decade, as political parties fought for control of the government,
office holders attempted to dictate appointments to the licensing council and to the supposedly nonpartisan public radio and television. The
Catholic Church is a strong presence in Poland, and Polish law charges
electronic media with the vague standard of respecting Christian values. In practice this standard is all but ignored. However, criminal
libel laws continue to allow for the imprisonment of journalists convicted of defaming the government or the president.

Prohibitive production costs have led Polish media groups to court
international capital. Consequently, foreign investors—primarily German and, to a lesser extent, French media conglomerates—play a major role in Polish media. By 1996, foreign money held a 56 percent
share of the dailies (a 12.5 percent share of *Gazeta Wyborcza* was sold
to the American Cox Enterprises, Inc.) and a more than 50 percent
share of the magazines. Polish law prohibits foreign investors from
controlling more than 33 percent of the country's broadcast media.

Romania

As VELVET REVOLUTIONS UNFOLDED in the surrounding countries, Romania experienced a bloody change of regime when long-simmering public discontent erupted into a full-scale coup in December 1989. The
eventual removal of Nicolae Ceauşescu came at an extreme cost of
life. Rule by his successor, Ion Iliescu, was also marked by abuses of
power.

Nonetheless, Romanian print media experienced extraordinary
growth in the years following communism, with the number of publi-

cations quadrupling from 495 at the end of 1989 to 1,800 in 1994. Of these publications Romania Libera was the first to establish itself in the wake of the revolution as a truly independent paper, one of the most widely read dailies in the country with a run of 1.2 million copies in January 1990. After 1992, however, the realities of production costs in a stumbling economy caught up with Romanian publications, forcing many to fold and others to cut back dramatically. By 1994, *Romania Libera*'s circulation had dropped to 150,000.

Romanian Television and Romanian Radio broke with the Communist Party after 1989 and were re-established as supposedly independent public services. It was soon clear, however, that Iliescu had every intention of abusing the country's electronic media, with the *Index on Censorship* reporting in June 1990 that the dictator's influence on state television "reveal[ed] a persistent misuse of power."

In May 1992, the government relented slightly and passed an Audio-Visual Law that made possible the licensing of private radio and TV stations. Throughout the following year, 82 radio, 50 broadcast television and 196 cable licenses were granted, although only 16 television stations actually broadcast that year due to financial and logistical obstacles (and all the licenses were for local and regional broadcasting as the state maintained firm control over national radio and television capacities). SOTI Television (Romanian Society for the Creation of an Independent National Television Company) begun in September 1990 and granted permission to broadcast on one of Romanian Television's channels, was the only one of these early stations able to make a national impact. By June 1994, however, while in the midst of political and financial turmoil, SOTI's license was revoked. In 1996, this country of 22.6 million people had 4.6 million TV and 4.7 million radio receivers.

After Iliescu's defeat in the 1996 elections (of which the dictator had blatantly attempted to control the media's coverage), several private TV stations were formed, the most significant of which was PRO-TV. The station, which quickly became one of the country's most popular, uses journalists trained in Western institutions. Observers credit it with raising the standard of reporting in Romania. And while journalists continue to be prosecuted under criminal libel laws, political interference in media declined sharply in 1997 under Emil Constantinescu's new government.

Slovakia

As THE CZECH REPUBLIC MOVED steadily in the direction of privatization of its media, Slovakia turned decidedly in the opposite direction towards state control and public media groups. Since breaking with the Czech Republic at the end of 1992, the Slovak government has reluctantly passed legislation to allow for privatization. But the public, state-influenced media have been the dominant source of information throughout the past decade.

Until May 1992, when a Radio and Television Council was established, applications for broadcast licenses by private groups had floundered in the bureaucracy of a government that has yet to confront the question of postcommunist media. Limited regional TV transmissions began in 1993, and several small cable channels emerged in the following years although they have been greatly hindered by a disjointed cable infrastructure with no national capabilities. In 1994, in a country with 5.3 million people, there were 950,000 radio receivers and 1.2 million television receivers. In 1995, the satellite station VTV began national broadcasts, although its news reporting varied little from state-run TV due to its close alignment with the ruling HZDS (Movement for a Democratic Slovakia) party.

HZDS displayed open contempt for independent reporting, especially during a 1998 election campaign when it actively denied independent reporters equal access to information. The party went so far as to amend the country's election laws to allow only state-funded media the right to broadcast reports of political activity a month prior to election and to ban the publication of pre-election opinion polls two weeks prior to an election. As the election neared, a company aligned with HZDS purchased Markiza—a TV station supportive of HZDS-opposition groups—and immediately fired the director and news editor. Despite such efforts, the four-party SDK (Slovak Democratic Coalition) defeated HZDS. SDK continued the cycle of politically biased press when it promptly named a new director of state TV who in turn replaced pro-HZDS editors and programs.

Relative to the country's broadcast media, Slovak print media have experienced greater diversification with the appearance of several new magazines and newspapers and privatization of some former state-controlled titles. Like electronic media, however, print media has been marked by strong political and government influence. Many publications suffered from plummeting circulation in the years after 1989 due to the faltering economy and the tumultuous political environment. *Pravda (Truth)*, the communist organ that had enjoyed a circulation of 400,000 in 1989, had dropped its run to 165,000 by early 1995. Three new newspapers supported by either government subsidies or party aligments rose in the aftermath of the revolution. Such equations proved flawed, however. The subsidized *Národná obroda* (*National Renewal*) has been completely redesigned, and the party papers have failed. By the close of 1995, 19 dailies had survived in Slovakia's media environment.

Joel Rubin is assistant editor of Media Studies Journal.

9

Naked Bodies, Runaway Ratings

TV Nova and the Czech Republic

Jeremy Druker

AN INVESTOR SURVEYING CENTRAL and Eastern Europe in the early '90s would have thought the Czech Republic the last place where a television channel featuring naked bodies and severed heads would boom. Led by Václav Havel—a playwright turned president who had helped lead a peaceful revolution in 1989—the country exuded calm intelligence and education, with past and present luminaries such as Milan Kundera, Antonín Dvořák and Franz Kafka. An appreciation for high art, music and culture was not confined only to the elite, but disseminated throughout society at large.

Today, 10 years after the Velvet Revolution, the image has changed considerably. The turning point was February 4, 1994, the day TV Nova went on the air. Almost overnight, the first private television station in Central and Eastern Europe grabbed an enormous market share. Using glitzy marketing to promote a lineup built on American films and television serials, Nova easily attracted viewers away from stodgy Czech public television (CT), the successor to communist-era Czechoslovak Television. Nova's runaway ratings victory led many to reassess their previous perceptions of a cultured nation that could withstand crude imports. And those who viewed the station's sensationalism as destructive to the fragile transition to democracy looked around for someone to blame.

THE RISE OF NOVA DATES back to the beginning of 1993. Czechoslovakia had just split into two independent countries, and the Czech government announced that it would accept project proposals for a commercial station. The new channel would assume the frequency freed up by the dissolution of the old state Czechoslovak network. Advised by experts from the BBC and elsewhere, regulators placed 31 conditions on the license operators as a way of guaranteeing that the station could not become a mere vessel of trashy, dubbed foreign productions.

The project submitted by CET-21, Central European Television for the 21st Century, seemed to have everything. A group of Czech and Slovak intellectuals—including former government spokesman and future Nova chief Vladimír Železný—would provide the brains, while an American company, Central European Media Enterprises (CME), would provide the financial brawn. CME had cash and connections: its top executives were Ronald Lauder, heir to the Estée Lauder cosmetics empire, and former diplomat Mark Palmer, both of whom had served as ambassadors in the region (in Austria and Hungary, respectively). Plans called for entertainment programming but also stressed high-quality educational and news programming.

Compared with other countries in Central and Eastern Europe, where politicized battles for licenses would soon take place, the process in Prague went fairly smoothly. CET-21 won the 12-year license, with a general recognition that it had been the best project. CME immediately injected nearly $10 million into buying a building in downtown Prague, outfitting a flashy, sophisticated studio and hiring a staff of mostly fresh faces—part of a conscious attempt to immediately distance Nova (which means *new* in Czech) from Czech public television.

Perhaps most importantly, the station quickly gobbled up the rights to dozens of American sitcoms, dramatic series, soap operas and films— shows like "Dallas," "Beverly Hills 90210" and "Days of Our Lives." The station lined up local entertainers to do variety shows, attempted a few hard-hitting investigative programs (a novelty at the time) and served up sensationalistic, glossy news coverage. Six months after its February debut, Nova already had twice the viewership of public television. In less than a year, Nova was generating profits—making the launch one of the most successful in television history worldwide.

The money has continued to roll in since then, and today Nova controls a remarkable three-quarters of the Czech advertising market.

Profits in 1998 were $54 million. More than 50 percent of Czechs watch the station—among the highest levels of viewership in Europe. Meanwhile, only roughly 25 percent watch CT1, the main public television channel. Prima TV—another private station without the bankroll or skilled management that Nova boasts—has roughly 10 percent of the market. CT2, the second public television channel that runs culturally and intellectually oriented programming, achieves ratings in the high single digits.

A MAIN INSTRUMENT IN Nova's continued domination was "Volejte řediteli" ("Call the Director"), the weekly program of General Director Železný, a name now synonymous with crafty opportunism. In 1968, during the Warsaw Pact invasion ordered by the Soviets to quash the country's experiment in "socialism with a human face," Železný was one of several Czechoslovak television employees who stayed at their posts to broadcast shots of the tanks rumbling through Prague's streets. He was fired two years later, in a period when Communist hard-liners were cleaning house of people associated in any way with reform. Until the Velvet Revolution, Železný's television contributions were limited to screenplays written under a pseudonym; he was not, however, a dissident along the lines of Havel or Poland's Adam Michnik.

With Nova, Železný would appear on his half-hour Saturday afternoon show to explain programming decisions (why he moved "Baywatch" to Thursdays, why Nova shouldn't support art films), question how CT won broadcasting awards despite the unpopularity of its shows and answer fawning queries from viewers ("Why don't you wear bow ties anymore? You looked so good in them."). Železny is a master communicator and though many of his gestures would seem as scripted as the letters he chose to read, he gave every appearance of being the smoothest public figure in the country.

But Železný would also use "Volejte řediteli" in a much more controversial way: as a soapbox to rail against the station's regulators (the Czech Radio and Television Council, a board that has chastised Nova for a series of infractions) and to bitterly criticize the competition, including publicly financed CT. Jan Čulík, an expert on Czech media at the University of Glasgow and one of Nova's fiercest critics, has written: "The purpose of 'Volejte řediteli' is to mesmerize the ordinary Czech viewer and to manipulate him into absolute submission. It is a self-promotional program, where Železný will say anything, often absolute manipulative rubbish, in an attempt to increase the viewing figures for his station." More disturbing has been Železný's excursions onto Nova's main news program. In 1998, he appeared on the nightly news to defend his son, a convicted rapist. And in April of 1999, Železný, embroiled in an ugly dispute with his American partners, took nine minutes of the news to explain his side while CME received a mere 30 seconds.

NOVA'S FORMULA FOR SUCCESS HAS changed little from the early days for two simple reasons: it sells spectacularly well, and no one has forced the station to live up to its earlier promises. Under communism, Czechs had prided themselves on mischievously working around the rules of the regime; now they despair that many of their fellow citizens adjusted such skills to capitalism all too well. Nova is but another example of profiting from holes in the system, a phenomenom that has appeared in privatization and tax collection.

In a situation that parallels the entire post-1989 transformation of Czech society, the legal framework provided too many loopholes and ineffective regulation. In a span of two and a half years, under pressure from various lobbying groups—including cable companies—the parliamentary media commission relaxed broadcasting restrictions. That included removing all 31 conditions that had regulated Nova. Commission members viewed television broadcasting as only another business, which did not need a special set of rules.

Intellectually minded Czechs contemplate Nova and lament how housewives sit mesmerized in front of "Melrose Place," how gruesome murders lead the nightly news and how their children spend summer evenings watching trashy action flicks instead of playing games outside—all, they allege, contributing to society's overall degradation. People in Prague, ashamed to see the myth of a special Czech cultivation shattered, say country bumpkins form Nova's core viewers and boost its numbers. And they usually blame Železný, not the media commission that took a *laissez-faire* approach, for letting it happen. They say that Nova's boss—an art collector and classical music buff with a doctorate in social science—took the easy way out and went lowbrow. In part, this hand-wringing over Nova represents a nostalgic yearning for the better aspects of life under communism, when "family values" supposedly took precedence over the destructive influence of commercialization (read Americanization) and capitalism.

Yet with a little prodding, Nova's critics admit that they too have also given in to an urge for mindless programming at the end of a hard day, demonstrating that "average" Czechs, as the intellectuals call them, aren't the only ones watching Nova. And they couldn't be. In 1998, for example, 86 percent of the country's citizens said they watched the station, making it clear how quickly Nova's "innovations" can reverberate throughout society. Take "Počasíčko," the late evening, three-minute weather forecast. After a news update (typically filled with a flaming car crash and a rundown of the world's calamities), a young woman strolls into a room—completely naked—and then slowly clothes herself according to the next day's weather. If rain is forecast, for example, her reverse striptease ends with an umbrella. (Men also appear on the show, but not frequently enough for some of Nova's female viewers, who would complain to Železný on "Volejte řediteli"). The show has become part of modern Czech lore.

Detractors also grudgingly agree that Nova's success has remade the media scene, contributing to the creation of a dual system of commercial and public television broadcasting—something that has yet to be established in all the other countries of the former Soviet bloc. There is now clearly a choice. At noon on Sunday, for example, you can watch public television's "V pravé poledne" ("High Noon"), which spends an hour on a pressing issue—the country's entrance into NATO, pension reform, rising unemployment—with various experts in what is usually a tame debate. Or you can switch on Nova's "7 čili Sedm dní" ("Seven Days"), a CNN "Crossfire" clone, where two politicians, usually bitter rivals, take a quick, heated run through the week's events. In general, the competition from Nova has undoubtedly forced Czech Television to make its programming more lively and varied.

NOVA'S POPULARITY HAS ALSO FORCED Czechs raised under 40 years of communism to realize that the country's most powerful media outlet is private and, even more importantly, independent. In 1998, some commentators accused Nova of providing former Prime Minister Václav Klaus' Civic Democratic Party with positive, pre-election coverage in exchange for Klaus' dropping a costly libel suit against the station. But such suspicions have been rare over the last five years. More often than not, the station's thirst for scandal has not spared any party or politician, including President Václav Havel. A charge with more substance concerns Nova's hesitancy to do news stories on its main advertisers. Last year, former star reporter Kateřina Kašparová, who was fired after clashing with management, published a tell-all memoir entitled *Pravda Přichází z Novy* (*The Truth Comes Out of Nova*). Her allegations about the station's self-censorship were seconded by other former Nova reporters.

Further proof that Nova is beholden to no political party emerged with the 1998 creation of "Kotel," which roughly translates to "Cauldron." The weekly program places a top politician down in a ring, surrounded by bleachers filled with a typically angry horde, bussed in from all over the country. Unlike the staged debates of the "town meeting" type in the United States, "Kotel" makes politicians squirm and face tough questions (the moderator is particularly good at pointing out when they don't answer). Hate the show as they might, politicians realize it's one of the most popular programs on TV and know they can't refuse an invitation. The debates are rarely deep, but they revolve around politics and the economy and, in that sense, rise far above Jerry Springer themes. And in a country suffering from political elitism—where those in power continue to make decisions without grass-roots participation—the audience's direct interaction with politicians on "Kotel" is a notable exception.

Buried amid the soap operas and movies are other innovative programs. Investigative shows tackle governmental corruption and legal injustice, as well as offer practical advice so people don't get conned by the charlatans that have appeared in the milder Czech version of Wild West capitalism. Afternoon talk shows target young people but don't sink to the exploitative level of their American models. A well-produced morning program—"Snídaně s Novou" ("Breakfast with Nova") features sprightly, young hosts whose guests often include representatives from nonprofit organizations and foreigners working in the Czech Republic. The exposure is important, because most of the country's media give short shrift to civil society and mention foreigners only when they are involved in criminal activity—a neglect that contributes to lingering xenophobia.

The current affairs programs, have, however not been without their own scandals. Twice in 1997, Nova newsmagazine shows depicted the carefree life that Romani (gypsy) asylum seekers were supposedly enjoying, first in Canada and then in Great Britain. The programs lacked balanced sources and ignored the many obstacles that asylum seekers face. But thousands of Czech Roma, who face widespread discrimination and occasional violent skinhead attacks, took the bait and left the country.

THOUGH CHOICE AND VARIETY NOW EXIST—a big improvement over a decade ago—when it comes to hard news, what kind of choice is it? Nova does break some stories—especially about financial wrongdoings—but usually does not rise above a simplistic style that avoids deeper investigations of the country's problems. Disgruntled viewers can always watch the competition, where they won't hear the precise and detailed injuries of accident victims ("severed head" is a Nova favorite) or gossipy news about celebrities and politicians.

But switching channels won't help them find a high quality information source. News on public television is competent but uninspired, providing a staid alternative to Nova's gloss (though crime coverage on CT has followed Nova's lead, inching up over the past few years). CT rarely scoops Nova and tends to spend too much time covering trivial governmental debates—a lasting legacy from the pre-1989 communist era. Efforts at reform have largely led nowhere, with the greatest disappointment the fate of Jakub Puchalský, a 28-year-old journalist, who was picked from among many candidates to head the station in 1998. Armed with ambitious plans to overhaul the station and institute BBC-style programming, Puchalský's age—seen by some as a potential asset in jump starting change—apparently backfired when CT veterans, backed by some vocal politicians, rebelled against any innovation.

CT's failed reform—coupled with Nova's sensationalistic news—means Czechs have virtually no first-rate outlets for national news and analysis. The press leaps from scandal to scandal, often providing politicized coverage and depending far too much on the leak of the day. The current lack of freedom-of-information legislation—which will finally take effect in 2000—has allowed bureaucrats to stymie investigative reports, which were already a luxury for much of the financially troubled Czech media.

A recent poll found that 89 percent of Czechs realize the importance of freedom of the press for a well-functioning democracy, but less than 50 percent feel the media provide them the information they need. The same research showed that most people believe that public radio and television provide far more accurate and reliable news than commercial stations. Yet such feelings apparently aren't strong enough to dig into the extraordinary popularity of Nova's news, which routinely routs its CT competition. People do watch CT when, for example, a big foreign story breaks, but revert back to Nova on slow days when entertainment seems more important than information.

DOES THAT MEAN THAT THE NOVA phenomenon has somehow changed the cultured Czechs? Or that now people will watch trash even though they realize it's not good for them? The image of refinement may have been an exaggeration—this was a country of television enthusiasts long before Nova arrived—but the station's success showed that American-style commercial programming can triumph even in unlikely places. Nova is both a reflection of the commercial invasion and poor taste that flooded the country in the early '90s and a contributor to that influx. Watched by so many viewers, the station has contributed to a general dumbing-down of society, though not as much as the intellectuals complain. And the station's negative news and sensationalism have added to what Havel calls the "poor mood" of the country, amid rising unemployment and other bumps along the road of economic reform.

These criticisms only irritate Železný. He interprets Nova's promotion of mass culture as a healthy development that knocked the intellectuals from their self-appointed roles as saviors and determiners of national culture. "Suddenly, Czechs proved that they are normal Europeans and not so vulnerable to the efforts of Czech intellectuals," he said in a June 1999 interview. "I hate the idea that Czechs are not mature enough and that they must be treated like a very special species that needs a careful transformation period to teach them the basics before they feel the impact of bloody capitalism." He scoffed at the need for license restrictions. "In a small, fragile emerging market in a postcommunist country, any regulation is an additional burden to the many burdens that are already present in the country."

Železný reserves his greatest scorn for his intellectual critics. "I am an intellectual. My library has more than 9,000 books, and I'm a founder of the Franz Kafka Society of Prague, but I should never be in the position to have the right to impose my thoughts on ordinary people." As far as Železný is concerned, he is only giving people what they want. "The intellectuals and regulators care about the ordinary people," he says sarcastically. "They feel that they have the right to know what is good and what is bad for ordinary citizens. But citizens don't care about this care of intellectuals."

Whether he felt he deserved that right or not, Železný's influence on his fellow citizens was unchallenged—until April 19, 1999, when CME, now almost the 100 percent owner of Nova's operating company, fired him. The American company claimed that Železný had started stripping Nova's assets and had broken an agreement not to compete with CME, though the validity of those charges remains far from proven. A few weeks earlier, CME had announced a merger with Scandinavian Broadcasting System (SBS) that would create Europe's largest broadcaster, comprising 18 television stations in 13 countries. The conflict may have arisen as CME, in preparation for the deal, tried to gain a firmer hand over Nova and Železný, who had been able to act largely unencumbered over the past five years. Or perhaps Železný had grown tired of sending virtually all of Nova's earnings back to CME, which needed the station's cash to prop up the rest of its broadcasting empire in Central and Eastern Europe. Hit hard by failures in Poland and Hungary, CME lost $34.7 million in 1998, according to a company press release. The mudslinging combatants filed a number of lawsuits and appeared resigned to a long court battle with an unclear conclusion. While CME owns Nova's operating company and its assets, Železný is the majority shareholder in CET-21, which controls the nontransferable license and the Nova name.

Železný's departure from Nova was a shock to everyone. Even his opponents had praised his managerial skills and his personal triumph in creating a successful station from scratch; he also managed to become one of the richest people in the country. "An era ends when one individual personified a whole institution and outwardly behaved like the caring father of all viewers," wrote media critic Mirka Spácilová. "In the future, every person who sits in Íelezný's seat will be 'only' a director, a polite executive manager, whose name people speaking over a beer will barely remember."

Železný and Nova will, in contrast, be remembered for embodying the Czech Republic at the end of the 20th century. As Jan Čulík has written: "The Czech parliament wished to have an intelligent, semi-commercial television station which would not be dependent on foreign interests. It ended up with a foreign-owned, extremely powerful, down-market broadcaster, operating forcefully in an unregulated environment." Instead of assuring that commercial television would partly fulfill a public service role—not too much to ask for a license worth hundreds of millions of dollars given away for free—government officials let Nova go strictly for profit. Not an awful goal in a country learning the capitalist way, but a risky one in a nation passing through disorienting times without a strong media.

Jeremy Druker is director and editor in chief of Transitions Online, *an Internet magazine covering Central and Eastern Europe and the former Soviet Union.*

10

Gazeta Wyborcza at 10

The progress of Poland since communism

Adam Michnik

To UNDERSTAND THE HISTORY of Poland is to believe in miracles. Consider this: if you supposed in 1984 that in five years' time Poland would regain its liberty and independence, you would really have to believe in miracles. However, the Polish nation, Catholic and God fearing, didn't really have faith in this miracle. After all, who among us, at *Gazeta Wyborcza*, thought back then that soon enough we would come to work in a large and important daily newspaper, respected both in Poland and around the world?

Without a shadow of a doubt everyone, in some way, desired an independent Poland, and everyone, in her own way, labored for it. But in all political camps there was no shortage of people with base morals and little faith, political opponents and hooligans, traitors to the national cause and troublemakers in the service of platitudes. Still, they performed a miracle: Poland regained its freedom, and every Pole has the right to a moment of happiness in the "recaptured garbage heap" of history. We at *Gazeta Wyborcza* were not and are not objective observers of Poland's struggles. We were and remain active participants in the debate on Poland.

WHY DID COMMUNISM FALL IN POLAND? Was it pushed by the election of Pope John Paul II and his memorable pilgrimages to Poland? Was it occasioned by the policy of the American presidents Jimmy Carter and Ronald Reagan, who used human rights as a weapon of American politics against totalitarian communism? Did Mikhail Gorbachev deal it a fatal blow when he tried to modernize the Soviet empire?

Each of these factors had an essential significance. But another factor was decisive: that Poles wanted to dismantle the system of dictatorship, and those Poles who served the dictatorship knew how to negotiate to this end with those who rebelled against it in the Great Polish Velvet Revolution.

The Round Table talks in early 1989 between the Communist government and its opponents negotiated the path to freedom and independence. With the consent of all the players on the Polish political scene, the government led by Tadeusz Mazowiecki was formed—the first noncommunist government in the Soviet bloc. Ten years later we look back with gratitude on that government and the people who supported it. It was a government of hope. In the midst of desperate economic collapse, a government of consensus and unity was formed to build the framework of freedom and sovereignty after years of dictatorship and subjugation. And it was this very government and this prime minister that soon became the target of an unforgivable attack initiated by those who condemned closing the book on the past, those who demanded an "acceleration of democratization and vetting of communists" and "completing the revolution." At the head of this attack stood the symbol of Polish resistance, the Nobel Peace Prize winner and leader of Solidarity, Lech Wałęsa—a man of brilliant intuition and shameless self-adoration, a natural political talent and arrogant autocrat. Wałęsa did not want to and could not wait. Is that why I still think of Wałęsa with a mixture of warmth and aversion, admiration and fear? He did not respect partners; he only recognized loyal courtiers. He craved presidential power the way a drug addict craves cocaine.

Wałęsa's genius was based on his acute perception and articulation of popular dissatisfaction. Solidarity activists were frustrated: they expected the Solidarity union to become the new "leading power," appointing university rectors and directors, chairmen, ministers and province governors. Disaffected workers felt they had won their freedom through strikes only to come face to face with the specter of unemployment. Catholics were frustrated, as they had expected that, after the fall of "Communist Poland," the time of a "Catholic Poland" would come. Those discriminated against under the dictatorship felt cheated for they had anticipated compensation but instead looked on as the Communist Party nomenklatura was enfranchised.

NEW GOVERNMENTS WANT TO BE liked—they like to hand out money. But Mazowiecki's government stood by finance minister Leszek Balcerowicz's strict economic policy. Now we can plainly see that Poland owes its present prosperity to that decision. At the time, however, demonstrations were held under the slogan "Balcerowicz is the Dr. Mengele of the Polish economy."

We at *Gazeta Wyborcza* always backed Balcerowicz's policy. We had trouble with this. Most of us entered the epoch of freedom holding the deeply embedded ethos of defending workers' rights, their dignity and their interests. The ideal of emancipating the workers, rooted in the socialist tradition and Pope John Paul II's encyclicals, was in direct conflict with Balcerowicz's policy. Instead of independent workers' authorities came privatization; instead of pay raises came price hikes and belt tightening; instead of social security came the specter of unemployment. We often asked ourselves: are we not betraying our ideals? Ten years on we can look back and answer: No. We did not renounce our dreams; we only renounced our delusions. We believe, here and now, that there was no other road for Poland to take than the rocky path of Balcerowicz's shock therapy. Along this path—though littered with mistakes, inconsistencies and scandals—Poland experienced an economic boom and social progress never encountered before.

The harsh logic of a market economy is often accompanied by the market's cold cruelty, the ruthless business mentality, the rigor of technocrats and the abasement of human dignity. In such moments we recall and will continue to recall that our ultimate goal is Poland's liberty and social freedom, to create a civic society where everyone has the right to live with dignity. We realize that the free market is an inevitable part of transformation. But by no means should we consider the enrichment of some and the poverty of others to be the result of divine justice. On the contrary. We should keep a check on the rich and provide the poor with aid and the opportunity to escape their poverty.

A tough free-market policy and rapid modernization led to a conservative backlash and populist reaction. In Poland, populism came in
various forms: the success of the populist émigré Stan Tyminski in the
1990 presidential elections, the harsh anti-capitalist and anti-European
pronouncements of many church authorities, the show of support for
the postcommunist parties in the May 1993 parliamentary elections.
The rate of reform was slowed, but there was no return to a command
economy. The populist-conservative reaction also took an anti-communist form, drawing from clericalism and ethnic nationalism. The
voice of Radio Maryja, owned by a Catholic missionary order, was an
extreme and perhaps the most dramatic articulation of these attitudes:
fear of the unknown, of Europe and foreigners; ill will toward ethnic
minorities; the fear of being responsible for one's own life; the fear of
poverty, unemployment, uncertainty, drugs, pornography and the sexual
revolution. Radio Maryja voiced, often using crude and unrestrained
language, the fundamental issues of those who felt wronged and fright-
ened.

We have described crushed and unfortunate people in *Gazeta
Wyborcza*, usually using journalistic language, but we have always
declared ourselves—in the language of commentary—on the side of
the reformers. We understood that a defensive backlash is a natural
consequence of modernization. That is why we were for the policy of
social dialogue, compromise and the law regulating employer-employee
relations. At the same time we knew that where dialogue ends, the
destruction of the democratic principles of the law-abiding state begins.

CONFLICT BETWEEN A GOVERNMENT with a policy of transformation and
the trade unions that defend workers' interests is just as inescapable as
compromise between the two is inevitable. Ten years of transformation has shown that, without society's consent, Poland cannot be reformed, and that this consent can only be won through dialogue and
compromise. We believe that a compromise on the economy is a pri-
ority because economic growth is the prerequisite for Polish achievement both at home and throughout the world. The economy should be
a jointly guarded area, taken out of the framework of political conflict.

From the beginning, since 1989, we at the newspaper have supported a united Poland, a republic—a homeland for all its citizens, a
state based on compromises and not on the domination of one political

camp, nor on a relentless battle and a never-ending settling of scores. We did not want Solidarity to become the new "leading power"; we did not want the once compulsory conformity to Marxist-Leninism and the Soviet Union to turn into conformity to the Catholic church or Western capitals.

We saw in other postcommunist countries how aggressive national-ism took the place of dominating communist ideology, and how old demons returned. We saw how the bloody conflict in Yugoslavia was born, erupted and lives on, where yesterday's Communists were trans-formed into today's aggressive nationalists and where former demo-crats spoke in the language of ethnic fascism. We also saw how Chris-tian clergy blessed ethnic massacres. We saw how nationalism, born of communism and anti-communism, seized Russia and other coun-tries of the former Soviet Union; with unease we listened to the out-bursts of Greater Russian chauvinism from Vladimir Zhirinovsky and Gennady Zyuganov. We witnessed the bloody riots in Romania, the dissolution of Czechoslovakia, the burning homes of African refugees in eastern Germany. We saw all this, and we must do all we can to prevent similar scenes from being repeated in Poland. That would be the death of Polish freedom.

This is why we have warned and shall continue to warn against the discourse of national hatred and against the ideology of ethnic exclu-sivity. We have condemned and will continue to condemn the ethnic conflicts that have surfaced in Poland's border regions—the Polish-German conflict in the Opole area, the Polish-Ukrainian dispute around Przemyœl, the Polish-Belarussian problems around Bialystok and Pol-ish-Lithuanian tensions in the Suwalki region. We have condemned the abuse of the Roma. We have also warned against anti-Semitism, which stupefies Poles and blights Poland's image abroad. We agreed with Jerzy Turowicz, editor in chief of *Tygodnik Powszechny* (*Univer-sal Weekly*), when he wrote to Father Stanisłeaw Musiałe: "Dear Staszek, I read your distinguished—and very important!—*Gazeta Wyborcza* interview with true admiration. You are 100-percent correct when you write that nationalism and anti-Semitism are the greatest weaknesses of the Polish Church. . . . It's true that more people in the Church are beginning to understand this (also thanks to you!), but there is still a long road ahead!"

Only by traveling this road can Poland's good name in the world be defended against damning generalizations.

We have been advocates of new relations between states and nations in Central and Eastern Europe. With this intention in mind we have printed many Russian opinions, including those of Russian democrats, to whom the world has much to be thankful.

It is an honor for us to call so many fine Russians friends of our newspaper. We also have reason to be proud because we are shedding new light upon the tangled history of Polish-Ukrainian relations. We consider work on behalf of Polish-Ukrainian reconciliation to be one of the great accomplishments of Polish politics, in which *Gazeta Wyborcza* has played a part. We believed that the most effective path to the West and to NATO and the European Union to be internal stabilization, good neighborly relations and an active regional policy. That is why we report extensively on the Czech Republic, Slovakia and Hungary, on Lithuania, Latvia, Estonia, and on Ukraine and Belarus.

FROM THE VERY FIRST ISSUE, we at *Gazeta Wyborcza* had great respect for the Catholic church. We recognized the tremendous role the church played throughout Poland's history and its great contributions during the communist dictatorship and at the Round Table. We admired the great cause of Pope John Paul II. Despite all that, and despite exercising caution in criticizing certain Episcopal declarations, we have often been accused of enmity toward the church. We regarded and continue to regard these charges as unjust.

We never claimed to be a Catholic newspaper, though we always considered ourselves friends of the church. We opine, in the words of philosopher Leszek Kolakowski, that "the power of Christianity does not manifest itself in theology nor in its monopoly on creating canons to regulate all areas of life. Its power is revealed in the fact that it can build barriers against hate in people's consciousness. In essence, mere faith in Jesus the Redeemer would be in vain and worthless if it did not carry with it the resignation of hatred, no matter what the circumstances; if after the words 'forgive us our trespasses' Christians did not have to go on to say 'as we forgive those who trespass against us.' This resignation from hating is the challenge Christianity presents which remains today."

It is from this kind of Holy Scripture that we came to understand the church. That is why we are disturbed by voices filled with hatred and contempt, fired by the spirit of revenge and embarked on a crusade against those who think differently—all in the name of the Gospel and under the sign of the cross. We were determined to show another side of Christianity and a church of ecumenical faith and hope, compassion and dialogue, forgiveness and reconciliation. We were and are people of dialogue but not of blind obedience, of criticism but not malevolence. Ours is the first daily newspaper to include a regular column on the Catholic church and religion.

There was a time when working with *Gazeta Wyborcza* was viewed unfavorably by the church. Therefore we wish all the more to thank all those people of the church who offered us their thoughts, articles and essays with courage and understanding. The church embodies simultaneously both the best and the worst of Poland. We were lucky in that we had the opportunity to associate with the best.

OFTEN, WE AT *GAZETA WYBORCZA*, and particularly myself personally, have been accused of being too soft on the perpetrators of the former regime. We have been criticized for not settling accounts and not taking part in vetting or decommunization and, as a consequence, of blurring the boundary between good and evil, truth and lies. One critic called this "a friendship pact with Cain." The 10th anniversary of *Gazeta Wyborcza* seems a good occasion to respond to these accusations.

For many years we belonged to the anti-communist opposition. Many of us spent a good bit of time underground or in jail, on the margins of public life, discriminated against and humiliated. On the pages of underground newspapers we vehemently denounced the communist regime. Only in 1989, during the Round Table talks, did we acknowledge that there was light at the end of the tunnel for Poland. Then we realized that the route to Polish democracy was to follow the Spanish way—that of evolution from dictatorship to democracy via compromise and national reconciliation. This approach assumes there will be no retaliation, no vanquishers or vanquished, and that future governments will be chosen by ballot.

We realized that we, members of the democratic opposition, KOR and Solidarity, were particularly winners. But from this moral high ground we rejected sweet revenge on yesterday's enemies. We said yes to amnesty and no to amnesia. The historian, essayist and artist were to pass judgment on our cursed past—not the prosecutor or investigator. We understand the building of a democratic and sovereign state as a process of reconciliation, of bringing together Poland Discordant: Communist Poland and Solidarity Poland. That is why we were against all attempts at decommunization and vetting. We consider decommunization, meaning discrimination against former Communist Party activists, to be anti-democratic. We see the analogies between decommunization of Poland and the de-Nazification of Germany as misdirected. Gomulka, Gierek and Jaruzelski were not the same kind of people as Hitler, Himmler or Goebbels. They were dictators, but not mass murderers and to blur these definitions is wrong.

Naturally, we often wrote about the communist era while hardly disguising our heartfelt antipathy. But even while condemning the system and its practices—particularly the mixture of lies and violence—we attempted to understand those caught up in it. To put it in another, more Christian, way: we differentiated the sin from the sinner. We did not want to demonize the supporters of the former regime, though we repeatedly wrote of the demonic nature of totalitarian dictatorships; nor did we want to "deify" the anti-communist opposition, though these were often our friends from Solidarity, the underground or prison. We wanted, despite obvious biographical, political and ideological differences, to seek that which binds.

This is the source of our resistance to vetting people on the basis of security files. Of course, we cared if Communist informers become ministers, ambassadors, etc. However, we felt that the data held in security files cannot decide whether a citizen is suitable for work in government administration. We did not believe the secret service archives to be an accurate source of information. These documents were used as instruments of police blackmail, to compromise those people who were inconvenient to the authorities. A prime minister wanting to know more about a co-worker can examine the material, but it should not be used to create a political circus.

REPORTING ON POLISH POLITICS and taking part in Polish polemics, we realize that mere politics do not life make. We wanted, therefore, to create a newspaper that is sympathetic and helpful.

We brought democracy and human rights right down to the grass roots with, for example, the two-year "Give Birth Humanely" campaign, which changed the face of Polish maternity hospitals. We demanded that staff show pregnant women respect and empathy, instead of the impersonal or even boorish treatment often handed out. We championed uninterrupted contact with the newborn and the presence of family members at birth. We asked readers to send in letters and surveys rating maternity hospitals, on the basis of which we compiled guides and rankings. Both medical staff and authorities at first scoffed at the campaign, but just a few months later hospitals entered a heated race for a better place in the ranking. We effected a change in consciousness, and the term "give birth humanely" entered everyday language. Specialists even believe that the rapid drop in the infant mortality rate was in some part thanks to the humanization of the birth process.

Gazeta Wyborcza also stepped in to defend the children of alcoholics and condemn domestic violence and violent television programs. We saved state orphanages by organizing a massive fund-raiser, and we supported the creation of family-style children's homes. We encouraged readers to "escape from the housing projects" in our "Live Humanely" campaign.

Several times we have directly lobbied for changes in the law. After the unexpected cancellation of the housing tax break in 1997, we collected thousands of signatures to urge the ombudsman to appeal against the taxation bill. We have covered the most difficult issues and those bound by social taboos such as sex education or, recently, the moving series "Why a Hospice Shelter." The newspaper regularly tries to convince Poles to live healthier lifestyles—to quit smoking, to eat properly, etc.

For years we've offered a steady stream of tax and financial advice, not to mention innumerable guides to construction, renovation, decoration and buying an apartment in *Gazeta Dom* (*Home Gazette*) or buying a car in the *Auto-Moto* section. We also print sample tests to help students prepare for standardized exams. Recently, our coverage of social reforms has been very popular, especially as there is a lot of confusion surrounding the changes. The most popular series are "How to Get Medical Treatment in This Mess" and "Choosing a Pension Plan."

Readers are also quite attached to our local supplements. They include lost pet listings, tongue-in-cheek competitions for the biggest pothole and hundreds of movie and theater ticket giveaways. Anyone can bid a fond farewell to a loved one in the obituary pages while some of our 20 local supplements print pictures of newborn babies in the "Welcome to the World" section. The supplements chronicle city life and include amusing stories such as that of the months-long search for a warthog that escaped from the zoo.

The supplements always keep a watchful eye on the local authorities. The series of articles "Cities Inside Out," published before the 1998 local elections, were the first summary of the achievements and failures of municipal authorities. The supplements also got involved in the tussle over the reorganization of Poland's regional administration map, organizing local referenda not only in those places threatened with losing their status as a province capital.

WE HAVE ALWAYS BEEN PROUD OF our roots in the opposition, KOR and Solidarity. But we never wanted to be either an organ of Solidarity or part of it. For we wanted to work for a democratic Poland, and not for successive Solidarity union bosses or for any other political party. When Lech Wałęsa and the Solidarity National Commission banned us from using the Solidarity symbol on our masthead, we painfully accepted the decision. Today we see it as a positive move—a trade union should be a trade union, and an independent newspaper an independent newspaper. The important thing is for the union to be wise and the newspaper to be absorbing and honest.

The first issue of *Gazeta Wyborcza* stated: "This newspaper has come into being as a result of the Round Table agreement, but we are publishing and editing it ourselves, and we alone are accountable."

"We do have links to Solidarity, but we intend to present the views and opinions of all society, of opposing trends."

Did we keep our word? We leave it up to our hundreds of thousands of readers to answer that question.

We believe that the prerequisite of our credibility is independence, political and material. We have built up this independence over 10 years, receiving many complements and diatribes along the way. Today is a fitting time to thank both our critics and our friends.

For nearly two centuries Poles symbolized martyrdom and bravery in the eyes of the world, but the Polish state and the Polish economy were spoken of with contempt. Today the world sees not only Polish heroism, but also the wisdom of Polish policy and the success of the Polish economy.

Today, Poland is no longer a lamentable object of pity in defeat, but respected, admired and envied in victory. This is also a good moment to remind ourselves of the downtrodden: the unemployed and the homeless, those impoverished and wallowing in apathy; those who do not take part in elections but strike and block roads for fear of an uncertain tomorrow. All are an intrinsic part of Poland and Polishness. Their fate should be a matter of common concern. Our attitude toward the downtrodden is, we believe, an essential measure of contemporary Polish patriotism.

What does patriotism, for that matter, mean to us at *Gazeta Wyborcza* today? We looked on with aversion when Solidarity members requested compensation for the years they spent in prison and others demanded compensation for time spent in concentration camps. Both have a right to compensation, but we believe that patriotism consists in not taking advantage of all our rights, in being able to offer communism's debts toward a free Poland.

That is our first instinct: to demand the truth and the righting of wrongs, while renouncing retaliation and veterans' privileges. Our patriotism is not a stick with which to beat those who have a different view; it is not to be used as a method of extortion by tossing around slogans about the homeland. What we need is common reflection for the common good. Our patriotism does not endorse any one political party to take possession of the state, be it postcommunist or post-anti-communist. Our patriotism is the firm conviction that Poland is the common homeland of all its citizens. Only the nation—meaning all the republic's citizens—can give the authorities a mandate. Any governing group that explains its right to rule through services performed in the past, no matter how great, is on the path to dictatorship. Our patriotism consists in opposing dictatorship. It also consists in memory. We try to remember that Poland was lost in the past not only due to foreign aggression, but also to internal discord and the drive for personal interests, and to an inability to compromise.

We are glad that Poland's happiest decade in the last 300 years also happens to be the best 10 years of our lives. The joy of this decade was created not only by *Gazeta Wyborcza,* but by all of democratic and independent Poland.

Adam Michnik is editor in chief of the Warsaw Gazeta Wyborcza, *the first Polish nongovernmental newspaper.*

11

Transforming Hungarian Broadcasting

Struggles for independent media

Péter Molnár

IT IS DIFFICULT TO TRANSFORM A political dictatorship with a state-controlled economy into a liberal democracy with a market economy. The creation of new institutions is not enough. The culture, the mind-set, the imperatives of the people who give them life must also develop, particularly for the media.

In Hungary, where Western investment in general is high compared to other former Soviet bloc countries, the liberalization of radio and television during the first half of the 1990s was slower than in other nations of Central and Eastern Europe. In other countries of the region, large private broadcasters began functioning while we in Hungary—where the constitution requires a two-thirds parliamentary majority for laws concerning freedom of the press—were engaged in a protracted debate on drafts of legislation that would govern our postcommunist broadcasting system.

At stake in Hungary was our ability to create a mixed broadcast system, with public and private broadcasters, in which the media would be free from political pressures. In this effort, the postcommunist socialists in the MSZP (Hungarian Socialist Party) and conservative nationalists in the MDF (Hungarian Democratic Forum), despite their differences, discovered a shared appreciation for politically controlled

103

broadcasting. The liberals in the Hungarian political system—the SZDSZ (Alliance of Free Democrats), heirs to the spirit of democratic opposition to communist rule, and FIDESZ (Alliance of Young Democrats), before their turn to conservatism—maintained a vision of independent media but remained a minority in this fight.

The debate on the Hungarian media law had two phases. The first, which lasted from 1990 to 1992, formed part of the so-called media war—a bitter dispute along party lines over the degree of government presence in Hungarian broadcasting that ended in a legislative debacle. Negotiations resumed in 1994 after the parliamentary elections. In late 1995, a broadcasting law was passed. Although it has been cursed on innumerable occasions since, its fruit is competition. Today, Hungarians can choose between programming on three distinct national television stations. This was the most important goal we achieved. Public television, however, is in ruins. Why did it happen? Did it have to happen?

THE CAUSES FOR THE MEDIA WAR may be found in the media policies of Hungary's different political parties. The chances for creation of a law liberalizing the media seemed to fluctuate according to the changing relations of power between conservative, liberal and socialist parties. (I was a part of these power struggles: as a liberal member of parliament from 1990 to 1993 for FIDESZ and from 1994 to 1998 for SZDSZ, I sat on a parliamentary committee on media.)

At first, the governing conservative parties appeared to be relatively open to a law limiting government influence on the media. It all began with promise. Initially, in the liberating atmosphere that surrounded the fall of communism in 1989, news programs on MTV, the public Hungarian Television station, suddenly became more interesting and informative—until, in a brief move that hinted of things to come, the socialist MSZP and conservative MDF temporarily delegated a supervisory committee to oversee MTV. Nevertheless, there were still hopeful signs: in a blessed moment of lucidity brought on by the shared experience of free elections in 1990, the six parliamentary parties agreed to appoint two widely respected social scientists to head Hungarian Television and Hungarian Radio (MR). Everyone regarded the BBC model as the one to follow, but the two presidents proved too autonomous for the government.

In the minds of the conservative governing coalition of the early '90s, the specter of liberal media power became increasingly strong.

Conservatives inveighed against the "threatening" and "conspiratorial" liberals. They attacked them for being deficient in national spirit and reluctant to promote the good image of Hungary abroad.

The two liberal parties that troubled the conservatives were FIDESZ and SZDSZ. Together with the postcommunist socialist party MSZP, which was showing some restraint following the election in 1990, they tried to create legislation that would firmly exclude government influence on the media. The right-wing government (and after 1994 the dominant part of the socialist MSZP as well) regarded the liberals' efforts to create independent media as part of a liberal media conspiracy rather than as legitimate efforts to expand Hungarian democracy. Thus, as a rule, the very politicians who proclaimed themselves champions of the national good did not, in fact, promote the best interests of the country.

As the conservative nationalist parties that constituted the government became more and more unpopular due to their outdated and aggressive politics, they increasingly blamed the messenger—the media—for their own mistakes. The conservatives became less inclined to give up the possibility of controlling the media. This tendency overshadowed debates on the regulation of public media—MTV, MR and Danube Television, a satellite public channel—and debates on guarantees of autonomy for the Radio and Television Office that would evaluate applications for frequencies. Because of the delay in distributing frequencies to private enterprises, MTV had a monopoly on nationwide television and therefore was strongly targeted by governing political forces.

PARALLEL TO NEGOTIATIONS ON MEDIA LAW, the government made repeated assaults on MTV and MR. In one morning session of my parliamentary committee, at the behest of the conservative Prime Minister József Antall, we were to hear from the nominees—who were nominated by the prime minister without previous negotiations with the oppositional parties—for the newly created vice presidential positions for public radio and television broadcasters. Prime Minister Antall's purpose was transparent: he wanted to control the presidents, who were attempting to follow the BBC model of impartial programming, by placing the vice presidents inside the institution. Virtually all the opposition representatives walked out in protest. Antall later carried out his plan but with other candidates.

In the frosty atmosphere of that afternoon, one of the government's representatives stated it flatly: the prime minister alone should have the power to appoint and dismiss the president of the Radio and Television Office. In the absence of a tradition of self-restraint, the prime minister's unchecked power to fill leading regulatory positions with power over the media posed a threat to freedom of the press. The prime minister, however, stuck to this position and resisted all attempts at compromise. For radicals to his right, liberal media policies smacked of decadent, libertine American culture. Once, the liberal representative Miklós Haraszti referred to the American FCC as an example that might be followed. The statement had an unusual effect on one of the vice presidents of the conservative nationalist MDF. István Csurka (whose weekly newspaper, *Magyar Fórum*, used openly anti-Semitic rhetoric in debates on media from 1992 on and who later founded the neo-Nazi Party of Hungarian Justice and Life that won a small number of parliamentary seats in 1998), muttered "FCC" with obvious distaste, left the room and took no part in subsequent legislative sessions on media.

The vote on the awkwardly compiled media bill took place in the last days of 1992. The voting about the numerous amendments lasted many hours. The opposition voted down the crucial parts of the bill that required a two-thirds majority. Ultimately the amputated bill received not a single "yes" vote.

With legislation stymied, both policy-makers and the press accepted the notion that allocations of frequencies and the introduction of new stations (with the exception of local ones from 1993 on) would have to wait until the passage of a broadcasting law. The only voice to break the near silence on the airwaves was the steadfastly liberal Tilos Rádió (Radio Forbidden), a pirate non-profit radio station in Budapest that, by 1991, had had enough of waiting and began broadcasting. The group presented a fine model of civil disobedience, broadcasting on the run while the authorities vainly pursued them. Thanks to a government order, they gained the opportunity to become legal. Moreover, they benefited from provisions in the 1995 media law fostering broadcasters who provide alternatives to commercial and public radio and television. In 1999, Tilos Rádió is the flagship of Hungary's nonprofit radio stations.

FROM LATE 1991 UNTIL 1994, the governing conservative parties, over-come by their frustration with criticism, used unconstitutional tactics against the presidents of MTV and MR, such as revalidating a communist government order issued in 1974 prescribing government control of public broadcasting—deemed unconstitutional by the Constitutional Court in 1992 but upheld until the media law was passed in 1995. On the initiative of the prime minister, the cultural affairs committee held hearings that were broadcast in summary form on television. According to plan, the parliamentary majority judged the two presidents unsuitable to fill their positions. It was no use for the president of MTV to refute the charges against him with a multitude of documents, nor did it help the president of MR when he walked out in protest at the beginning of the very first hearing. The only reason they were not dismissed immediately after the "show trials" was that the president of the Republic refused to give his approval.

Indeed, the government used budgetary pressure as well, freezing part of the allocation for MTV, for example. Finally, at the end of 1992, the government succeeded in forcing the two presidents to resign, partly by placing the budget of MR and MTV under the authority of the prime minister's office. This measure was judged unconstitutional by the Constitutional Court, but only after the election in 1994 and the decision was of no help to the ousted presidents of MR and MTV.

The vice presidents who were to manage MR and MTV until the 1994 elections turned them into the government's mouthpieces, dismissing 129 experienced employees of Hungarian radio on political grounds and canceling the more liberal news programs of MTV.

All of this had a boomerang effect in the 1994 elections. Hungarian voters, nostalgic for the relative security of communism, voted out the conservatives and gave 54 percent of the seats in parliament to the socialist MSZP. The backlash against the conservatives was due partly to their media policies: the brutal propaganda put out by the conservatives reminded voters, ironically, of the information manipulation of communism. Angered, they turned against the conservatives and voted for the socialist MSZP and liberal SZDSZ.

THE 1994 ELECTIONS REDREW THE HUNGARIAN political map. The liberal party SZDSZ, with almost 20 percent of the seats in parliament, entered into a coalition with the MSZP in the interest of achieving eco-

nomic stability and improving foreign relations frayed by the nationalist sensibility of the previous administration. It was a strange alliance:
the SZDSZ, founded by members of the democratic opposition of the
1980s and creators of the underground press, became partners with
former Communists.

When the 1994 governing coalition was formed, the new political
situation seemed encouraging. I trusted that my liberal party, SZDSZ,
would support a law laying the foundation for media autonomy. I
hoped that the socialist party would follow suit even as a governing
party. And I assumed that the conservative parties then in opposition
would naturally support a law limiting the government's media power.
If not, we could still count on a more than two-thirds majority from
the liberal-socialist coalition. But my optimism was again a vain hope.

There was some momentum at the beginning. The liberal SZDSZ
succeeded in making privatization the central question. Despite the
fresh experience with media being taken over by the government,
getting debate focused on privatization was difficult. The recently
emerged private companies—with the exception of nonprofit radio
stations—had no organizations that could represent their interests. I
even recommended to various television and radio companies that
they establish commercial associations to lobby for them. Many did.
In parliament, however, the SZDSZ remained alone in striving to create a wide-open media market and simple, independent supervision.

At this point the opinions of the Hungarian right and left coincided
again. Their common denominator, in itself a refutation of the para-
noid charge of liberal media power, was their shared desire to retain
state control over the media. Both wanted to guard the public mind.
Both wanted to keep the media in their own hands, not only to break
the imagined power of the liberals, but also because of their paternalist
sensibility.

In late 1995, the media bill eventually passed. Soon after, in 1996,
the Hungarian parliament created—to the greater glory of the left-right
platform—boards of curators to oversee public media. At least one
representative of each party sits on the supervisory boards of MTV,
MR and Danube Television. Legislated political control causes serious
damage in each body. The boards supervising national broadcasting
are, practically speaking, incapable of appointing presidents with in-
vigorating ideas. A similar structural paralysis afflicts the ORTT (National Radio and Television Board), where decisions on frequency
allocation at times obviously violate due process.

The politicized state of the boards pleases both the left and the right; there is no immediate solution in sight. Even if a much more liberal supervisory structure were written into law, it would succeed only if it were matched by regulators who would act in a fair and reasonable manner. Obviously, we must try to create supervisory bodies that help to develop the political culture of liberal democracy. The regulatory paralysis produced by the left-right platform has thus far thwarted this experiment, but the task remains open.

To the frustration of the liberals, Hungary has developed an open media market but not an enlightened system of media regulation. With the creation of the ORTT, distribution of frequencies to private broadcasters began—a positive result of the 1995 media law. At the same time, MTV, the public television broadcaster, became the first victim of faulty regulations—a negative result of the 1995 media law.

The essence of the left-right platform was to secure direct participation by parliamentary political parties in media supervisory bodies. Through the National Radio and Television Board, the resulting structure endangers even the independence of the private media, which are already overregulated by the law and hindered in adjusting programming to viewers' and listeners' demands. Applications for nationwide frequencies for private television stations were evaluated on political grounds, not according to the prospects for their content and the amount they bid for access to the airwaves. What we may hope, nevertheless, is that the real radio-television market that has developed will sooner or later compel more rational regulation that will allow less room for arbitrary decisions and encourage more self-restraint on the part of the powerful media curatorships.

IN 1999, THE NATIONAL COMMERCIAL television stations each have a one-third market share. In contrast, the national MTV's share is down to only about 10 percent. In the curious competition between public and private television, the media boards of curators are like ankle weights that MTV must wear in competition as well as in training.

The new coalition of right-wing parties, after 1998 governing with a narrow majority, voted only their own candidates onto the supervisory board of MTV. Using other tactics, the right-wing parties also took over the boards of MR and Danube Television. The still strong MSZP protests, but if it comes into power, it might again support regulation that violates freedom of the press. The liberal SZDSZ—

which allowed itself to be placed on the defensive too much in the previous coalition and has now shrunk to the status of a small party—also protests in vain against the governing coalition's takeover of media boards. MTV's debt grows while its ratings slide.

The political will and the measure of consensus necessary to lay the foundation for the institutional autonomy of the Hungarian media are lacking. The right-wing parties are "in possession" again and have again made national television into government television. They seem unperturbed by the fact that they are increasingly speaking to themselves alone when they hold forth from MTV's sparsely watched shows. This may be the final act in the 10-year tragedy of public television. In today's competitive market, one can no longer act as if it were the early '90s, when the majority of citizens could choose only between MTV's two programs. Low ratings might even make unliberal politicians more likely to ignore MTV. Paradoxically, such benign neglect could give MTV a better opportunity to become a genuine provider of public service television.

The media market has created a world that operates according to its own nature and the choices of viewers and listeners. This is the essence of the transformation in all new democracies where only government-controlled media functioned before the transition. Once this change has taken place—in Hungary relatively late, but strongly—the genie cannot be squeezed back into the bottle.

An illustration: At a meeting of experts in 1994, someone said worriedly that if a certain recommendation were to be implemented, it would set the media loose—that is, let them become independent. The target of the criticism replied succinctly: "But we wanted to set the media loose, didn't we?"

Serious public broadcasting, however, can be created only if the necessary two-thirds parliamentary majority understands the need to support, for the benefit of democracy, the autonomy of the media and the validation of professional measures of quality. As long as the fear of free media infects the left and the right, causing them to commit neurotic acts, institutional reforms will have no chance—not even on paper.

Péter Molnár teaches at the Media Center of ELTE University in Budapest. He was a member of the Hungarian parliament from 1990 to 1998.

12

Lessons for the Media from Foreign Aid

*Journalists in newly democratic countries must
chart their own course.*

John Maxwell Hamilton

THOSE WHO THINK IT THEIR DUTY to ask Bread and other Blessings daily
from Heaven, should they not think it equally a duty to communicate
of those blessings when they have received them," Benjamin Franklin
wrote. "But a Commercial Nation particularly should wish for a general Civilization of Mankind."

Many would be surprised to know that one of America's pioneer
journalists was also among the first to point out the virtues of foreign
aid; many more, no doubt, would be amazed to realize that in the last
decade journalists have gone beyond rhetorical support for assistance
to unprecedented levels of direct involvement. But inspired by the
opportunities for democracy building in the former Soviet bloc, journalists have ventured abroad to provide training and advice, and occasionally a little direct material support, to help build free, independent
press systems.

Moreover, their recent foreign aid programs have taken on the aspects of government-run foreign aid programs. In fact, the U.S. government funds many of these free-press initiatives. This makes it worthwhile to step back for a moment to review general lessons learned
from the last 50 years of general economic assistance abroad and to
ponder how they may apply to nascent media foreign aid.

FOR STARTERS, BE PATIENT. Early in their history Americans viewed themselves as having something to offer the rest of the world. With the exception of a few people like Franklin, Americans viewed this gift as a passive one. The United States, an editorial in *The Illinois Gazette* said in 1825, is "a country manifestly called by the Almighty to a destiny ... of holding up to a benighted and struggling world the great example of a government of the people by the people themselves."

This government by the people was not about to loan money for industrialization projects or even famine relief. In the 1890s, Congress voted down legislation to use a U.S. vessel to transport privately donated food to starving Russians. Opponents of the aid considered it unconstitutional to uplift other nations with American citizens' tax dollars. The first serious government-funded foreign aid did not come until Lend-Lease in World War II. Bilateral and multilateral economic assistance came after the war.

This history of reluctant material assistance helps explain why the federal government has treated foreign aid the way doctors treat appendicitis. Operate, get patients on their feet, do a checkup a few weeks later to make certain that everything is OK. Congress funded the Marshall Plan to rebuild Europe as "aid to end aid." In 1961, it created the U.S. Agency for International Development as a temporary organization, and it remained so until the late 1970s.

We now know that development does not come simply by getting the prices right, to use the lingo of economists, or some other simple one-step solution. Development is a slow process, with many setbacks. It is also tied to a variety of subtle factors. Women's literacy, for instance, is one of the best ways to promote economic productivity and reduce runaway population growth.

These lessons apply in building free press systems. Our free press is closely linked to our vigorous free market—to prosperous companies eager to advertise to a population that has money to spend and regularly reads newspapers and turns on the news. Journalists in newly democratizing countries are not likely to adopt our fact-based reporting until their bosses, seeing how that approach will attract more advertisers, insist upon it.

In Eastern Europe to do a story shortly after the Berlin Wall, I encountered one example after another highlighting the problems of turning back decades of central economic planning. "I have a whole wall of books," Karol Szwarc, secretary of state in Poland's considerably diminished Central Planning Office, said in an interview. "Everybody tells you how to make socialism more perfect. But there is not a single book to tell you how to move from socialism to capitalism." Even the language needed overhauling. Poles, he lamented, used the same word for stocks and bonds.

Retreaded journalists who toiled under the heavy-handed communist system see press freedom as an opportunity to vent, rather than an opportunity for responsible, balanced reporting. As Alexis de Tocqueville said of those who brought down the French monarchy, revolutionaries "didn't have any idea of the dangers which always accompany even the most necessary revolutions."

William Dickinson, longtime editor with *The Washington Post* now holding the Manship Chair in Journalism at Louisiana State University, went to Romania through a Knight Foundation International Press Fellowship. "There's a saying in my part of the United States," he wrote back to the International Center for Journalists, which administers the Knight Fellows program, "that you can take the boy out of the country but you can't take the country out of the boy. Romania is still trying to exorcise the habits and systems that characterized 45 years of hard experience."

The media in these countries "need to realize that being independent does not necessarily equate with being in opposition," as international media consultant George Krimsky puts it. "It's OK to support the government when it is right."

All of that said, the remarkable aspect of contemporary media development in Eastern and Central Europe is that it has come so far so fast. From its very beginnings, the United States embraced free enterprise; it did not acquire the professional press values we cherish today until the end of the 19th century. Early journalists were nothing if not partisan, often in vicious, irresponsible ways.

The best way to view development is as an unending process for everyone. By way of example, we Americans have plenty of media problems of our own. At the moment we worry, among other things, about the increased emphasis on the bottom line and the impact of Matt Drudge on the quality of our civic discourse. Indeed, many journalists are eager to go abroad to train foreign journalists because they are fed up with journalism practices in their own news organizations.

THIS OCCASIONAL DISENCHANTMENT with our own newsrooms leads to a second lesson: we don't have all the answers, and in any case, we need to help journalists abroad solve their own problems.

Secretary of State George C. Marshall understood this when he said in 1947 that it would be "neither fitting nor efficacious" for the United States to draw up a plan for European reconstruction. This was the genius of the European Recovery Program, as the post-World War II Marshall Plan was formally called. Americans would help after the 16 European nations worked out a regionally acceptable scheme. The resulting plan laid the groundwork for European economic and political integration.

The same approach was not used elsewhere, however. "We did not see the prerequisites for a collaborative approach" with developing countries, Marshall Plan architect George Kennan commented when I interviewed him in Berlin at the 40th anniversary celebration of the Marshall Plan (a remarkable celebration because in a speech to commemorate the occasion Kennan foresaw the collapse of the Berlin Wall). When newly independent Third World countries hauled down the flag of their colonial masters after World War II, few had anything like an adequate cadre of highly trained government bureaucrats. Taking a paternalistic attitude, donors supplied the development plans as well as the development money.

Whatever the rationale for the second approach at the time, media assistance must adopt the first strategy. Journalists in newly democratic countries have a better chance of succeeding if they chart their own course.

There are practical reasons for this. American journalism cannot be pulled up by the roots and transplanted in foreign soil. The press systems in advanced industrialized nations differ in some respects and still serve their publics. The Swedish government, for instance, nurtures diverse points of view by funding small-run publications with distinct voices, something the United States would never stand for. We should expect similar differences in newly democratic countries.

One way to foster local problem solving is the creation of journalism associations. Media competition is intense in former Soviet bloc countries. Anxious about the survival of their own publications and wary of the Soviet-style labor system that locked them in unions, these journalists rarely get together the way their American counterparts do to think about best practice. Much work is needed before journalists in newly democratic countries understand that by collaborating they have a much better chance of beating back government restrictions that hurt them all.

The Independent Journalism Foundation, among a few other institutions, operates in-the-field training centers for working journalists that sometimes include special training for students. This is very useful. But mindful of the need for truly indigenous training, media assistance organizations should also focus attention on universities.

American journalists who think j-schools in their own country are too theory oriented should take a long look at journalism education in Eastern and Central Europe and the former Soviet Union. The university media departments I have seen really ought to be called philosophy departments. Typical professors have no journalism experience and little pragmatic knowledge of what free-enterprise journalism is all about. Students frequently graduate without ever having written a news story.

The Freedom Forum, which has increased its presence abroad in a variety of valuable ways, is starting an International Initiative for Journalism Education that may go a long way toward helping. While American scholars will be tempted to see this as a way to carry out research with colleagues abroad, such pursuits should be secondary to upgrading professional journalism training.

The future of good journalism in these countries lies with eager young men and women who are not burdened with the past but armed at a tender age by their own schools with the outlook and tools to do the daily job of gathering news responsibly.

It also lies, contrary to much newsroom wisdom, with teaching governments how to interact constructively with the media. "There are numerous countries in the world where the politicians have seized absolute power and muzzled the press," David Brinkley said 25 years ago. "There is no country in the world where the press has seized absolute power and muzzled the politicians."

Perhaps the press is never a danger to freedom, as Brinkley suggested. But it is also true that a free press does not operate in a vacuum any more than any other institution in a developing country does.

Over the years development experts have learned the hard way that foreign assistance doesn't work if the government is not supportive.

Agricultural advisors can show farmers how to increase crop yields, but farmers will not grow more if the government artificially keeps food prices low.

The parallel with media assistance is this: it is not enough to teach journalists how to fire tough questions at government officials. Government officials must learn how to answer the questions. Our media system works as effectively as it does because journalists and the people they cover volley back and forth energetically and often to mutual advantage.

Training officials to manage their media relations is not merely a matter of showing them how to protect their political flanks. They must learn how to create political constituencies that bring positive change. This is important in fledgling democracies that are retooling their economies.

Consider the simple idea of asking the public to pay for heating their apartments. Payment for services is necessary for wise use of energy (if you are not paying for heat, you do not conserve it) and in order to develop revenue streams to repair and upgrade services. But communism taught the public to expect free heat; and in any event, "liberation" for many of these people has meant freedom to look for— and often not find—work. Many people feel much poorer than they did before they tore down the Berlin Wall.

Leaders in these countries need the media to bring about such badly needed socioeconomic change and at the same time ensure their own political survival. If they do not learn to work constructively through a free media, no one should be surprised if they are tempted to douse the lights in troublesome newsrooms and resort to the crude propaganda of an earlier time. It is even less likely that many governments will stop charging ridiculously steep broadcast licensing fees, controlling newsprint and distribution networks, or passing laws limiting the amount of advertising that a newspaper can run or the amount of its assets that a company can spend on advertising to reach consumers.

As MUCH AS GOVERNMENTS NEED to work with journalists, donors need to work together effectively and efficiently.

Foreign aid has continually searched for true north and never found it. In the beginning, development experts concentrated on national economic growth, believing the benefits would trickle down to poor people. When this did not work, donors directed aid at the potentially productive poor, which worked better but was more complicated. More recently they have had to address overarching structural fiscal reforms to deal with overwhelming Third World debt and other economic imbalances.

Simultaneously, donor governments have switched their attention from one country or region to another depending on what seemed expedient, promising or necessary at the moment. At one point, about 30 years ago, the U.S. Agency for International Development directed roughly one-half of its assistance programs at Vietnam.

Contemporary media assistance has exhibited some of these same traits. The most obvious problem is media experts congregating in a few countries. When Great Britain's Institute for War and Peace Reporting sent me to Bosnia, it had trouble finding people to train when I got there. At lunch with a leading Bosnian editor one day, I offered to provide a handsome scholarship for master's degree training at our journalism school to any promising reporter he might select. He had so many different offers for help on the table that he didn't even give this one serious consideration.

Crowding advisors in one place invites a quick-fix mentality, rather than the stick-to-itiveness that is really needed. Beyond that, a developing nation has only so much absorptive capacity, an aid expert's way of saying that you cannot stuff development into a country the way you can corn into a goose.

By focusing attention on a few countries *du jour*, we have ignored many others that are desperately interested in training and assistance, and ready to use it effectively. "The Cold War is over," Maj. Gen. Joseph Garba, a Nigerian diplomat, said a few years ago, "and Africa lost."

Bratislava is more attractive to many would-be media advisors than, say, Lagos, but both need help. And if free press is a value worth promoting in the Slovak Republic, it is equally worthwhile to promote in Nigeria and everywhere it is welcome.

Years ago, multilateral development banks and countries with bilateral aid programs began meeting annually to work out aid strategies for each recipient country. These gatherings also provided an opportunity for collective lobbying with governments on needed economic policy.

Journalism assistance organizations would benefit from similar mechanisms. One possible approach for helping avoid duplication lies in the International Journalists' Network operated by the International Center for Journalists. Their Web site IJNet.org posts information on media development lessons learned, reports who is doing what and lists knowledgeable contacts in the field. Admittedly, nongovernment assistance groups are less inclined to get together for sharing sessions than are government ministries, but they can coordinate more closely than they do now.

Funders, of course, can help by insisting on such cooperation as a prerequisite to funding initiatives. "The good ones already do," says Whayne Dillehay, ICFJ's vice president. "But much more attention needs to be given to cooperation."

And cooperation might help donors get more out of foreign aid for themselves.

IN 1861, KING MONGKUT OF SIAM offered to send elephants to President Abraham Lincoln to help him win the Civil War. In 1931, the people of the Cameroons collected $3.77 for the relief of "the starving" in New York City. These reverse foreign aid activities may seem comical to us. But it would be a mistake to discount that others can help us while we help them.

To the extent that economic assistance in the last century has created prosperity, it has enlarged trading possibilities for our manufacturers and farmers. When aid has paid more attention to the environment, it has helped reduce such problems as global warming for all of us. The list of this sort of example could go on at length, but focus for a minute on the benefits of media assistance.

Economic prosperity in the information age is linked more than ever to free press systems. As noted above, economic prosperity creates growth within countries and among countries. As one of the world's leading trading nations, we have an economic interest in promoting a free press abroad.

Free press systems benefit American journalists and their institutions directly. Because of their duty to inform their customers, journalists have an interest in securing as much access to the rest of the world as possible. Countries with free press systems afford more access than those without. Also, well-trained foreign journalists can aid our media organizations. There is no good purpose here for reciting all the reasons (many of them bad) for our increasingly inward-looking media companies. Suffice it to say that foreign journalists can provide us with valuable reporting at a reasonable cost.

Reminding ourselves of this is important because long-term foreign aid is predicated on self-interest. Humanitarian sentiment has motivated Americans to provide disaster relief but has not provided a sufficiently strong motivation to promote significant development assistance. The United States ranks dead last among the industrialized countries in the percent of its GNP directed at aid, 0.12 percent. If media assistance is perceived as nice but not essential, governments, foundations and media companies are unlikely to step up with enough resources over a long enough time to get the job done.

FINALLY, MEDIA ASSISTANCE IS SO important that the media must take the lead in making it work.

For years government and multilateral development agencies showed no inclination to pay attention to media. The World Bank was notorious for thinking about the economy without considering the political ramifications of its palliatives for aid recipients. That has begun to change. The Agency for International Development especially has discovered media training.

Unfortunately, bilateral and multilateral development authorities have little experience in the media. After years of tying foreign assistance to its political agenda, USAID officials are inclined to do just what one would expect. They support media organizations overseas aligned with U.S. policy. It helps when a large aid organization works through an intermediary like the Eurasia Foundation, which gets aid to the grass roots without a lot of paperwork, although it has little in-house media expertise.

Also troublesome, many government and nongovernment groups fund journalism training when they are really interested in something else. Motives range from the sublime (equipping journalists to cover family planning better) to the you-know-what. Internews proudly announced this year that it was helping launch a home improvement television program for Bosnians. Internews says this is part of its "overall program of support for independent media in Bosnia." USAID is funding it.

For these reasons journalists should be chiefly responsible for conceiving and carrying out media assistance. Government and nonmedia foundations can help with funding, and they should. But more money must come from media companies, who should help pay for equipment as well as training. The International Media Fund filled this material assistance role admirably while it was in business; its successors have done much less. Media companies also can help by giving paid leave to staffers who are willing to help their brethren abroad.

"As military policy is too important a matter to be left ultimately to the generals, so is foreign aid too important a matter to be left in the end to the economists," wrote eminent political scientist Hans Morgenthau in the early 1980s. Now, at last, when development experts are recognizing that a strong media is essential to development, we can usefully take Morgenthau a step further.

Journalists were among the first to call for foreign aid. As the ones who know and care most about a free press, they should make propagation of independent media their special aid mission. The task is too important a matter to be left to anyone else.

John Maxwell Hamilton, a former foreign correspondent, is dean of the Manship School of Mass Communication, Louisiana State University. He served in the U.S. Agency for International Development and at the World Bank.

13

Wall Fall Profits, Wall Fall Losses

The media and German reunification

Stephan Russ-Mohl

FOR MANY EXPERTS IT IS UNDISPUTED that the media—specifically West German TV—played a major role in the revolution that culminated in the opening of the Berlin Wall. Before 1989, 80 percent of East Germans could watch West German programs. "The class enemy entered the living rooms every evening," Communist Party functionaries used to bemoan. TV shaped the expectations of the ordinary GDR citizens as to how much nicer it ought to be living in a colorful capitalist market economy instead of a gray "workers' paradise."

There is no doubt, that television—as well as other modern technologies, like Xerox machines—had their impact on spreading revolutionary activities in the former Eastern bloc. Simply by reporting what was taking place elsewhere, TV was igniting the protest movement. And because TV cameras were everywhere, they served also as a shield against brutality by the police or armed forces that might otherwise have undercut protest activities.

However, one should be cautious with monocausal explanations: if TV really played a major role, it would be hard to explain why revolutionary activities appeared much earlier in Poland, Hungary, Czechoslovakia and even the former Soviet Union, before they finally took off in East Germany—which was most directly, and without any language barrier, exposed to a broad variety of Western TV programs.

ONCE THE WALL CAME DOWN, there was more than a new world to be discovered by East Germans; there was also an old one, broken into pieces, with very little from it left to give further orientation. Whatever East Germans knew about the West, they knew from watching West German TV—news, soap operas, advertisements—a media world of its own that had little to do with the "real world" they were heading for. Now, for the first time, they could also read uncensored newspapers and magazines—previously forbidden and only rarely smuggled across the border. West Germans, in turn, could participate in the journalism of East Germany. The consequences of these changes for journalism, politics and culture in a unified Germany are at once momentous and subtle—and likely to be visible for years to come.

Initially, there was an overwhelming interest in print media from the West. The mood was euphoric on both sides; only a few skeptics disclosed doubts whether something like reunification might work at all. Many East German intellectuals had envisioned a "third way" between capitalism and socialism, and dreamed of building a new society that would somehow combine Western riches with Eastern job security and equal distribution of wealth. The great majority of East Germans, however, hoped and expected simply that they would catch up within a short time and would have, like their West German "brothers and sisters," consumer goods, travel and other pleasures that make everyday life more enjoyable. Some West German intellectuals suggested a slower pace of reunification, but they were disregarded. The business elites in West Germany and in Western Europe were eager to take over the new markets, and the political establishment imposed, on the East, the West German system that had worked nicely for the last 50 years. German intellectuals familiar with basic economics played word games and spoke of the "Wall fall profits" that entrepreneurs and adventurers would gain.

Currency reform transformed generally worthless East German savings into valuable West German deutschmarks and helped many East Germans immediately get one of their most desired consumer goods: their own car. The trade unions, reaching for new members in East Germany, quickly demanded equal pay for East German and West German workers.

No longer did anyone in East Germany compare his situation with developments in Poland, Czechoslovakia, Hungary or Russia. The only measure that counted was how "to keep up with the Meiers" next door, how they were doing compared to their well-off West German compatriots.

THE CULTURAL CLASH WAS foreseeable and inevitable. The West Germans were willing to share—but not too much. Mainly, they wanted to provide help for self-help. Besides that, many West Germans were looking forward to getting back some of their lost riches in the East, in particular real estate. East Germans did not want to give it back. Socialized by socialism, many of them expected that West Germans would more generously share their riches. From their point of view, the East Germans had suffered more and longer from World War II. To Easterners, it was now the West Germans' turn to sacrifice more than just a moderate tax hike to the East.

Indeed, there were a lot of benevolent West Germans who not only invested but even moved eastward. They dedicated several months or even years of their lives to the *"Aufbau Ost"*—to help rebuild the East. But there were, of course, also adventurers, fortune hunters and shameless speculators for immediate "Wall fall profits" invading East Germany like a plague of locusts.

Nobody really knew how to proceed. There were no policy "recipes" for reunifying a country with two completely different political and socioeconomic systems. Trade unions were unwilling to take into account the big productivity and skill differences between the two labor forces. Consequently, East German workers' salaries rose overnight, surpassing those everywhere else in Eastern Europe, but workers' productivity was unchanged. The markets in Eastern Europe, where East German goods were traded traditionally, broke away within months. East Germany was left with a long-lasting structural crisis.

The West German government poured billions and billions of tax money into East Germany. A large share of this money consisted of welfare benefits that probably prevented civil upheaval but otherwise did little to improve the long-term prospects of the economy. East Germany was not ready for the economic takeoff it had dreamed of. The structural crisis lead to agony, discontent and unemployment rates of more than 20 percent—previously known in Germany only during the world economic crisis of the late 1920s. The successors to the formerly ruling Communists of the SED, the Party of Democratic Socialism (PDS), saw their share of votes in local, regional and national elections skyrocket. West Germans could not understand why so many Easterners entrusted their fate to their former oppressors.

Of course, there are many factors that can explain how too high expectations were transformed into disappointment and frustration. But it would be a mistake to assume that the media did not contribute to this process in their own way. Certainly they reported widely, some of them even without comment or criticism, Chancellor Helmut Kohl's unrealistic promise during the election campaign of 1990 that within a few years there would be "flowering landscapes" of prosperity in the former GDR. This, however, can be seen as the media's main function: to report news as well as unrealistic promises from relevant sources. As long as journalists place such news in context, there is no reason to blame the messenger if promises don't become true. But there are other reasons why the media played a double-edged role in the unification process. To understand it better, we have to take a closer look at what happened to them in East Germany after the fall of the Wall.

As long as the wall was there, watching West German TV was the favorite pastime for East Germans. After all, their own TV programs were pretty boring. After the communist order fell, its highly centralized television and radio network was liquidated. Within two years, most of the once 14,000 people working for State Television of the GDR were laid off. Since then, all national networks of any importance (ARD and ZDF as public television, SAT.1, RTL and ProSieben as private networks) were and are dominated by West German headquarters, West German (or Austrian) CEOs and mostly West German editors in chief.

As part of the "federal" system that had become a trademark of German public broadcasting during the 50 years after World War II, two new regional public television and radio stations were founded in the East: the Ostdeutscher Rundfunk Brandenburg and the Mitteldeutscher Rundfunk. They belong and contribute to the public ARD network, but they also provide regional news. Two more of the West German public radio stations, the Norddeutscher Rundfunk and the Sender Freies Berlin, started additionally to serve East German publics in Mecklenburg-Vorpommern and in East Berlin. A national public radio network, Deutschlandradio, was established by a fusion of the West German Deutschlandfunk, the West Berlin-based RIAS (Radio in the American Sector) and the leftovers of the East German Deutschlandsender Kultur.

Besides that, East Germany opened up for new private, local and regional radio and TV stations. For example, in Brandenburg can be found 27 commercial TV city channels. The strongest ones work together to create the Brandenburger Fernseh-Netz, a network of local stations that cooperate in selling commercials as well as in providing regional news to their audiences. But their share of overall TV programs in Germany remained marginal. As they did before the Wall came down, East Germans continued to watch West German TV.

PRINT MEDIA, HOWEVER, present a completely different picture. In the GDR, besides the two national party newspapers, *Neues Deutschland* and *Junge Welt*, regional SED-party newspapers had the strongest market position. All of them were sold by the Treuhand organization, which had taken over "the people's" leftovers of the bankrupt GDR economy in order to find new private owners for them.

Unfortunately, Treuhand had other things in mind than a media policy that might have created competition among newspapers and could have helped at least some of the many startups of the early '90s survive despite the old and mighty Party papers. Its bureaucrats handled the newspapers as if they were selling screw factories. They wanted nothing but to stimulate investment and save as many jobs as possible—even those in the newsroom that belonged exclusively to partisan Communists. The 14 monopoly papers were sold to experienced new owners, meaning big players from the West German media industry. And those media companies did not do what would have been in the public interest, but rather what seemed most profitable for them: they brought in new leadership from the West, built up new, modern printing facilities and laid off as many people as Treuhand would allow. And they killed their newly founded, inexperienced and smaller competitors by dumping prices. Besides that, they kept most of the original newsroom staff. The result, as the *Neue Zürcher Zeitung* reported recently referring to research done by Beate Schneider: 70 percent of the reporters and editors working today for East German newspapers were on the job before 1989.

East German regional newspapers lost about one third of their former circulation, but nevertheless they increased their market share in the total East German newspaper market from 63 percent pre-1989 to 78 percent in 1999. Today, newspapers like the *Freie Presse* in Chemnitz

(450,000 circulation), the *Mitteldeutsche Zeitung* in Halle and the *Sächsische Zeitung* in Dresden (both 400,000 circulation) are among the largest newspapers in Germany. The two most important national papers in the old GDR, the *Neues Deutschland* (pre-1989 circulation more than 1 million) and the *Junge Welt* (pre-1989 circulation more than 1.5 million) have survived so far, but they have been marginalized: *Neues Deutschland*'s circulation is down to 70,000 and *Junge Welt*'s to 14,000.

In the print media market, including journals and newsmagazines, not a single West German publication really gained ground. East Germans continue to read East German papers and magazines—or no paper at all.

THERE MAY HAVE REMAINED A FEW traits of a capitalist economy that were not reported adequately to East Germans before or since 1989: that there can be high unemployment, that you need certain skills as well as capital-intensive machinery, equipment and infrastructure to get started, that to a certain degree it is the old game of survival of the fittest and the smartest, that you have to take care of yourself instead of letting the state push you around. It was surprising how rapidly many East Germans picked up the "lingo" of capitalism, but it takes a lot longer to live and behave according to the new rules of self-reliance and responsibility. The media provided a lot of advice, and a completely new genre, the so-called *Ratgeberjournalismus*—consulting journalism, that gave advice on such subjects as opening a bank account and understanding tax laws—flourished in East Germany.

Television programs, however, became quite superficial. By 1989, West German TV had been for the last four years on the road to commercialization—which meant less and less in-depth coverage of political and economic developments. Some researchers, like the media watchdogs from *Medien-Tenor*—a sister organization of the Washington based *Media Monitor*—argued that even the public television networks, which still had a market share of close to 50 percent during the early 1990s, simply neglected developments in East Germany.

It was a *"Wirtschaftswunder,"* or "economic miracle," to watch how rapidly telephones systems, highways, shopping malls were built everywhere in the East. But little of this good news was reported. After the revolutionary years when East Germany absorbed so much attention, the national media had moved on to other stories and rarely covered the nitty-gritty details of implementing reunification.

IN CONTRAST, LOCAL AND REGIONAL newspapers in East Germany were focusing mostly on East Germany and echoing a lot of lamentations. Indeed, *ostalgia*—nostalgia for the East—became surprisingly hip during the mid-'90s. East Germans (*"Ossis"*) started to commiserate with each other, and it became popular to view West Germans (*"Wessis"*) as colonialists who had taken over the East. In a time of rapid change, there was little that people in the East could cling to—so they grasped at their newspapers, which emphasized localism and provided an identity.

But there is another explanation for the increase of misunderstandings and misperceptions after 1989: very few journalists had moved from West to East. Most who did ended up in command positions rather than in day-to-day reporting. In the rank and file survived many editors and reporters who had inhaled communist ideology in the so called Red Cloister of Lipsia, the one and only journalism school of the GDR, which was under complete control of the SED. Journalists in the GDR were supposed to serve in the communist propaganda machinery and had to be 150 percent partisans. This meant that even the secret police, the Stasi, did not care very much for newsroom operations. Newsrooms were simply considered "off limits" for the enemies of the socialist empire. The Stasi affiliation of journalists in some of the regional monopoly papers of the GDR was recently analyzed by three historians, Ulrich Kluge, Stefan Birkefeld and Silvia Müller, but they found little evidence of extensive secret service activity. Of course, every newsroom was infiltrated by Stasi members, but there was not much for them to do: "In the area of mass media the conformity with the socialist system was so high, that the Stasi did not need to put in extra work to ensure control," the historians concluded.

While West Germans during the 1970s were obsessed with keeping all kinds of "Communists"—kids of the 1968 student rebellion—out of public office and journalism, such issues were handled differently after 1989. Most public officials as well as university professors who had served the SED regime had to go, but many newspaper journalists could stay in their jobs as long as they had not been involved in direct collaboration with the Stasi.

Quite a few of them continued to write at least in a way that did not harm the postcommunist, leftist PDS. "Journalists are much more dedicated to criticizing the new political order than to criticizing the GDR past," says Claus Detjen, who came from West Germany to become the publisher and editor of the *Märkische Oder-Zeitung* after the Wall fell. On the other hand, Detjen, who retired last year from his post at the East German regional paper, is probably right in stating, in *Die politische Meinung*, a conservative party journal, that the work of these journalists has been part of the success story of East German newspapers since 1989: by concentrating on local news, and by relying on reporters and editors who were struggling themselves for survival in the new order, they provided "identification" to their readers—and they "went their way into the new era and the new society at a pace the readers could keep up with." On the other hand, these journalists may have contributed to the high level of dissatisfaction and frustration that persists in East Germany, and that helps explain how the PDS could gain so much support.

THE FOCAL POINT OF the opportunities and calamities of "media reunification" in Germany can be seen most clearly in the media market in Berlin, particularly the newspaper market. Contrary to the realities in most other parts of East Germany, Berlin is the most competitive metropolitan media market in Germany. But if one takes a closer look, even Berlin consists still of two markets: the one in former East Berlin and the one in former West Berlin. In Berlin everything seems to move more rapidly, yet nothing moves at all. This paradox was especially apparent during the decisive two years of the government's relocation from Bonn to Berlin.

Everything is moving: more and more of the international correspondents are settling down in Berlin. All the big television networks are at least building up major dependencies in Berlin, SAT.1 is moving its headquarters to the capital, and the all-news channel n-tv, Germany's CNN, is based in Berlin. After several unsuccessful and unprofessional startups of local TV, the new TV Berlin will probably flourish. There is a steady coming and going between dozens of local and regional public and private radio stations that compete for market shares and survival.

Ten newspapers are available daily. Six of them are run by three of the largest German media chains, Axel Springer AG, Gruner + Jahr (a

Bertelsmann daughter) and the Verlagsgruppe Georg von Holtzbrinck. Each of them would like to become the parent company of the future *"Hauptstadtzeitung"*—the flagship newspaper that will dominate, like *The Washington Post* in the United States, not only the regional newspaper market of the capital, but will also become the authoritative voice from Berlin, renowned nationally and internationally. The papers competing for this rank are *Die Welt*, Springer AG; *Berliner Zeitung*, Gruner + Jahr; and *Der Tagesspiegel*, Holtzbrinck.

Publishers have developed strategies and invested millions of *deutschmarks*, but they also engage in a continuous process of trial and error and price dumping. Even the editors in chief are replaced much more frequently than in any other more stable newspaper market—and every newcomer tries to "reinvent" his newspaper anew. Although all 10 papers have improved significantly in the long run, publishers' tactics occasionally jeopardize and counteract their strategies.

Prices for street sales as well as for classified ads are in the cellar. Only in Berlin can a high-quality regional paper be bought for less than one *deutschmark*. Nowhere in the world can the effects of competition, even of ruinous competition, be better studied than here—except, perhaps in London, where Rupert Murdoch is still fighting for larger market shares.

On the other hand, nothing is moving. Even in Berlin, most of the publishers' and top editors' positions are still held by West Germans (with the exception of *Neues Deutschland*). Unmet is the challenge to integrate minorities into newsrooms—though Berlin has become the most multicultural city of Germany and is home to hundreds of thousands of foreigners: Turks, Russians, Poles and Italians. Nowhere else but in Berlin do East Germans and West Germans cooperate, as rank and file, in the daily routines of news gathering.

Though each of the three aspirants for the rank of *"Hauptstadtzeitung"* has come from a different starting point, none of them has won much territory: *Der Tagesspiegel* is still the intelligentsia newspaper, which is read by the elites in West Berlin, the *Berliner Zeitung* has remained the market leader in East Berlin, and *Die Welt*, though it moved from Bonn to Berlin several years ago, does not yet have a local base in Berlin, though it is the only one of the three that is a national paper with a strong position in northern Germany. The target for each of the three, to get to the Olympian standard of quality seen in papers such as the *Frankfurter Allgemeine*, the *Süddeutsche Zeitung* or the *Neue Zürcher Zeitung*, is still out of sight.

Publishers in Berlin have become very nervous. Two of the three most prestigious local papers have been in red ink for many years, and most of the others have seen a drop in circulation. Year by year thousands of newspaper readers seem to disappear in the Bermuda Triangle and never return.

THUS, COMPETITION WILL REMAIN stimulating, and there will be turbulence and surprises in the future. Competition will continue among the media and will affect a handful of German cities that would like to become Germany's media metropolis. In Germany, as in the United States, it is probable that only one of the three or four best national newspapers will be located in the capital. Berlin is unlikely to become the media capital of its country in the 21st century. It will have to share the rank of a big player with other places such as Hamburg, Munich, Köln—and even Gütersloh, where the headquarters of Bertelsmann are located in the middle of German nowhereland. With this arrangement, the federalist structures of postwar Germany will be reflected in the future.

Due to its geographic location, however, Berlin seems to be predestined to play a major role as a turntable in European East-West relations. Berlin-based media, especially newspapers, could intensify their coverage of Europe, particularly Eastern Europe, and thus contribute to reducing the mental barriers and anxieties that persist between East and West. Unfortunately, Berlin so far is not well prepared for such a function, neither "medially" nor mentally.

The problem is that citizens in both parts of the new capital were "locked in" for such a long time—East Berliners behind the Iron Curtain, and West Berliners in their artificial, insular world that was surrounded by barbed wire, militia and the Wall. It was one of the sad experiences of newspaper editors during the years after the Wall had come down: after a few weeks of curiosity, readers in both parts of the city started to lose interest in the other side. West Berliners complained that the *Berliner Morgenpost* and *Der Tagesspiegel* offered them too much news from East Berlin, while the East Berliners disliked how many stories in the *Berliner Zeitung* dealt with West Berlin. Readers whose attention had been focused for 50 years on only a fraction of their city were now overwhelmed by sudden changes. They reacted as most of us would react: like snails withdrawing into their shells, where they feel safer than "out there" in a rapidly changing environment. Citizens who are so busy with their own small world find it difficult to take a closer look at what is happening elsewhere. This may be not only the problem of Berliners, but also of Germans elsewhere as they approach the 21st century.

Ten years is not enough to make up for 50 years of ideological and cultural separation. "East Germans are different," concluded Germany's major media trade journal, *journalist*. "They watch more TV and listen longer to radio. They read local subscription newspapers more frequently, they buy neither tabloids nor the national quality papers. And they are less enthusiastic about magazines."

For now, East Germans continue to rely mostly on their own print media and consider major TV network news as alien to their needs and self-esteem. Someday TV soap operas and sports like soccer and car races, which are enjoyed in both parts of the country, may provide the glue that holds the two cultures together.

How to succeed with media in Germany's East? The answer that Jochen Wolff, editor of the most successful newly founded East German magazine, the tabloid *Super-Illu*, offered in 1991 still stands: "*Denke Ost und handle West*," or "think like Easterners and act like Westerners." It might still be the right answer in the year 2011.

Stephan Russ-Mohl, a professor of journalism and media management, is the director of the Journalisten-Kolleg at the Freie Universität Berlin.

Part 3

NEW STORIES

The revolution passed, as Havel said, from poetry into prose.
—*JAY ROSEN*

14

Civil Society and the Spirit of 1989

Lessons for journalism, from East to West

Jay Rosen

WHEN THE BERLIN WALL FELL, there was only a shrunken, ill-fed and retreating army behind it. No guns boomed, no tanks rolled. If anything should make us wonder about the power of words, ideas and convictions in politics, surely it is the experience of those who longed for open and democratic societies and who saw their wishes fulfilled amid the epic events of 1989.

Ten years later, the meaning of those days is still unclear to us. But if we do not look to the ideas that mattered in Eastern Europe, before and after its velvet revolutions, then we are certain to miss what they can yet teach us about our own quest for democracy and the journalism that is done in service to it.

Among the lessons we should retain is the importance of "civil society," an idea—and a reality—that pointed the way to democracy's rebirth in the East, while illuminating its troubled condition in the West. This same idea, under a variety of headings, has lately influenced the American press. One example is the movement for public (or civic) journalism, which I have been engaged in, but there are others.

CIVIL SOCIETY IS AN IN-BETWEEN TERRITORY—neither the state in its official capacity nor citizens in their private affairs. It is a middle ground between the two. In this civil space we can picture strangers becoming citizens, and readers becoming publics. We can imagine debate and discussion, conducted not by princes but by free-thinking and reasoning people who form associations, claim their voice, argue among themselves and refashion their common sense. Civil society is an open sphere. It may be guaranteed by law, but it is not equivalent to the rule of law. Governments rise and fall against its backdrop. Politics flows into it and feeds off it. Journalism finds its audience there, and much of its purpose.

Although it has something in common with the "free market" (namely freedom), civil society is not another name for the private economy or the marketplace of ideas. It brings people together, voluntarily, so that they might discover themselves in number and work on common tasks—which could be practicing their religion, organizing a trade union, or heading up an organization such as the Red Cross, as presidential candidate Elizabeth Dole has done.

Like the Red Cross, Charter 77—the movement of intellectuals and activists that bedeviled the communist regime in Czechoslovakia—was a classic example of civil society. One of its founding members, Václav Havel, was lifted to the Czech presidency by appealing to a principle of legitimacy that originated in the civil sphere, where people spoke up to say, "We want a chance for a decent life." At his first inaugural, Havel announced: "My people, your government has been returned to you." He could say that and be believed because his authority derived from the Czech and Slovak people, imagined not as the Communist Party of Czechoslovakia—which had completely discredited itself—but as a civil society demanding a change in the nature of power.

"Havel to the Castle!" shouted the crowds in Prague, using a street term for the president's office. They knew what this meant—not a new boss, but an end to being bossed by a corrupt and unaccountable regime. Government could no longer be based on the claim that the Party and the people were one and the same. The time for that fiction had passed.

Havel, in effect, negotiated the Party's surrender on behalf of an emergency alliance of forces called the Civic Forum. His authority, murky to nonexistent in law, was primarily moral: he had suffered in jail for his principles—human rights, political freedom and ordinary decency—and it was evident to all that he would not abandon those principles at the critical hour. But where could such a thing be made evident? In civil society—a free space created and claimed by people. Havel and other courageous figures had tangled for years with the state. But the place they created lay outside the state in a social setting where people could, as he put it, live in truth, rather than swallow the lies of a hollow and ruthless regime.

In reclaiming their basic freedoms, the dissidents of Eastern Europe declared that a civil society now existed behind the Iron Curtain, whether or not the state agreed to have it. Solidarity in Poland, which was banned but could not be stopped, achieved the same result as the Civic Forum. The union was helped immeasurably by the Catholic Church, the one countervailing force to the government in Poland. Human rights organizations, some of them international in scope, played their part—as did *samizdat* publishing, underground theater and even rock music.

It is worth remembering that Solidarity was, among other things, a newspaper. Ordinarily, we would say that it *published* or put out a newspaper, but there was nothing ordinary about the act. The simple fact that the paper appeared and circulated meant that Solidarity stood for more than a struggling trade union. It was also an underground power capable of breaking into print, when print was supposed to be the stronghold of the state. It is no accident that one of its key figures, the writer and intellectual Adam Michnik, is today the top editor of the leading—and most profitable—newspaper in Poland, *Gazeta Wyborcza*.

A DIRECT LINE CONNECTS THE underground press of the 1970s to the free press of today. As Michnik well knows, one connecting thread is civil society, which he wrote about, helped bring into being and now tries to serve as the editor of a daily newspaper. A similar thing happened in the former Soviet Union. Whatever else *glasnost* was, it was made real and vivid to citizens in an explosion of journalism—in newspapers liberated from Party restraint. Here again, civil society was born alongside an independent press. Proof of its existence was found through the press. It was not only that people had real news for the first time. It's that *glasnost* in its early forms suggested other reforms that could (and did) follow.

But then a curious thing happened. After civil society "won" in

Eastern Europe, normal politics and global markets descended on the emancipated nations. The revolution passed, as Havel said, from poetry into prose. Political parties that could compete without threatening violence, a free press with economic support, a legal system to guarantee rights and compel justice, leaders who could serve with honor, a private economy released from state control—all these had to be created under intense pressure and high expectation. Civil society had to be won all over again.

Meanwhile, those who had grown accustomed to subservience, corruption and hopelessness in public life lacked many of the "democratic dispositions," in the philosopher Jean Bethke Elshtain's phrase, that are required of citizens responsible for their own fate. One result of this deficiency was the quest for revenge on collaborators in societies where virtually every person collaborated in some way. Another was the murderous appeal to ethnic nationalism.

Such events confirmed that civil society is essential to democracy, before and after the revolution. But we have to understand the notion in a variety of ways, without losing the common thread. Civil society is a middle space between the state and private life. A moral space from which leaders emerge with their authority earned. A free space for art, politics, culture—and journalism. A social space where churches, unions and other voluntary associations flourish. A civil space on which elected governments stand. A cognitive space where people come to think of themselves as citizens, able to live together despite stresses and strains. And finally, an imaginative space, where nations are formed or reformed in response to historic events.

All of these things should matter to journalists, even those who are far removed from the struggle for basic liberties. Ask yourself this: Which is now the bigger threat to independence and enterprise in the American press—an overweening government or a hypercommercialized and fragmented society? Obviously it is the latter, but that is the sort of problem to which our First Amendment tradition rarely speaks.

"Freedom of the press is guaranteed only to those who own one." A.J. Liebling's famous crack underlines what should be evident to all: journalism can be lost to the private sphere as surely as it can be crushed by public power. It thrives in a middle space, the civil sphere—but only when this territory is healthy, active, strong enough to draw people in as citizens. That was the insight on which the movement for public journalism was founded. Those involved (including myself) think the press can do more to strengthen civil society without abandoning its role as truth-teller, chronicler or critic.

But public journalism is just one expression of this impulse. Many newspapers around the United States (*The Dallas Morning News* is an example) have lately been expanding their coverage of religion. Undoubtedly they think there are readers to be won. But behind that belief is another: public life includes more than politics and policy. Religion is "public" (although it is also private) because it orients people to one another, gets them out of the house, engages them in a collective enterprise. Communities cohere around it. Values are formed there. And Americans are a religious people. By enlarging and improving their coverage of faith and values, newspapers are recognizing that such a vital feature of civil society cannot be neglected, despite the secular leanings of the newsroom staff.

ANOTHER CIVIL SOCIETY VENTURE in recent years involves the interrelated problems of credibility, fairness and the collapse of professional standards. The Committee of Concerned Journalists announced its formation in 1997, co-chaired by Bill Kovach of the Nieman Foundation and Tom Rosenstiel of the Project for Excellence in Journalism. In its founding statement, the Committee proposed to "summon journalists to a period of national reflection" during a critical moment for the craft, which seemed to be showing a "lost sense of purpose."

Also in 1997, the American Society of Newspaper Editors announced a three-year credibility study, "a long-term effort to better understand and reverse the damaging erosion of our credibility with the public." The Freedom Forum entered the same year with its Free Press/Fair Press initiative, designed to "make journalists aware of the depth of public concern" on that issue.

Several things impress me about these efforts. The first is that they understand how the press is dependent on public trust, which is a verdict won not only in the marketplace but also in civil society, where discussion and debate take place and attitudes are formed. Second, all three initiatives are the work of civil society groups; government and industry are not the actors here. Foundations, professional societies, committees of concern—these institutions aspire to a "civic" identity. They are not angling for state power or private profit. Whether they succeed or fail in their task, their work is a good thing to have happening in civil society.

Why? Because certain problems (public trust is one) do not lend themselves to government action or private enterprise. They are appropriate for the middle sphere. Clearly, we do not want the state involved in creating trust in the news. Companies in the news business have some reason to care about trust in the product, but only to the degree that news is the product they want to deal in. There are now many competitors to serious journalism within the nonfiction sector of the media business. In docudramas and in tabloid television, on talk radio and on the Internet, in publishing houses and in Hollywood suites, making "stuff" from the real has become the daily work of millions who will never be called journalists—or care about being called journalists.

BY ITSELF, THAT SHOULD NOT WORRY US. Democracy thrives when more people get in on the action, including the action involved in making money and reporting the news. But when the question is whether serious journalism will get made anywhere in the mess, then amid all the companies and competitors in the marketplace we need another kind of competitor moving around in civic space. We need a Committee of Concerned Journalists, a company of the like-minded, which is the only kind of company that can say: this is not just a business we're talking about.

Anchored in civil space, voluntary and free standing, efforts like the Committee of Concerned Journalists and ASNE's credibility project—along with a host of others—make sense only when civil society makes sense as a field of action. If everything is going to be determined by government policy or the next election; if consumption patterns or corporate cultures are fully in charge, it is senseless to call journalism to account for its lost credibility or to summon journalists to a period of reflection. At worst, such actions may paper over problems by suggesting that puny responses have meaning.

But those who think that honest efforts to reform journalism have meaning (and may do some good) think this because they have concluded that not everything is determined by government or private enterprise. Civil society has a say in the matter. And whenever journalists speak up as professionals, or act through their associations, they are not only speaking to civil society; they are creating it themselves by committing their energies and institutions to a common task.

Will it work? I don't know. We never know how much life there is in civil society ventures until we undertake them. That is why they are grounded in faith, hope, trust and the commitment of the unembarrassed.

Which brings us back to 1989.

If there is one lesson in that date for small-d democrats in every country, it is to never be surprised by our good as well as our bad turns on the wheel of history. Despite all expectations to the contrary, normal politics returned to places like the Czech Republic, starting in 1989. Civil society was restored in countries that had done everything they could do to destroy it. No counsel of realism could have predicted such a result. That is why President Havel refuses to take that counsel even now, when he has to be realistic about everything.

What he is saying to us goes something like this: Surprising, even astonishing changes can come to a free society, and to one that wishes to be free, if they spring from the intelligence and decency of a people whose civic capacity has been awakened and put to the test. The same, I believe, is true for journalism. It can better itself by recognizing where it truly lives.

Jay Rosen, a 1990–91 Media Studies Center fellow, is an associate professor of journalism at New York University. His book, What Are Journalists For?, *will be published by Yale University Press.*

15

Poisonous Neglect

*Environmental issues are undercovered in Central
and Eastern Europe.*

Reshma Prakash

THE BEAUTIFUL SNOW-CAPPED mountains and clear blue streams seen as
you climb up the highway from Sarajevo to Velíka Kladuša on the
Bosnian-Croatian border can almost make you believe that there never
was a war here. But not for long. There is nothing deceptive about the
ghost villages that still dot the countryside with their bombed houses,
collapsed roofs, gouged concrete and bullet-riddled walls.

It's been almost four years since the Dayton Peace Agreement
brought fighting to an end in Bosnia and Herzegovina, but despite
clearly visible signs of destruction, people still can't tell you what
damage the war did to the environment. With reconstruction and return on their minds, there are few people who can speak authorita-
tively of the state of the rivers, the air pollution, the contamination of
the soil and the long-term effects of a damaged environment on people's
health. The same holds true for the news. The environment is too
"soft" a topic in the face of hard-nosed reporting on the return of
ethnic minorities, the composition of local police forces or the behav-
ior of international peacekeeping forces.

By comparison, the media did give extensive coverage to one of the
biggest environmental stories to come out of the region—the nuclear

143

disaster that was Chernobyl. One would think that because the issue had received so much attention that public awareness would be high. But curiously, though more than a decade has passed since the accident at the nuclear plant, journalists traveling to affected regions find people still unaware of the dangers posed by radiation. There are many people who obviously have never had access to media reports on the matter. Sleawomir Grunberg, a Polish-born filmmaker who now lives in the United States, has made a documentary called *From Chechnya to Chernobyl*. It tells the story about a contaminated village called Raduga in Belarus. The government has been relocating people, mostly refugees from Chechnya and Armenia, into abandoned villages on the border of the area most severely contaminated by Chernobyl. In spite of radiation levels that are 20 times higher than the recommended safety limits, the relocated people are drinking and fishing contaminated water and growing crops on contaminated soil, seemingly unaware of the mortal danger they face.

The region of eastern and Central Europe, the focus of this article, is an area rich in biodiversity and blessed with beautiful rivers, waterways, mountains and forests. But it is also a region cursed by a gross neglect of the environment combined with little public awareness of the issues. The presence of people living in the shadow of history's worst nuclear accident, unaware of the hazards posed by radiation, says much about both governmental neglect and the media's ability to fulfill any kind of watchdog function. Public interest in and knowledge of the environment are intertwined with the past, present and future of reporting on the environment in Central and Eastern Europe.

Decades of neglect and mismanagement by past Communist authorities in Central and Eastern Europe have left behind a bitter legacy of polluting power plants, coal mines and chemical factories, badly designed hydroelectric projects, depleted forests, dying lakes and a host of other environmental catastrophes. According to the International Union for Conservation of Nature, by the end of the 1980s, one-third of the forests were damaged in Bulgaria; 70 percent of rivers were heavily polluted, 40 percent of sewage untreated and half the forests dying or damaged in Czechoslovakia; 95 percent of the rivers were polluted, leukemia rates were soaring and half the farmland was damaged by high acid levels and metals pollution in Poland. The statistics for the rest of the region were equally dismal.

While knowledge about the environmental and health consequences of government policy was often sketchy in Central and Eastern Europe before the fall of communism because of government censorship, the environment curiously emerged as an area of resistance in fights against the old regime in Czechoslovakia and above all in Hungary, where opposition to a dam project became the flashpoint of protests against the communist government.

In 1977, Hungary and Czechoslovakia agreed to build a giant complex of dams, canals and power stations on the Danube River between Gabčikovo in Czechoslovakia and Nagymaros in Hungary. Environmentalists warned that damming and diverting the Danube would disrupt a natural water purification process, flood forests, drain wetlands and dry up wells in Hungary. The environment was a relatively "safe" subject for the media to report on compared to other more political matters. In Hungary, what started as an underground movement by activists soon spread and received massive public support, swelling the ranks of opposition to the regime, a process fueled by media reports on the movement. Mass demonstrations before the Hungarian parliament just days before the regime fell in 1989 marked the high point of these protests. The environment was clearly one of the major factors leading to the Velvet Revolution that brought down communist regimes across the region.

BUT PARADOXICALLY, THE FALL OF hard-line regimes and the ushering in of a new era of experimentation in free-market economics and popular sovereignty may have led to a decline of interest in the environment. The enormous economic and political changes generated in these societies has put the environment on the back burner even though the media, once restrained by state control and with no access to information or independence, have fewer restrictions now. Some countries, such as Hungary, Poland and the Czech Republic, have relatively independent media, while others such as Albania and Moldova have had mixed success. But this freedom has not translated into more interest in the environment. Rather, more freedom has meant that the environment now competes with other issues for media attention, and it hasn't held up too well.

This is mainly because, throughout the region, concern for the economy often overrules environmental issues. Should a polluting factory be shut down for environmental reasons or kept going to save thousands of jobs? The choices are unclear. What with the precarious state of the economy and the troubles of adjusting to market rules, the media show scant interest in environmental stories. As these countries undergo economic privatization and political restructuring, coverage of problems such as unemployment, inflation, corporate bankruptcies and low growth rates generates more of a response from the public than the environment.

"It's true, media attention to the environment has declined," said Gábor Szabó of Hungary, an environmental reporter with HVG, a publication whose name roughly translates to *World Economic Weekly*. "In the prior regime everybody was a green. Often, reporting on the environment became a fight against the government, like when we wrote about the dam. But now, there are lots of ways to show dissatisfaction against the government. The environment is not the only game in town."

Journalists in the old days had to more or less accept whatever the "greens" said because they had no way of independently verifying the information they received. Now, said Szabó, reporters are beginning to be influenced by Western standards of unbiased reporting and are beginning to think more critically. When journalists come across an environmental story now, they don't automatically assume that those opposing the government are right, he said; journalism is getting more sophisticated. Reporters these days make an attempt to figure out whether the environment is just being used as an excuse by vested interests, and they evaluate the merits of the case based on what's good for the country, said Szabó.

The level of media coverage also seems to correspond with the presence of environmental organizations. While the environmental movement today is relatively well developed in Hungary, Poland, Slovakia, the Czech Republic and to some extent the Baltic states, it is very much in its infancy in states such as Romania, Bulgaria and Albania. In areas where there are strong environmental organizations with good public outreach programs that provide people with reliable information, there is also more media coverage of the environment.

CONSEQUENTLY, SOME TOPICS GET more coverage than others because the media finds it easier to get access to certain kinds of information. An additional reason why this may happen is that some stories are more sensational—people falling ill and clear cases of the previous regime's negligence are obvious favorites.

Interest in environmental hot spots such as the "Black Triangle"—the infamously polluted area of the former East Germany, Poland and the Czech Republic—is high. For instance, there have been numerous reports on the province of Katowice, often known as Poland's industrial wasteland, and its alarming rates of infant mortality, lead poisoning among children, increasing incidence of cancer and reduced life spans. These trends are often attributed to industrial pollution and contamination—Poland's air pollution is among the worst in Europe.

The Danube delta is another "hot" topic. Cross-border contamination of water evokes great interest, and there are many internationally funded projects connected with the Danube. The dam project saga that began with the communist regime is far from over and continues to grab media attention. When the Hungarian government under the new regime dropped its plans for constructing the dam, the Slovak government decided to go ahead with it in Gabčikovo, leading to a bitter dispute between the two countries. Hungary unilaterally abrogated the original treaty agreement to build the dam complex and appealed to the Hague International Court of Justice for intervention. The court's verdict—that the original agreement was legal but that Slovakia didn't have the right to split the Danube unilaterally—satisfied neither government, and the issue remains unsettled.

Problems associated with the nuclear industry and the dangers posed by old plants, outdated technology, faulty construction and contaminated sites have attracted media attention as well. The latest nuclear issue to grab headlines is the Czech government's decision in May 1999 to complete construction of a controversial nuclear plant started by the communist regime back in 1987. The Temelín nuclear plant has triggered intense debate within the country and elsewhere in Europe. Neighboring Austria is concerned that the plant would present a major nuclear safety hazard, a view echoed by a resolution passed by the European Union.

Such reporting on the environment, though, is mostly local. Larger international issues such as global warming and water scarcity aren't popular with the media, and there are few in-depth analyses of such international trends. These are some of the environmental stories that do get missed. Environmentalists often complain about the lack of media attention to "serious" issues but acknowledge that it may be due to the fact that the environment is often viewed as a luxury, or even an esoteric, item in these societies.

THE FACT THAT MEDIA OWNERSHIP has been moving from the state into private hands may be partly to blame as well. Editors, too, like the rest of the region, are increasingly ruled by the market. As the media learn to operate more on the profit motive, the stories that sell are the stories that rule. Editors reason that when people are worried about their jobs or the stability of a government, environmental stories will not compel people to go out and buy a particular magazine or watch a particular channel on television.

"The emphasis is on scandal and sensational news, even when they are reporting on the environment," said Olavi Tammenäe, executive director of the Tallinn, Estonia, branch of the Stockholm Environment Institute. "What is neglected is awareness building and education about the environment. While there is an emotional connection to the environment, there isn't a deep understanding of the issues concerned."

Another reason why certain issues get little publicity is that information on the environment is still hard to come by. Journalists complain about the difficulty of gaining firsthand knowledge of issues, often having to rely on unsubstantiated rumors or reports from third parties. While many of the Central and Eastern European nations have rules requiring that industries report on their by-products, for instance, the authorities have not been able to monitor every one of them. So a lot of industries still get away with very little accountability for their actions. Without access to records on what the level of emissions are from a particular factory, the media have no way of backing up their stories with hard, scientific facts. Or, with little access to a toxic inventory, mainly because few exist, it is difficult for the media to determine if an industry's waste is toxic and if it is being disposed of in a safe manner. The same lack of transparency applies to the environmental costs of a privatization deal or how much a company is spending on cleaning up the environment.

"Finding out the details of the environmental impact of projects is very difficult. Very often, the economic ministry is completely in favor of projects that may be harmful. More often than not, even the environment ministry doesn't have the necessary records so the media can't even turn to them," said Tom Popper, a project manager with the Media Information Service of the Regional Environment Center for East and Central Europe. "There is no tradition of disseminating information in this region. Institutions first need to be built up to do this. This is a completely new idea that will take time to develop. Interference with the process of media reporting is routine in certain areas. There are practically no freedom of information acts, but libel laws are very much in place. In places like Serbia and Croatia, journalists can and have been arrested for their work."

HOWEVER, MATTERS ARE SLOWLY improving. Not all the news is doom and gloom. Pursuit of European Union membership may hold out cause for hope in countries such as Poland, Hungary, the Czech Republic and Slovakia. Some environmentalists, in fact, point to the European Union as just the break they're looking for.

"These countries feel that their economic future depends on acceptance into the EU," said Tom Pluta of the World Environment Center in New York. "But access to the EU depends on how well they can harmonize their laws with EU standards. They are starting to feel pressure from the outside to change their laws, and a lot of this will surely relate to the environment. Also, if these countries want to attract investment from multinational companies, they will have to adopt industry standards called ISO 14000 that relate to the environment. These standards have a community relations clause that requires the release of information to the public. This should really go a long way in making information accessible to the media, something they've had problems with in this part of the world."

Another encouraging development is the fact that freedom of information laws are being drafted with the help of the international community under what is known as the Aarhus Public Participation Convention, an international convention on public access to environmental information, signed by 36 countries in 1998 and likely to enter into force around 2002. Except for some nations such as Serbia and Russia, most countries in Central and Eastern Europe have signed the convention. According to the convention, governments are not only required to make environmental data available generally, but also to release information specifically requested by the public in a manner similar to the United States' Freedom of Information Act. All citizens have the right to access environmental information and participate in policy formulation, says the convention, and have access to legal redress if these rights are not met.

But there are certain exceptions—national defense, the conduct of international relations, intellectual property rights, competitiveness of industry—that governments could no doubt use to deny information.

When a government is coming down hard on those who oppose its policies, an international convention may not be of much help even if the government has tried to present a positive image abroad by signing it. Some analysts, though, are optimistic: they think it could work by putting some outside pressure on such governments and by giving domestic forces an extra arrow in their arsenal.

INCREASINGLY, THE PRESS IS ALSO being fortified by the rapid spread of Internet facilities. The recent crisis in Kosovo is a case in point. While much of the world's media focus has been on the fighting, the refugees and their travails, there have been some reports drawing attention to other aspects of the latest war in the Balkans. According to the Regional Environmental Center for Central and Eastern Europe, the current conflict in the Balkans has several environmental faces: the destruction of industrial and infrastructure facilities, causing increased pollution; sanitation problems for refugees and for populations where the infrastructure is overloaded or damaged; and an overload on environmental institutions, including NGOs, that may lead to their breakdown.

Newspapers in the West have been very slow in picking up this angle of the crisis, but the Internet, the Worldwide Web and e-mail flooded the information gap on the environment very early in the conflict. Reports of air, land and water pollution from the bombing of chemical and pharmaceutical factories, toxic fires, the use of depleted uranium in weapons and the destruction of fragile natural habitats have, in fact, led to furious debates on various sites on the Internet. While much of this debate is political and some no doubt nationalistic, fed by propaganda, what cannot be doubted is the widespread environmental damage, said Jim Detjen, president of the International Federation of Environmental Journalists. What also cannot be doubted, he said, was that the Internet provided a marvelous resource for the local media.

The past decade has shown that while it normally takes a crisis to get the media to focus on environmental issues—a problem that is, no doubt, international—the media in Central and Eastern Europe still show signs of being hampered by the historical baggage of the communist era. The pattern is by no means uniform, for some parts of the region have fared better than others. While it is encouraging to see that the Internet is breaking through some of the barriers that still exist, one must remember that access to Internet facilities among the public is still low compared to the West. That is certainly bound to improve.

But as long as the media perceive that there is little public interest in the environment, the situation will be slow to change. One could argue that it is precisely the media that can awaken such interest, and endlessly argue about what comes first. The truth is, without building up and strengthening institutions that are dealing with the environment—that can provide reliable information on the issues and that can act as a legitimate voice for the environment—the quality of environmental reporting will continue to depend on the sheer ingenuity of individual reporters.

Reshma Prakash is a senior correspondent at The Earth Times.

16

How I Became a Witch

Nationalism, sexism and postcommunist journalism in Croatia

Slavenka Drakulić

I AM A WITCH AND I HAVE PROOF in writing. In the press, that is. How is that possible? In many postcommunist countries like Croatia, bizarre things are possible—among other things to be proclaimed a witch.

It happened in the winter of 1992. The war in Croatia was over and it had just begun in Bosnia. After years as a staff writer for the newspaper *Danas* (*Today*), suddenly I found myself without a job. A group of journalists loyal to Franjo Tudjman's party took over *Danas* and kicked out more than 20 journalists, considered to be among the best in the country. This was possible through the corrupt privatization of the state property, when the new nomenclature acquired factories, hotels, real estate as well as newspapers.

However, I was not particularly worried, because since the mid-'80s I was publishing in the European and American press, and my novels and nonfiction books were widely translated. But as I was perhaps one of the very few Croats with access to the foreign media, the new regime—and its cronies in the press, as well as all kinds of nationalists—was sensitive to my writing and to the kind of image of the new Croatia I could create there. In January of 1992, at a time of nationalist homogenization in Croatia, I published an essay in the international edition of *Time* magazine: "That is what the war is doing to us," I wrote, "reducing us to one dimension: the Nation. The trouble with this nationhood, however, is that whereas before I was defined by my education, my job, my ideas, my character—and, yes, my nationality too—now I feel stripped of all that. I am nobody because I am not a person anymore. I am one of 4.5 million Croats."

I did not have to wait long for the reaction. Soon the essay was translated in *Globus* (*The Globe*), the biggest political tabloid (a peculiar postcommunist breed of newsmagazine), and, in an article published along with my essay, I was attacked as a public enemy and a traitor. It is interesting that this tabloid was not controlled by the government, yet the atmosphere in the media was such that all but a few journalists succumbed to fierce nationalism.

These were not just innocent words. In a country at war, where Serbs disappeared overnight, to be considered a traitor carried a considerable danger. But this attack meant only getting the taste of the real witch-hunt that was in store for me.

Like in novels or movies where a mob points at one woman as a witch and then the Inquisition takes her case over, I found my name singled out in the Croatian daily newspapers in the article about the International PEN Congress in Rio de Janeiro. There, the American president of PEN asked his Croatian counterpart about the situation of the five journalists and writers, Jelena Lovrić, Vesna Kesić, Rada Iveković, Dubravka Ugrešić and I, because he knew that we were critical of the regime. (Aside from all being women, we had nothing more in common.) In his report to the press the Croatian PEN president mentioned the exchange. A female journalist for *Večernji list* (*Evening News*), the biggest daily newspaper in Croatia, wrote a comment about five pets of communism, privileged and greedy for revenge. She labeled us "witches from Rio," and the hunt started.

The next attack (again in *Globus*) was an example of a fascist-like prosecution and had all the attributes of a call for lynching. Under the sensationalist headline CROATIAN FEMINISTS ARE RAPING CROATIA, an anonymous "investigative team" spread their "proof" over two large-format pages. Clearly, we were labeled witches because we were *feminists!* And as such, it was our duty to write about the mass rape of Muslim and Croatian women, especially because we had "the access to the world media," as they put it. By not exposing the rapes, we committed the crime of "raping Croatia." We were described as spoiled, self-centered middle-aged women who had problems finding men, and if we had any they were *Serbs*. The "investiga-

tive team" constructed a table where our nationality, the nationality of
our parents and husbands, our marital status, number of children, education, real estate, countries we traveled to during the war and the
most "problematic" quotations from our articles could be seen at a
glance. In fact, only the addresses, the telephone numbers and the
number of abortions were missing.

This time I can't say that I was surprised. But the "accusation" was
so absurd and the entire article filled with such hate speech and preju-
dice that the only way to describe my own feelings is utter bewilder-
ment. The article had nothing to do with the mass rape of Muslim and
Croat women; it was only a pretext to publicly rape us, the five women.
It was also painful, for I knew people hidden behind the "investigative
team": they were my colleagues, and until recently we had worked
together.

IN MANY WAYS THAT article in *Globus* was a turning point. Journalism
in Croatia had been heading for some time towards smearing, persecution and public execution of all who dare to think differently. With a
few exceptions such as *Feral Tribune* (a fiercely independent political
weekly published in the city of Split) and Radio 101, an independent
Zagreb radio station, all media were ideologically united in their nationalism, hatred of the Serbs, hatred of "others," as it were. As the
Franjo Tudjman regime became identified with the new state itself, to
criticize it meant to criticize the new state. It was not possible to do so,
because one would automatically be considered a "traitor" to Croatian
independence. Even *Globus*, being independent, was not less nationalistic. Indeed, the article about "witches" perfectly fit its image.

What followed was a real public execution—even better, burning of
us five women at the stake. This was an extraordinary demonstration
of nationalism and sexism linked together. Perhaps the reason—apart
from a patriarchal culture—is the fact that in the late communist years,
the most critical journalists in Yugoslavia happened to be women. As
my fellow witch Jelena Lovrić once said, women have less to lose in
being critical—they can always go back to their other "profession"—
children and home. I don't know if women really are better at taking
political pressure, but in Yugoslavia journalism was a low-paid and
little-respected job. In the mid-'80s, women moved into print journalism, radio and television, and raised the standards. The pay didn't get
any better, but thanks to women, in the last years of communism in

Yugoslavia, journalism was more independent and more critical than in the last decade, at least in Croatia and Serbia. Was the attack on us partly male revenge? One could speculate about that.

In any case, there was hardly a day when some newspaper or other did not publish a vitriolic comment about the "witch case." Not only did our male and female colleagues join in calling us witches, but journalists, writers, intellectuals from both the government and the opposition made our story a test case. By attacking us, they would prove their own fidelity to the Tudjman regime. The smear campaign, fed by fear and opportunism, continued, with highs and lows—usually spurred by an article or interview that some one of us would publish abroad—for the next three years.

The most difficult thing for me was the lack of solidarity. Very few people defended us. No professional associations—writers' union, journalists' union, lawyers' association, human rights group—took up our case. I will always remember that terrible feeling of loneliness—that feeling of being all alone, exposed and that no one was lifting a finger. And I will always remember when I saw a former colleague cross the street to avoid meeting me. And when a longtime friend, sitting at the next table in the restaurant, pretended she didn't know me. The door to my home was spit on every single morning; my car was damaged; I got threatening telephone calls and hate mail; my daughter was harassed and so was my aged mother.

THE ABSURDITY OF THIS CASE, for me, was beyond belief: while the "investigative team" at *Globus* was preparing a "trial" against us, I was preparing an op-ed piece for *The New York Times* about rapes. My *Times* piece was written days, if not a week, before the *Globus* piece appeared, but because of the proposal and editing process at American newspapers it didn't run until December 13, just one day before *Globus* ran its attack. Within weeks of the *Times* op-ed, all major American TV networks were in Croatia, shooting reports on raped women, and I collaborated with some of them. Further, a week before the *Globus* article I had received a letter of intention from my German publisher, Rowohlt, giving me a green light to do a book of documents on rape. So while I was in fact dealing with the rape issue on several levels, at the same time I was being accused of ignoring it! At that point facts no longer mattered, because the snowball of attacks had too much momentum.

The case got so much attention by the international press that the 1993 international PEN conference to take place in Dubrovnik came into question, which, sadly, only played into the hands of those who accused us of trying to undermine the conference. A poll taken by the executive committee of international PEN found that the majority of its delegates would not go to Dubrovnik—they simply did not want to come to the country where women writers were called "witches." In the end, however, the committee allowed the Croatian PEN president to hold the "59th Congress" (in the less desirable location of Hvar rather than in Dubrovnik) even though there would be no formal assembly of delegates. And to our dismay, the controversy did not stem the attacks against us.

The consequences for all five of us women were severe. For several years none of us could either publish or work in our country, and two women even left the country to live and work abroad. Between 1992 and 1995, I published abroad exclusively. This, ironically, was taken as yet another proof of my anti-patriotic activity. Moreover, *Globus* continued to harass us and repeat that the "witch scandal" brought us to fame abroad, that we profited from it and used it as a spring-board to launch ourselves as victims of the regime. We took the only action we could. In the spring of 1993, we took the case to court and sued the paper and its chief editor. Six years later our individual cases are at different stages but all unresolved—not surprising, considering the fact that the independent media like *Feral Tribune* are crushed by the same "independent" juridical system that can't decide in our cases.

THE MEDIA SITUATION after this case has not improved; on the contrary, it has worsened: the pressure on independent media grew, as well as the control of the television. This, after all, is one of the reasons, together with minority rights, that Croatia is not accepted into European organizations such as the European Council or NATO.

Independence of the media is a good way to judge democratic development in a country. In that respect, Tudjman's regime is nothing short of a dictatorship. For example, it has been revealed by a witness that Tudjman personally conducted sessions to plan the elimination of *Feral Tribune*. Also, the first person who took the opportunity to sue *Feral Tribune* under the new law that permits public figures to ask for the enormous amounts of money for their "psychological suffering" was, in fact, President Tudjman himself. His family, as well as many other politicians, have followed his example.

Now there is no need to forbid publication of *Feral Tribune* or any other newspaper any longer. If it has to pay off $3 million in damages, it will mean its end. This is the new policy—perfectly legal and perfectly "clean"—to put financial pressure on the freedom of the press. Aware of the importance of independent media, a six-party opposition coalition is putting forth a condition to the government before it will discuss the new election law—or anything else, for that matter: first, allow the establishment of a private national television channel. But even that is no guarantee for a fair election campaign.

The five of us want not only an apology from *Globus*—we want money. If I win, I have decided to found an annual journalism award for the best and the bravest woman journalist. Perhaps it will be called . . . well, how about "Witch of the Year"?

Slavenka Drakulic, a free-lance journalist born in Croatia, is the author of three novels and four books of nonfiction, including Café Europa: Life After Communism.

17

Roma in the Hungarian Media

In unstable times, images with dangerous consequences appear.

György Kerényi

GYÖRGY MOLDOVA, ONE OF THE most widely read Hungarian writers, crams his volume of interviews with police officers with details of what Hungarian police and journalists call, in one word, *cigánybûnözés*, or "Gypsycrime." His book *Bûn az élet* (*Born to Sin*), which was serialized in one of the most popular Hungarian dailies *Magyar Nemzet* (*Hungarian Nation*) despite protests from Gypsy and non-Gypsy intellectuals, contains the following exchange:

"What happened?" asks Moldova.

"Seems to be a triple homicide at Rákospalota," says a police officer.

"Gypsies?"

The assumption embedded in the exchange is still alive in Hungary and its media. According to a 1995 survey, 67 percent of Hungarians are convinced that the inclination to commit crime is inherent in "Gypsies' blood." In European history, the label "Gypsy" connotes a deviant, unwanted outsider who is incapable of joining modern society. It is a term used in a derogatory sense by a powerful majority rather than one that people use to describe themselves. As a consequence of a rise in political self-consciousness since 1989, the people referred to as

Gypsies prefer to call themselves the Roma—a term derived from their own language, Romani, which can be traced to India. In times of instability—yesterday the world wars, today the transition out of communism—images associated with Gypsiness appear in the Hungarian media: the dark-haired criminal paraded in handcuffs, the swarming family of 10 living in squalor, the passionate musician. These images have dangerous consequences for the Roma—stifling exotic stereotypes, inferior citizenship and, at worst, physical violence.

The belief in Gypsy criminality that appears in the Hungarian media is a product of both contemporary reporting and old cultural and political patterns. Since the centralizing efforts of the Habsburgs in the 18th century, the Gypsy question has been a problem of politics, order and policing. Habsburg officials issued enforcement measures (which were fully realized only in communist times) that forced Gypsies to settle down, forbade them from keeping horses and wearing traditional clothing, and banned their language. Their children were taken away and given to Hungarian peasants to raise. Before World War II, in parliament, speeches were delivered on sterilizing Gypsies and gathering them in special camps. During the war came the Roma holocaust (*porrajmos* in Romani), when the Nazis killed thousands of Roma. Under communism, until the 1960s, the Roma had identity cards of a distinct color. Until 1989 Roma criminals (and their families) were registered separately with the police. Criminological researchers examined the finger and palm prints of Roma, using Roma children living in reformatories for the experiments.

UNDER COMMUNISM, THE ROMA were treated as coddled but unworthy members of state. Gypsies were not included in the compromise that defined the regime of János Kádár, the leader of the Hungarian Communist Party for 30 years after the suppression of the 1956 revolution. In return for Hungarians' accepting his dictatorship, Kádár broke with the Stalinist practice of ideologically based harassment in all areas of people's lives and gave people the possibility of slow but safe growth in prosperity. Sooner or later they could acquire their own little *Trabant*, a small apartment and a weekend garden. Roma, in contrast, had to get by on poorly paid, unskilled work far from their homes—with no opportunities for moonlighting—which made their integration into the market economy even more difficult. Some specially targeted social welfare programs, however, did reach them. Most of the isolated Gypsy quarters were liquidated. (In 1971, 65 percent of the Gypsy population lived without any of the basic amenities of civilization; by 1993 this figure was 14 percent.) Under the rhetoric of lifting up the Gypsies, the Roma could receive special housing subsidies and loans. Even as many of them were assigned inferior apartments in government-constructed housing that formed the core of miserable new ghettoes, these Gypsy "privileges" sparked jealousy in the Hungarian majority.

Meanwhile, the average Hungarian—growing ever wealthier by working simultaneously in the socialist first economy and the private second economy (at the cost of long work hours and high mortality rates) was flabbergasted to learn that his village was becoming increasingly accessible to Gypsies and that public housing was being assigned to them under the rhetoric of equal opportunities and a caring state.

Besides the stereotype of the idle Gypsy, another image appeared in the media: the unworthy Gypsy, who is unable to exploit opportunities provided for him while the Hungarian toils day and night to obtain anything. Under communism, unhappiness with state policies to aid the Roma was enhanced by the negative stereotype of the Roma promulgated in the official press. Newspapers and magazines published articles on Gypsies burning the parquet floors in their new flats, keeping pigs in the bath tub, and generally offending the norms of "socialist coexistence." These myths successfully obscured painful facts, such as Roma life expectancy—which was 10 years shorter than that of the typical Hungarian.

The stereotype of the pampered but unworthy Gypsy took roots in the media in the best days of socialism and has recurred ever since. The socialist media's role in the perpetuation of the stereotype was twofold. It supported the integration of the Roma into Hungarian society (which was carried out by the authorities without regard for the circumstances and the needs of Roma) but also strengthened the myths around them. By connecting the ideas of coddled and criminal Gypsies, the media turned prejudices against Gypsies into strong anti-Roma attitudes.

PREJUDICES GREW VIRULENT UNDER socialism, when the "everyone is given the chance of thriving" ideology was hammered into the public mind. News reports emphasized how much wealth the state expended in lifting up the Roma. While the media of the Kádár era basically sought to avoid conflict, the tendency to emphasize efforts to elevate the Roma only served to set them up for a fall. In the 1980s, when the communist order was headed for collapse—when unemployment first threatened people who had been used to full employment, prices rose and people had to wait many years to obtain apartments—the number of articles depicting Gypsies in a bad light began to increase. Rising unemployment hurt the Roma worst of all. Nevertheless, the media tried to cement crumbling national unity with opposition to the Gypsies.

In 1989 in the city of Miskolc, the city council wanted to assign a housing project to Roma originally living in the city center. During the three months preceding the decision on building the housing project, 45 percent of the articles on Gypsies in two regional papers, both belonging to the Communist Party, dealt with the connection between Gypsies and crime. The proposed project, which consisted of 30-square-meter flats, was to be situated on the bank of a river polluted with quicksilver, one kilometer from the last bus stop. The proposal was defeated only after a struggle.

After the fall of communist rule, negative attitudes against the Roma only intensified. Consider the case of Tiszavasvári. In 1997, the town became well known all over the country through coverage of a controversy over a segregated graduation ceremony for Roma students. The courts found "segregated graduation ceremonies" an offense against the students' personal rights and sentenced the local government that maintained the school to pay 100,000 HUF (U.S. $400) compensation per student—much less than the sum demanded by the parents.

The segregated graduation ceremonies brought media attention to Roma life in Tiszavasvári. Reporters also revealed that several times the police placed Gypsy enclaves under a 6 p.m. curfew, and a local government representative instructed the frustrated teachers struggling with the Gypsies, who lived in horrifying squalor, to "do with them whatever you want; we just don't want to see them in town."

IT IS NOT TOO MUCH TO ASSUME THAT tendentious coverage incited prejudices against the Roma, who—in Tiszavasvári or Miskolc just like anywhere else—are living in quasi-segregated misery. Generalizing from partial truths helps to develop the image of an enemy, arouses a sense of danger and incites—even without openly declaring—the need for the entire nation to join forces against a threat. When the communist order completely collapsed, the call to arms became explicit: TO

ARMS! said the headline of an article on the Roma in the national daily newspaper *Pesti Hírlap* (*Pest News*) in 1994.

In October 1991, the same paper published an interview with a high-ranking police officer with the title CRY, HUNGARIANS! In the article, the major (today a lieutenant-colonel) said: "The Gypsy burglar wreaks great havoc . . . he feels hostile towards those who own things, he is unable to digest it, he wants to ruin values . . . Gypsies cannot tolerate frustration, they simply do not have any tolerance . . . They would plunge each other into poverty, or strike each other dead . . . nowadays Gypsies in Budapest do whatever they want to. . . . It is a miserable situation that we cannot differentiate them from other individuals . . . there's no other solution than joining forces . . . repulsion toward Gypsies is a natural reaction of defense. . . . They have huge powers of self-preservation, they are prolific . . . more aggressive and tend to commit crimes. . . . Gypsies cannot be assimilated. Neither by force nor democratically . . . "

By the early '90s, criminologists had proved that crime is dependent on one's social status and not one's affiliation with one or another minority group. Nevertheless, a great number of articles warning Hungarians of the Gypsy threat appeared in newspapers and magazines. It is no accident that this process began when the economy was collapsing and the huge socialist system of social benefits was faltering, but the press was still under the control of political authorities. Accordingly, Hungary developed an image of the Roma that served the interests of those in power. In short, a scapegoat.

THE YEARS AFTER THE FALL OF communism saw turbulent conflicts over economics and the meaning of Hungarian national identity. They also brought a new dimension of the image of the Roma in the Hungarian media: scapegoat for a society going through a wrenching transition from communism to democracy and capitalism. In situations of conflict—and, according to a 1996–97 study by Gábor Bernáth and Vera Messing, in 1997 more than 60 percent of the reports on Roma were of this nature—the media usually deliver descriptions that suggest the threatened situation of the (Hungarian) majority. This attitude comes either from the people living in the Gypsies' neighborhood or from representatives of authorities, or is conveyed by the words and images presented by the journalist.

When the president of the Republic in 1994, Árpád Göncz, was about to submit draft legislation that proposed to legally restrict "hate speech," a right-wing paper published a commentary titled "They Shoot Hungarians, Don't They?" It traded on the idea that Hungarians are physically endangered, an idea grounded in the image of the blustering, violently complaining Gypsy.

Since then, there have been some improvement in this area: nowadays we can read about brown, dark-complexioned or even white criminals. According to the Bernáth-Messing survey, in 1996, 18 percent of the reports on Gypsies in daily papers were related to crime—a significantly lower percent than in previous years. In the case of criminals belonging to other minorities, the Hungarian media never refer to group identity. Indeed, at the beginning of 1997 the ombudsman of data protection and minorities described any reference to one's origins in warrants or criminal reports unlawful.

The drawing of a direct connection between Gypsies and crime has had pernicious effects, but the constant maintenance of a myth of Gypsies living comfortably on social welfare benefits available only to them may have done even more harm to the public image of the Roma. The situation of the Roma, opinions about them and their image in the press are developing simultaneously. The press both reflects and shapes the public opinion by constructing specific knowledge about the Roma. It cannot put an end to prejudices concerning Gypsies, but by the images it delivers it strengthens the significant physical and social distance between the Roma and the majority. Less frequent than the criminal or slacker Gypsy but just as obnoxious is the stereotype that connects Gypsies with epidemics or infections. The reporter meets Gypsies carrying meat they have stolen from the carrion well where dead animals are deposited in villages. The Gypsy children at Tiszavasvári are infected with lice. The journalist enters a stinking hovel where a pulmonic, deranged woman "is wheezing in his face"— all of these images can cause physical disgust in the reader.

IN A COUNTRY WHERE THE DIMINISHING number of Hungarians is a favorite issue of the nationalist right wing, these descriptions arouse ancient fears in readers. They raise the horror of "strangers" invading "us" and the prospect that sooner or later proliferating strangers will gain the majority. According to certain prognoses, the population of Hungary, which currently barely surpasses 10 million, will decrease to 8 million by 2050—at which time 15 percent to 20 percent of it will be Roma.

As the nationalist neurosis is traditionally intolerant of groups not belonging to the nation state, after the first free elections in 1990 most of the press continued to nourish the feeling of being threatened by a shrinking population, by Gypsies in the street, and by Romanians, Slovaks, Ukrainians and Serbs in neighboring countries. (Hungarians are a major national minority of Europe:
3 million of them live in neighboring countries, most of them under strongly nationalist governments.)

As a consequence of blinding nationalist and racist rhetoric, people do not believe their own eyes but always side with the anti-Gypsy forces. In 1999 the mayor of a country town—where last autumn a deranged teacher attacked some children in a Gypsy class with a knife—protested against one of the commercial TV channels. Before cheering citizens at a mass meeting, he said that the channel "made the settlement appear in an unfavorable light," because it recorded, with a hidden camera, how brutally the police treated the town's Roma. The mayor also demanded the reinstatement of a policeman dismissed after beating up a young man who had testified against the police.

The isolation of the Roma also grew because, during the transition out of communism, independent Roma organizations declared themselves close to the "anti-national" liberal parties whose founders had befriended them during communist times. But the conservatives defeated the liberal parties in the 1990 elections, and the Roma found themselves connected to a beaten political force. In the right-wing press, the Roma issue has been portrayed as one strongly colored by party politics. In the opinion of nationalistic conservatives, the liberal parties, who are seen as lacking in national spirit, use the Roma issue as a battering ram to weaken conservative Hungarians. (The liberal parties, however, think twice before standing up for Gypsies in public. They know the poll results and are well aware that they can lose votes by taking up the case of the Roma, while the Roma themselves are uncertain voters with strong nostalgia for the communist days when they enjoyed housing subsidies and social benefits from the government.)

IN HUNGARY, SINCE 1993, NATIONAL and ethnic minorities have had the right to establish self-governing bodies whose powers are confined to the fields of preserving tradition and culture. In news coverage, Roma policy-making is presented as the quarrels of bickering little children.

A pulp magazine reported on the election of the Roma national government with the title "Roma Squabble," another labeled it "Roma War," and a third referred to an agreement of two Roma organizations as "making peace à la Gypsy." In contrast, the policy-making of Romanian, Polish or Armenian organizations is depicted in the media similarly to that of Hungarians.

The liberal and socialist press, which claims to be sensitive to Roma concerns, often strengthens prejudices as well. Several reporters of the most widely read daily paper, *Népszabadság* (*Freedom of the People*), which is close to the socialists, previously worked for fiercely anti-Roma county papers. Even in sympathetic descriptions, where Gypsies appear as an underdeveloped stratum, existing in different states of necessity, their deprivation does not arouse solidarity because dehumanized reporting blames the victim. Facts refuting stereotypes of the Roma are treated as exceptions that prove the rule. "Positive" articles are often reversals of negative stereotypes, with titles such as "Gypsies Get Down to Work," "They Want Work" and sentences such as "who works to get his own, will not steal" or "not every Gypsy is a criminal." According to the Bernáth-Messing survey, in 60 percent of stories the Roma appear without any indication of individual roles—just as Gypsies. Cross-categorization (a Gypsy doctor, a Jewish bricklayer) weakens the strength of racial stigmas, but this practice is not common in Hungarian journalism. Only 25 percent of the Roma in the examined sample had the opportunity to speak directly; readers usually learned about their opinions through the interpretations of others.

Majority perceptions of minorities tend to treat individual members of minority groups as the representatives of the whole group. In Hungarian television, for example, pictures of Roma individuals are used interchangeably—regardless of whether they are connected directly to the story being covered. Ágnes Daróczi, a well-known Hungarian Roma politician, once protested against Hungarian public television after she had appeared on the screen in connection with an event in which she had no part. For the Hungarian reader or viewer, every sentence about one Gypsy person means 500,000 people.

In the Hungarian media, the Roma appear within a narrow thematic frame, usually in situations of conflict. We hardly meet any who are successful, professional or skilled workers. Only the Roma artist, painter and musician gain a place in the media—the exotic ones, successful because "they have music in their blood." "The only image of us they tolerate is that of the dancing slave," remarked Jenő Zsigó, president of the Roma Parliament, a civil organization of the Hungarian Roma. (Apart from this, the romantic image of the exotic, wandering Gypsies, still common in the West, has been pushed into the background in Hungary.) Gypsies are regular characters in Hungarian cabarets, mostly representing primitive criminals, but they have no roles in the soap operas or talk shows, which indirectly transmit cultural patterns and values. Neither can they be seen in commercials (not primarily because they cannot be taken into account as potential consumers, but because the ordinary viewer sees them and is reminded of problems). There are no Roma television anchors and they cannot be found in the "we asked the man in the street" columns of magazines. In Hungary, the half million Roma exist only as people with a Gypsy existence and identity. Being a Gypsy is an exclusive and indelible mark, which allows no other role.

THE ROMA CAN HARDLY DEFEND themselves against this stereotypical and prejudicial presentation. There have not been any legal cases against publications or television concerning the violation of rights of Roma individuals, and the number of Roma journalists who work in the mass media is less than 10. The situation is similar in politics. There are no Roma politicians in the parties or in parliament. The present government's ideas concerning Gypsies are beyond the influence of Roma civil organizations, including their national minority self-governing body.

Roma have been passive subjects of the majority's ideas concerning them for centuries, both in the media and in politics. The transition out of communism has not changed this. Whoever is in power employs various manipulations to prevent the Roma from becoming a strong enough group to promote their own interests.

The media are not, of course, responsible for unresolved social problems; its responsibility lies primarily in selecting the topics and defining the frames of social discourse. The biggest mistake of the Hungarian media may not be their often prejudicial, one-sided presentation of Gypsies, but their failure to treat the major unresolved issue of Hungarian society as it heads towards the European Union—the Gypsy question—with the appropriate weight and sense of context. The media fail to transmit that this is an issue not only for the Roma, but also for the majority—which will be judged by its relationship to the Roma. In late 20th-century Eastern Europe, we have seen what becomes of countries that violate the human rights of their inhabitants. The story of the Roma in Hungary is bigger than stolen chickens and children infected by lice.

György Kerényi is the editor in chief of Amaro Drom (Our Road), *a magazine of Roma issues.*

18

Business Reporting in Eastern Europe

New markets, new journalism

Mark M. Nelson

DEEP WITHIN THE CORRIDORS OF the massive Stalinist edifice that houses several of Romania's leading newspapers, the latest East European revolution is now well under way. After nearly a decade of concentrating on Romania's tormented politics and its steady stream of scandals, some newspapers here are slowly starting to change the subject. All of the half-dozen or so newspapers that are published in this colossal concrete wedding cake—built in the 1950s as combination publishing center and culture ministry and now known as "the House of the Free Press"—are building up a team of economics and business reporters. The same is happening at many other newspapers and broadcast media companies across the country.

It is a development that has long since taken hold in much of the rest of Eastern and Central Europe, which in this article refers to the area from the Baltics to the Balkans and eastwards up to the western borders of Russia, Belarus and Ukraine. Especially in the countries where the transition to the market economy has progressed more smoothly and rapidly, publishers are trying to come up with their versions of *The Economist*, *The Wall Street Journal*, and—right down to the pink paper—the *Financial Times*. They have created new Web sites, added business talk shows to the TV and radio lineup and produced documentaries on investment, corruption and privatization. And perhaps most important of all, the economics and business story has migrated from specialized publications into many of the region's larger-circulation newspapers and magazines.

In many ways, the shift towards business and economics coverage is motivated by a simple concept: the bottom line. Along with business and economics pages come advertisers who want to reach the educated, more affluent readers that those pages attract. The very people who follow stories on privatization, bankruptcies or exchange rates are also the people making buying decisions for their families and companies—the very target many advertisers are trying to reach. And here in Romania, where the average worker still brings home less than $100 a month, reaching higher-income audiences is a key to survival.

Sex still sells, but credible, understandable information about the economy may be more valuable. "We now have at least three pages of business and economics news every day," says Cristian Tudor Popescu, editor in chief of Romania's largest daily, *Adevărul* (*The Truth*), which under its old name, *Scînteia* (*The Spark*), was the mouthpiece of the central committee of Romania's Communist Party. "Some advertisers only want to place their ads on the business pages."

THAT IS NOT TO SAY that all that many newspapers in this part of the world have really figured out how to deliver lively, interesting economics and business stories. In fact, some of the results have been downright dismal, resulting in nearly unreadable articles full of numbers, jargon and often poorly documented scandals. In some countries, the press has no doubt contributed to the confusion about economic policy and the desirability of reform. Yet, newspaper editors across the region now seem to be realizing the value of improved coverage of business, finance and the economy, and are taking steps to improve their record.

"This is an important story for any serious newspaper these days," says Paul Raudseps, managing editor of *Diena* (*Day*), Latvia's largest daily. "And we're taking steps to make sure that we do it well." To gear itself up for the new demands, *Diena* editors have organized economics training courses for their business staff and beefed up coverage of markets, private businesses and corruption.

Expanded business coverage is also a sign of the dramatic economic changes that have taken place here in the 10 years since the angry mobs escorted Nicolae Ceaușescu and his wife to their grue-some end. In the more precocious reformers of the region—Poland, the Czech Republic, Hungary, Slovakia, Slovenia and Estonia—inter-est in business and economics came soon after the changes and were a by-product of successful policy reforms. Indeed, some observers say they saw interest in economics and business from newspaper readers as a kind of leading indicator, a sign that these economies were on the verge of sustained economic growth.

"Business reporting was an important element of the transition," says Adam Michnik, the famous Solidarity activist who is now editor in chief of one of the great successes of the Polish transition, *Gazeta Wyborcza*, Poland's largest daily with a circulation of 591,000. "The business sector has seen a lot of growth and change, and the relation-ship between business and politics has been a fascinating story."

Those developments may finally be coming for the slower-moving countries as well. While Romania, Bulgaria and Albania are still strug-gling to turn around the 6 percent to 7 percent declines in economic growth they suffered last year, all three are starting to see significant changes within their media markets. And the countries of the Balkans, which have spent much of the last decade engulfed in the wars of Yugoslavia's breakup, may now benefit from the NATO-imposed peace and Western-financed rebuilding effort. In any case, many media ex-ecutives report a growing demand from both local and foreign audi-ences for more information about the economic and business environ-ment.

PERHAPS THE MOST important force helping to change the role of the business and economics press in Central and Eastern Europe is the suddenly growing interest of foreign investors. That interest developed painfully slowly, and still is a mere trickle compared to the sums that media companies invest in other parts of the developed world. Never-theless, a closer look at some of the success stories that have been produced in the region so far shows just how important those brave few foreign investors have been to changing the subject—and the journalistic mood—here.

Indeed, behind most successful newspaper ventures in the region is a major foreign investor, and it is hardly an exaggeration to say that investments by foreign media companies here constitute one of the most important transfers of knowledge to these societies that has taken place since the fall of the Berlin Wall.

Foreigners brought not only modern technology and editorial standards, but played a major role in helping solidify the media's independence. To a large extent, foreign funding has helped protect most of this part of Europe from the "Russia syndrome," where the major newspapers and television stations have fallen into the hands of a few wealthy local oligarchs who use the newspapers to promote their narrow industrial interests. Instead, many newspapers here have found foreign strategic investors with interests in the media, rather than a local "entrepreneur" interested in free advertising.

FEW STORIES ILLUSTRATE the potential of this region more clearly than that of *Rzeczpospolita (Republic)*, the former Polish government newspaper that today is one of the most authoritative voices on business and economics in all of Central Europe. Convinced that the transformation of Poland would be first and foremost an economics story, the newspaper in 1991 started making the changes that were to make it one of the most successful quality papers in the region.

Rzeczpospolita's rise was helped by a foreign investor, Groupe Hersant. the French media conglomerate, which in 1991 bought 49 percent of its shares and invested in improving the technology and management of the newspaper. (Hersant eventually acquired an additional 2 percent stake and sold its 51 percent interest in the newspaper in 1996 to the Norwegian holding company, Orkla Group.) Editors and journalists were sent off to London, Tokyo and the United States to get themselves trained in the new economy that Poland decided to create.

The investment paid off both for the new owners and for the staff at *Rzeczpospolita*, which now has 273,000 buyers and recently opened a new four-color printing plant. Known for its famous "green pages" of economics and business news, it has established new standards for editorial integrity in Poland and is a must-read for investors, business managers and financial-market professionals. It also enjoys a large readership of thousands of ordinary Poles who participated in that country's privatization process and have become share owners in the country's booming equity markets. And its pages are covered with advertisements from airlines, luxury automobiles and real estate companies that are thriving in the new Poland.

"Almost every paper in Poland has decided to cover the capital markets here," says Leonard Furga of the Warsaw Stock Exchange.

"Enough people are following the markets that, to be serious in the publishing business, you have to cover this subject."

Michnik, the activist-turned-editor of *Gazeta Wyborcza*, calls Poland's transformation "the Polish miracle" because of the country's combination of luck and good decisions in the early days of the transition. One of those decisions, made by first postcommunist Prime Minister Tadeusz Mazowiecki, was to get the government out of the newspaper business and to allow foreign investors to enter the broadcast market.

It was this decision that paved the way to the competitive newspaper environment where newspapers like *Rzeczpospolita* and *Gazeta Wyborcza* could thrive. Cox Enterprises, Inc., owner of the *Atlanta Constitution*, paid $5 million for a 12.5 percent stake in *Gazeta Wyborcza* in 1993. That stake had produced dividends of more than $1 million and was worth $60 million as of 1998, according to company reports.

THE POLISH MODEL HAS SPURRED on efforts in other countries, though the results are still less spectacular. Many countries have realized that they lack the legal and institutional infrastructure, the respect for the rule of law, that was so relatively quickly restored in Poland. Another reason is economics. Even in Poland, GNP per capita was still just $3590 in 1998, according to World Bank figures, less than a third of the level in countries like Spain, Portugal or Greece. Romania's economy, for its part, was still contracting and had a GNP per capita of just $1410, less than Thailand, Iran or Guatemala. At such income levels, major advertising markets are still a distant dream; some people can hardly pay a nickel for a newspaper.

"In many ways, investments in Eastern and Central Europe have been a sideline, not a preoccupation of the biggest media groups," says David Adair, a media analyst at HSBC Securities in London. "Investors see this market as a long-term play. It should change in the future, but they are not making a lot of money yet."

For now, some of the region's most serious economics coverage is found in small, specialized weeklies, many of them in English, about business news aimed mainly at the foreign community. The three leaders in this market, *Warsaw Business Journal, Budapest Business Journal* and *Prague Business Journal*, have spawned a whole school of imitators. Numerous such publications of uneven quality are also emerging in Romania, Bulgaria and even Albania. On a typical hotel lobby news rack in Bucharest, a visitor will find *Bucharest Business Week, Romanian Business Journal, Romanian Economic Daily, Romanian Survey* and *The Business Review,* all free, and all scurrying to get in on what they see as a promising emerging market.

SCANDINAVIAN MEDIA GROUPS, nevertheless, are taking the plunge, especially in the Baltics. Sweden's Bonnier Group has over the past few years invested in a variety of dailies and periodicals in Estonia, Lithuania, Latvia and Poland. Schibsted ASA of Norway is also moving into Estonia like a freight train, buying stakes in a wide variety of business and nonbusiness publications and broadcast media. Ringier AG of Switzerland invested in a number of business and economics weeklies and monthlies such as *Profit* and *Týden (The Week)* in the Czech Republic, *Capital* and *Success* in Romania and *Profit* in Slovakia. Bertelsmann AG has also made forays into the region, taking interests in daily newspapers and magazines in Poland, Slovakia, Hungary and Romania. Westdeutsche Allgemeine Zeitung, the big German publisher from Essen, created controversy by buying out close to 80 percent of the total print circulation in Bulgaria, including the country's two best-selling tabloids, *Trud (Labor)* and *24 Chasa (24 Hours).*

Rolf Sunden, vice president for finance at the Bonnier Group, says the company's expansion into the Baltics and Poland has a long-term horizon, and that profit growth there will be slow for some years to come. But he's convinced of the long-term promise. "This market can be very important in the future," he says, "and we want to be there even if it won't make us a lot of money for a while."

While foreign investors are important, Tarmu Tammerk, managing director of the Estonian Newspaper Association, worries about the possibility that the media will end up in too few hands to create healthy competition. "Plurality, which was so hard won, is still very fragile," he says. "In Estonia, we have markets where radio, television, the weekly paper, the morning paper and the evening paper are all from the same group. It's very easy to manipulate the political agenda in such a situation."

Yet he still thinks the overall effect has been, on balance, positive. When the Bonnier Group's *Äripäev (Business Day)* started practicing a code of ethics that forbade its journalists from taking payments in exchange for positive coverage of business groups, it created a new

model for the rest of the industry to follow, and the newspaper association adopted similar rules last year. "Self-regulation is starting to
happen," he says. "And these foreigners have played a role in helping
people realize that this self-regulation is different from self-censorship."

EVEN WHEN MEDIA COMPANIES FIND a solution to their financial problems, putting out a good business newspaper or a readable "Money
and Markets" page can still be exceedingly difficult in this part of the
world. Many of the region's most promising newspapers still have a
way to go before developing the professional, confident economics
coverage that the region so badly needs.

Editors say they have trouble finding journalists who are capable of
covering the economics story, can't keep them once they're trained
and suffer from the generally undeveloped information systems that
plague many of the region's slowest-moving economies. Otherwise
promising countries like Croatia are still in the hands of heavy-handed
regimes that spend more time persecuting journalists than trying to
create a stable market economy. Many of the countries in the region
have draconian libel laws and protections for leaders and politicians
that greatly curtail the abilities of journalists. The lack of regular reporting requirements by companies, the poorly developed information
infrastructures within government ministries and the long-established
traditions of secrecy also present huge obstacles to running a decent
newspaper.

"There is still too little informed political opinion about economic
policy," says Raudseps of Latvia's *Diena*, a paper that is 49 percent
owned by the Bonnier Group of Sweden. Yet that paper has begun to
enliven public interest in the subject by pointing out sweetheart deals
that were part of the country's privatization process and by trying to
explain the impact of various policies on regular people.

Many experts say that, for all its problems, the press is playing an
increasingly important role in helping mediate the many lingering con-
troversies and unsettled scores of the transition from communism. In
Romania, for example, the press has been accused of failing to clarify
the country's economic choices and of siding with conservative forces
unwilling to take the leap to a market economy. But today, many
experts see a major change under way. In the last two years in particular, Romanian newspapers have taken a lead in attacking the corrup-

tion that has undermined political stability here, says Dumitry Sandu, a sociologist at the University of Bucharest.

"In the anti-corruption fight, the press has been more successful than the judicial system," he says. "And I think they are playing a more and more constructive role."

This role could have probably been even more effective if newspapers in the region had been able to work in more stable economic environments or had had the capital to do their jobs properly. But because journalists are so poorly paid in the slower-moving economies, business journalism often turns into a shady affair: journalists simply sell their services to companies that want good coverage. In Romania, where many journalists earn less than $100 a month, the temptation to moonlight for the local business mogul is just too great. Some editors, frustrated with their inability to control such influences, have effectively banned coverage of private companies altogether.

Even in the more economically advanced countries, making business news readable and relevant to regular people is a major challenge. *Delo (Day)*, Slovenia's leading daily with 91,000 buyers, recently started *The Small Investor*, a free monthly that is sent to all 600,000 homes in Slovenia. It is trying to reach the growing market for readable stories about personal investing, consumer banking and other such business stories. But *Delo* Chief Editor Mitja Meršol says it is difficult to find journalists that are able to handle these topics with style and accuracy.

"We need to convey very basic information and know-how to the small investor without being patronizing," he says. "It's hard to find journalists and editors who can handle this task."

No event pointed out the wide gulf among Eastern Europe's economics papers as the August 17, 1998, announcement by Russia that it was going to let the ruble float freely and would declare a unilateral moratorium on its foreign debt.

That event, which came on the heels of the financial crisis in Southeast Asia, was to have huge consequences for all of Central Europe's fragile stock markets and would sour foreign investors on the region for months to come. But realizing these important local consequences and writing about them intelligently within a few hours requires a confident, well-managed newsroom staffed by well-trained professionals. Some papers didn't live up to the challenge.

In Poland, the Czech Republic and the other advanced parts of the region, the story found its place where it belonged—on Page One, with the analysis that helped people understand what to expect. Readers of *Rzeczpospolita* learned that this Russian devaluation would be the beginning of a rough slog for Poland, but that the damage shouldn't be exaggerated, since Poland had shifted much of its economic relationship toward the West. While Poland's markets slumped badly, the government still was able to proceed with the planned privatization of the Polish telephone monopoly a few weeks later.

In Bulgaria, readers of the country's business press got a better picture than did readers of some of the more popular publications. *Pari (Money)*, the leading financial daily with about 14,000 buyers, put the story (from AP and Reuters) at the top of Page One on August 18 and followed it up on the following days. *Trud* and *24 Chasa*, the Westdeutsche Allgemeine Zeitung properties, also had the story but at first gave it less prominence than it deserved; Bill Clinton and Monica Lewinsky were still stealing the headlines. *Trud* (circulation 440,000) didn't really catch on to the full implications of the story until August 22, when it lead page one with THE CRISIS HAS JUST BEGUN!

In Romania, meanwhile, Adevărul and many other major papers in the country ignored the story altogether and were to take several days to make sense of it. But that's just what *Ziarul Financiar (Financial Daily)*, Bucharest's spanking new pink daily, aims to fix. Started from scratch in November 1998 by a local media group and modeling itself on the *Financial Times*, *Ziarul Financiar* vows that Romanians will know where to turn for the next crisis.

"The newspapers here really didn't know what to make of this financial crisis," says Mihaela Lupu, finance editor. "But we are going to change this. We are going from 16 pages to 24, and our circulation is growing. Our readers ask many questions about business, banking. They really want to know. I'm very optimistic about the way things are going in this business, and about the future of this newspaper."

Mark M. Nelson, senior operations officer at the World Bank in Paris, manages economics journalism training programs in developing countries. For 11 years he was a staff correspondent for The Wall Street Journal *based in Europe.*

19

The Renaissance of Jewish Media

Imagining and organizing a future

Ruth Ellen Gruber

WE DON'T TELL PEOPLE HOW they should be Jewish, or even that they ought to express their Jewishness at all," says Konstanty Gebert. "We simply want to show them that Jewishness is something so interesting that they'll be sorry to miss a single issue of our magazine."

Gebert, is the editor in chief of *Midrasz*, Poland's only Jewish monthly, and his statement could serve as the magazine's motto.

Since its first issue came out in April 1997, *Midrasz* (which means "explanation," or the immense literature based on rabbinical commentary) has grown from an optimistic experiment into a respected journal that each month presents a lively mixture of commentary, cultural essays, poetry, fiction and hard news articles on current local and international Jewish issues—as well as Sabbath candle-lighting times and commentary on the Torah.

Nationally distributed, and with a print run of 3,000, it reaches a significant proportion of Poland's emerging Jewish community and is fast becoming that community's most important voice. Not only that, a reader survey in 1998 showed that as much as one-third of its readership was comprised of non-Jews.

The magazine is Gebert's brainchild. A longtime Jewish activist in Poland, Gebert was a well-known underground militant in the anti-communist Solidarity movement of the 1980s; at that time he wrote in

179

the underground press using the deliberately Jewish pen name of Dawid Warszawski. A nationally known journalist and commentator after the political changes, Gebert quit his job as foreign correspondent and columnist at *Gazeta Wyborcza*, Poland's largest circulation daily, to found *Midrasz*.

"I was waiting for years for a decent, Polish-language Jewish magazine to appear, so that I could write for it," he said. "It eventually dawned on me that if I didn't create one, I wouldn't have one!"

With its slick graphic design, meaty content and distinguished stable of writers, *Midrasz* is the latest—and one of the most prominent—of a new crop of Jewish publications and other information outlets in Central Europe that have grown up in the decade since the fall of communism.

These new—or in some cases revamped—magazines, newspapers, newsletters and bulletins—have arisen as the fruit both of the broad new press freedoms unleashed by the political changes of 1989–1990, as well as of the new efforts at Jewish communal revival enabled by the democratic transformations. Throughout the region now, one finds new Jewish schools and newly active synagogues, kosher restaurants and Jewish study centers, Jewish student clubs and modern homes for the elderly. It is in the pages of publications such as *Midrasz* in Poland; *Szombat* and *Múlt és Jövő* in Hungary, *Ros Chodes* in the Czech Republic and others in which the deep internal debates and discussions that have accompanied these tangible signs of Jewish revival are voiced—and fought out. How to confront the issue of who is a Jew. Is it possible to take on Jewish identity in mid-life? How to make Judaism relevant in today's spiritual marketplace. How to deal with the doubly damned legacy of the Holocaust and communism. How to train new community leaders and improve Jewish education. How to achieve restitution of Jewish property. How to chart future relations with Israel.

In addition to traditional media, Jewish communities, institutions, organizations and individuals in the region increasingly have embraced Internet technology to create Web sites, chat lists and other computer networks to debate these issues and get their message across. In some places they have also gained access to radio and television broadcasts. The exposure and the professional quality of some Jewish media outlets may indeed give the impression that communities are stronger and more influential than their numbers decree.

IT IS A FAR CRY FROM A DECADE AGO. Under communism, Jewish practice, expression and education were tightly controlled by the authorities. The level of constraint differed from country to country (and also
shifted in response to the general political scene). But, as a general
rule, topics regarding Jewish history, culture and the Holocaust were
taboo, off limits both in the mainstream media and in internal Jewish
publications.

An officially sanctioned Jewish media existed before the changes of
1989, but the permitted Jewish press in Central and Eastern Europe
were organs of the state-approved official Jewish communal organizations and thus tightly muzzled. In the early decades of communist rule,
they were virtual mouthpieces for the Communist Party: anti-imperial-
ism and anti-Zionism filled the pages. Although overt pro-regime propaganda was toned down in most places by the mid-1960s, and a
further relaxation occurred in some countries from the mid-1980s onward, conscientious self-censorship ensured that most Jewish publications remained dusty and irrelevant chroniclers of the mundane. They
echoed the policies of the central Jewish organizations, which had no
intention or desire to anger the Party or draw attention to real issues.
Poland's *Folks Stimme (People's Voice)* was essentially, a Jewish
version of the party's *Trybuna Ludu (People's Tribune)*; in Hungary,
Új Élet (New Life) was not much different from *Népszabadság (Freedom of the People)*. In Romania, just as the official media slavishly
fostered the personality cult of dictator Nicolae Ceaușescu the Jewish
communal newspaper slavishly served the parallel personality cult of
Chief Rabbi Moses Rosen. Full of news of the comings, goings, do-
ings and pronouncements of "His Eminence," it was referred to, cyni-
cally, as the "Rosenblatt." Just as Jewish topics became the subject of
semiclandestine dissident study groups, it was only in underground
samizdat publications that Jewish issues could be tackled or reported
in an open, critical, in-depth manner.

"The changes of 1989 brought about a democratization of the Jewish press," says Edward Serotta, a photographer who has documented
Jewish life in Central Europe since the mid-1980s and currently di-
rects the Vienna-based Central Europe Center for Research and Docu-
mentation: "Younger writers, some of them well-known *samizdat* figures, who had had no chance of directly addressing a Jewish audience,
looked for and found financial support from a variety of international
foundations and then started up Jewish journals, quarterlies and month-

lies. The landscape has now changed radically. There is a variety of publications that act, in essence, as forums for Jews to discuss identity, religion, nationality, relations with Israel and the rest of world Jewry."

Prominent examples of the new Jewish media can be found in three capitals—Budapest, Prague and Warsaw. All three cities are centers of a rich and lively mainstream press, and each is also the scene of a postcommunist revival of Jewish communal structures and life. The demographics of the Jewish community, as well as the means and manner of Jewish revival are quite different in each city, as are the publications under review. Together, however, they form a composite picture of the scope of Jewish media possibilities now open in central Europe—as well as the problems and challenges they face in staying afloat.

Many of the new publications limp along with far too little financial subvention, and it is not clear how long some of them will last. Some publications have staked out editorial positions that have not proved attractive to their target audience. Most, too, are not run or written by professional journalists. Indeed, one of the things that sets Poland's *Midrasz* apart is that its editor is a seasoned reporter with many years in the business, who knows how to make a publication attractive to a potential readership.

IT IS THE NATURE OF MANY JEWISH publications, in the West as well as the East, to feel that they have a service mission that goes beyond simply reporting news and providing commentary on Jewish issues.

Midrasz editor Gebert wants his magazine to play this sort of role in Poland. "I'm a great believer in Lenin's maxim that a newspaper is a great collective organizer," he says. "We're trying to get this Jewish community together again. There is no one single Jewish institution in Poland today to which all Jews can relate without antagonism, without problems. I'd like *Midrasz* to be such a—quote unquote—institution."

Since the fall of communism, hundreds if not thousands of people have stepped forward to reclaim Jewish roots in Poland. Poland's specific history, however, has made the process particularly problematic. Poland was Europe's Jewish heartland before the Holocaust, but more than 3 million of its prewar 3.5 million Jews were killed. Waves of anti-Semitism immediately after the war and an "anti-Zionist" campaign by the communist regime in 1968 forced most survivors to leave. Those who remained were considered the final remnants of a closed chapter; indeed, many of the elderly survivor generation who remembered the richness of prewar Jewish life, refused to recognize the newly emerging younger Jews, who stepped forward from the 1980s onward, as real Jews. Today, estimates of Poland's Jewish population range from several thousand registered members of the religious community, to 10,000 or 15,000 with some sort of Jewish affiliation, to as many as 30,000 or 40,000 with Jewish ancestry.

SINCE THE LATE 1980s, MUCH OF THE Jewish revival process in Poland has been underwritten by the Ronald S. Lauder Foundation, which has sponsored numerous educational and other programs for emerging Jews in Poland. *Midrasz* falls within this framework. It was launched in April 1997 with a generous Lauder Foundation grant, and the Foundation remains its principal source of funding. This means that *Midrasz* is not an organ of the official Jewish communal structure. Staff members insist that the Lauder Foundation has maintained a hands-off policy, and the magazine does not consider itself to be an organ of the Foundation. "So far it has not interfered whatsoever," says writer and editor Agnieszka Nowokowska. "We feel free."

The Lauder Foundation funds are essential, said Nowokowska, as so far the magazine has had difficulty selling advertising. "It is not clear as to whether there is a lingering reluctance on the part of businesses to be identified with a Jewish milieu, or whether they think it is not worth the effort because of such a small, elite readership," she said. Even the Israeli airline El Al, she said, refused to place an ad, because they already had a corner on the direct flights to Israel market.

Gebert works with a paid editorial staff of five in a one-room office at Warsaw's bustling Jewish center next door to the city's only synagogue. Staff members—like the content of the magazine—reflect the dynamics within the new Polish-Jewish community itself: "I'm religious; the rest of the staff is secular," Gebert says. "We're divided about Israeli politics, with both Likudniks and Labor supporters present. We are divided in the strength of our Zionist commitment, from a strong commitment to a very strong diasporic identity. So it would be very hard to nail us down," he said. "But we don't want to be nailed down. We want to be as pluralist as possible."

Editorial content is a mix of local and foreign current events, feature stories, commentary, literature and practical information. The target audience, says Gebert, is threefold: committed Polish Jews, "Poles of Jewish origin" and members of the Polish intelligentsia, whatever their religious or ethnic background. "Of our three target groups, the second is the largest and most important," he says. "The decisions that this group will make about the nature of their identity will have a defining impact on the future of Polish Jews. We want to influence these decisions." About 40 percent of copies are distributed through subscriptions; the rest are sold in quality bookstores. Each edition sells out.

Midrasz articles are written in a provocative as well as an informative manner. A 1997 cover story on kashrut in Poland, for example, produced angry letters from some readers who were unhappy with what they called the "separatedness" that keeping kosher implies. The cover illustration was a satirical cartoon, and that issue of the magazine also "outed" kashrut problems at a restaurant in Cracow that advertises itself as kosher. A story in another issue lambasted one of Warsaw's main bookstores for selling anti-Semitic publications. *Midrasz* features numerous articles on sensitive Jewish identity problems, many of which provoke a lively response in the letters column. One such article dealt in general with Jews who converted to Christianity—an important and delicate issue in Poland, where thousands of Jewish war orphans were raised as Catholics by foster parents. A related article was an intensely personal account written by a Roman Catholic priest who only discovered in 1978, 12 years after his ordination, that he had been born to Jews killed in the Holocaust and raised from infancy by Catholic foster parents. The article included a picture of him, wearing a skullcap, with newly discovered Jewish relatives in Israel. But *Midrasz* also runs commentaries on the weekly portions of the Torah, which have become popular with readers. And its literary section has attracted well-known names among the Polish-Jewish literary elite, and also some non-Jewish figures, as essayists and reviewers. In November 1998, *Midrasz* co-sponsored Poland's first Jewish book fair.

"We want to generate controversy," Gebert says. "We want to show that Jewishness is not all Shoah, anti-Semitism and *Fiddler on the Roof.* We have no fear of running out of new ideas. . . . We are being read. We are being argued about," he adds. "And if someone decides not to read us anymore, that means he cares about his own version of Jewishness so much that he will not stand ours. From a Jewish perspective, that's not so bad."

BUDAPEST IS HOME TO CENTRAL Europe's largest Jewish community: as many as 80,000 or more Jews may live in the Hungarian capital, the vast majority of whom are highly assimilated. There are nearly a score of functioning synagogues; three Jewish day schools with a total enrollment of some 1,500 pupils; two old-age homes and several senior centers; kosher restaurants and shops; and a modern Jewish community center that houses clubs, a computer lab and various activities. The sheer size of the community makes Hungary the only country in the region with a really substantial internal Jewish market. *A Jewish Guide to Hungary*, put out in 1997 by Budapest's Jewish Museum, listed more than a dozen Jewish publications. They ranged from newsletters published by various organizations to the official communal biweekly organ *Új Élet* to the intellectual cultural quarterly *Múlt és Jövő* and the independent cultural monthly *Szombat*.

Szombat (Sabbath), founded in 1988 in the waning days of communist rule, is similar in format to *Midrasz*, featuring a mix of foreign and domestic news, features and commentary, but it has been less successful finding a role as a respected Jewish voice. This is due in part to the ambiguous nature of Hungary's assimilated Jewry, but also to *Szombat*'s aggressive independent stand, which does not just air debates on controversial issues but also raises vocal criticism of official Jewish communal structures, organizations, policy and individual community leaders.

"Our stand is based on double roots," says editor in chief *Gábor T. Szántó*, an essayist and author of fiction. "We are Jews, but we belong to the European intellectual tradition. We have neoconservatives, liberals, traditionalists. We try to open the door as wide as we can, but most official Jewish leaders do not like to air such debates. Everyone has tried to hide from the questions of what kind of Jewishness do we need to build after the Holocaust and communism. So we try to make ourselves an alternative forum . . . but very few of our readers try to respond to our articles if they are critical of the leadership. It's a taboo to criticize them. It's forbidden to criticize other Jews, because, so they think, the 'goys' could use this against the Jews."

Szombat comes out 10 times a year and is published by the private Federation to Maintain Jewish Culture in Hungary. Only 1,700 copies are printed. About 600 are distributed to subscribers; the others are sold in shops and Jewish institutions. *Szombat*'s readership is almost totally within the internal Jewish community, but the magazine's gadfly—some say finger wagging—attitude has alienated some potential readers, drawn criticism from community leaders and contributed to marginalizing the magazine to some extent. The magazine is in continual financial crisis: for several months last year it had to print its covers in black and white because it did not have enough funds for color printing. Principal funding comes from state sources, including the Culture Ministry and the National Cultural Foundation, and independent foundations. "Jewish money is the smallest part, not more than 15 percent of our total 1998–99 budget," says Szántó. "We are too critical to get official or private Jewish contributions."

Szombat's focus is also seen as too narrow—too Jewish—by most prominent Jewish intellectuals, who prefer to write for the mainstream media. Fees paid for articles are also low, averaging one-third to one-half of the national average. These problems are recognized by the editors. "There are a lot of media outlets in Hungary now," says Szántó. "There are a lot of places where one can publish articles on Jewish topics. We have to fight to get good writers to contribute. There are few who want to publish in a hard-core Jewish paper."

Ivan Sanders, a Hungarian-American Jewish intellectual and respected translator of Hungarian literature into English, agrees. "*Szombat* is in opposition to the official Jewish community line," he says. "Its editors are critical and on top of them, so in this sense it serves an important service." But, he adds, "Jewish writers tend to look down on the magazine. A few prominent writers publish there, but there is still a lot of resistance; Hungarian Jewish writers do not want to [risk being] ghettoized intellectually."

THE HUNGARIAN JEWISH INTELLECTUAL quarterly, *Múlt és Jövő (Past and Future)*, has fewer problems in attracting prominent intellectual figures, mainly because it sets itself up to be a detached intellectual and cultural journal dealing with broad themes and ideas rather than concrete day-to-day issues. It also publishes a considerable selection of foreign-language scholarly and literary work translated into Hungarian.

Founded by writer and sociologist János Kőbányai in 1988, *Múlt és Jövő* attempts to carry on the tradition of an earlier, highly influential Jewish publication of the same name, which flourished from 1911 until the Nazis marched into Hungary in 1944. "The main aim of the magazine is to reunite what once was broken: to provide a review appearing on a continuous basis and to manifest and celebrate the existence of the Jewish intellectual potential, once almost expelled from Hungarian culture," Kőbányai has written. "Current politics and the so-called struggle against anti-Semitism are strictly forbidden in the pages of the magazine."

Múlt és Jövő has managed to attract several very influential intellectuals as regular contributors, including the internationally known Hungarian-born sociologist Ágnes Heller. *Múlt és Jövő* also publishes books and enjoyed a real coup last year by publishing Heller's hugely successful memoirs. *Múlt és Jövő* presents the staid appearance of an academic journal. It targets much the same audience as *Szombat*, but its different approach means that the two publications do not compete. "People who are really interested buy both," says Sanders.

THE PRAGUE JEWISH MONTHLY *Ros Chodes* differs from the other publications under review in that it is the official organ of the Jewish Community and reflects the positions of the community leadership. It is the direct heir to *Věstník*, the Jewish community bulletin that resumed publication after World War II in 1945 and was published throughout the communist period. Jiří Daníček, the current president of Prague's official Jewish communal organization, is its editor in chief. Changing its name from *Věstník (Bulletin)* to *Ros Chodes* in 1990 symbolized the new democratic conditions following the Velvet Revolution. *Ros Chodes* means the new moon, marking the beginning of a new month. "Over the past decade, we have tried, and still try, to make *Ros Chodes* more attractive to our readers, more readable," says editorial staff member Alice Marxová. This has included not just vastly broadening the content and upgrading the graphic design to include photographs and color reproductions, but also introducing more lively and immediate feature material, including interviews and personality profiles.

Ros Chodes remains a cross between a feature magazine and a community newsletter. Its content emphasizes "straight news" and information, including book reviews, cultural notes, religious tradition, and birth and death notices rather than critical essays or commentary on local problems. Articles tackle a wide range of issues, including Jewish identity, nationalism and property restitution, but the tone is nonpolemical, and articles are not critical of community policy, institutions or leaders. "Problems are reflected, but not directly," says Marxová. "Differences of opinion are expressed in interviews with individuals and also in the letters-to-the-editor column."

About 3,000 to 4,000 Jews belong to Jewish communities in the

Czech Republic, about 1,500 in Prague; another 3,000 live in Slovakia. Some 2,300 copies of *Ros Chodes* are printed, about 300 of which are distributed in Slovakia. The magazine was the organ of the combined Czechoslovak Jewish community before the breakup of the country in 1993, and, although its publisher today is the Prague Jewish community, its masthead still calls it the organ of Czech and Slovak Jews. The main audience is the internal Jewish community, but Marxová says that there is a relatively large readership of non-Jews who purchase *Ros Chodes* at selected bookstores. As in Poland, non-Jews have expressed interest in aspects of Jewish life that were taboo under communism.

All of these publications broach issues that are of interest not only in Eastern Europe but in the rest of the Jewish world as well—including the United States. In 1998 and 1999, the American Jewish Committee published selections from *Midrasz* and from *Szombat*, in order to illustrate the scope and quality both of these magazines and of the issues under consideration. These publications demonstrate the vitality of Jewish life in former communist Europe in ways that can be readily grasped by American readers, notes Rabbi Andrew Baker, the American Jewish Committee director of European Affairs.

The issues aired in the postcommunist Jewish press are the same as the concerns debated in the Jewish media in other countries. In addition, the postcommunist Jewish press faces the same pragmatic problems that confront Jewish media in the democratic, pluralist West: how to find funding, how to increase circulation, how to upgrade professional standards, how to secure advertising, how to balance community service and institutional backing with editorial integrity. The new Jewish media in postcommunist Europe reflect both the general changes since the fall of communism and the specific concerns of Jewish communities and individuals. Jews in Central and Eastern Europe are trying to construct—or reconstruct—identities and ensure a Jewish future in a region where, until a decade ago, such a future was virtually unimaginable.

Ruth Ellen Gruber, a columnist for The New Leader, *is the author of several books on Jewish culture in postcommunist Central and Eastern Europe.*

20

Struggles for Independent Journalism

Ten years of learning and teaching,
from Poland to Yugoslavia

Jerome Aumente

THE FIGHT FOR A STRONG independent press in Central and Eastern Europe, despite stubborn dictatorial opposition, has reached significant milestones and generated important lessons for global media assistance elsewhere.

When the former Soviet bloc nations rejected communism and asked the West to help create independent news media, democratic nations responded with a concerted drive to provide bootstrap aid. In its scope, the effort has no counterpart in recent history. Trace an arc from 1989 when Poland became the first nation in Eastern Europe to elect a noncommunist government to the present-day media in Serbia in 1999 and we see stunning changes.

Poland's underground *samizdat* produced hundreds of titles during martial law from 1981 to 1989. Many efforts were limited to flimsy, tissue-thin mimeographed sheets passed hand to hand. Some, however, evolved into permanent publications such as *Gazeta Wyborcza*, today one of the country's most respected mass circulation dailies. A decade later, independent media in Serbia use the Internet to instantly distribute news reports worldwide with laptops, satellite links and clandestine Web sites created by international computer wizardry to elude censors.

Despite technological advances, there is striking similarity to the task at hand when you survey the Balkans and surrounding countries and measure the resources needed to bring viable, independent print and electronic news media to Serbia and Montenegro, and also to Bosnia and Herzegovina, Croatia, Albania, Macedonia, Romania, Bulgaria, Ukraine or Belarus. There is a numbing sameness to the task, heartbreaking in the suffering once again endured, with Serbia the latest tragic example.

Journalists continue to be harassed, jailed and killed. News outlets are peremptorily shut down. Valiant attempts to break away from state-controlled news media are met with repressive laws that censor, fabricate charges of criminal libel or block legitimate applications for broadcast frequencies.

Cronyism rewards party faithful, and independent media are hit with punitive taxes. Print media often feel the choke hold of paper supplies, printing presses and distribution networks closed to them. Universities must reinvent themselves to become trusted and legitimate training grounds for future journalists.

While hardly matching the sticker price of even a few Stealth bombers or the cost of a week's aerial bombardment, money from the United States and other Western nations since 1989 to aid media in Central and Eastern Europe has been substantial: tens of millions of dollars spent by governments, foundations and media organizations. Programs first developed in the former Warsaw Pact nations continue today with the NATO-Kosovo crisis and assistance to war-ravaged Bosnia and Herzegovina. Earlier lessons—learned in Poland, Hungary, the Czech Republic, Slovakia and the former Soviet states—about creating independent media present useful clues for today's challenges: how to sustain an independent press in a fragile, market-driven economy, train a new breed of questioning rather than passive journalists and strip away press laws that shackle the news media.

Secretary of State James Baker jump started media assistance in Central and Eastern Europe in 1990 with a pledge delivered at Charles University in Prague of U.S support for independent media in the region. Thus began a string of media assistance projects ranging from a specially funded East European task force in the U.S. Information Agency (USIA) to later creation of the International Media Fund (IMF) and expanded media support programs through the U.S. Agency for International Development (USAID), USIA and its U.S. Information Service offices at embassies. ProMedia, the Professional Media Program of the International Research and Exchanges Board (IREX) in Washington, received $19 million from USAID for media assistance to 10 countries in the region from 1995 through this fall, with millions more up for competitive bid.

The Soros Foundation, through its Open Society Institutes and foundations, is a heavy spender in the region. Its most recent annual report of 1997 shows support for media and communications at $2.7 million in the former Yugoslavia; nearly $1 million for Bosnia; $1.3 million for Croatia; $1.1 million for Romania; and amounts varying from a quarter million to $1 million each in Poland, Hungary, Albania and Macedonia. In 1997 alone, Soros gave $13.7 million in Russia for media projects, additional millions in Central and Eastern Europe for publishing assistance and $2.6 million for a network media program.

The Freedom Forum spent millions creating and operating journalism libraries in the major capitals of the region, giving journalists and students Internet and computer resources, and running training programs, professional fellowships and conferences. The focus on the media in Central and Eastern Europe spawned the Independent Journalism Foundation with its successful media training centers in Prague, Bratislava, Budapest and Bucharest. The International Center for Foreign Journalists in Washington grew with the opportunities for hundreds of journalists from the region. Universities, such as Rutgers University, the University of Maryland, the University of Missouri, Columbia University, Indiana University, New York University, California State University-Chico, and University of Georgia, developed media programs in the region, many of which continue to this day with their own curricula enriched by research and overseas training.

AS DIRECTOR OF THE JOURNALISM Resources Institute at Rutgers University, I conducted media needs assessments in Poland, the Czech Republic and Slovakia in 1989 and 1990 for USIA and the IMF. This led to major funding and the design of a ladder approach of assistance: first, provide essential, first-tier journalism skills quickly; second, begin longer-term institution building; and third, create a turn-key approach to transfer resources to domestic professionals as foreign assistance is phased out.

First came basic print and broadcast journalism workshops, followed by establishment of a Media Resources Center in Warsaw, then teams of American journalists assigned for longer consultations with newspapers, radio and television. Later we helped create a now thriving School of Journalism at Jagiellonian University in Cracow, a public radio station run by the Cracow Academy of Engineering and specialized reporting training. We favored indigenous projects run by native Poles and institutions to continue the programs after we left. Simultaneously, Polish journalists came to the United States for short- and long-term study fellowships.

Many factors, including a transformed economy once Poland accepted needed but painful market reform, propelled it to prosperity, and with it the independent news media. Still, the early infusion of sustained media assistance from abroad helped provide the media structure to ride this economic tailwind.

Today, Poland, with 40 million people, is a media success story with a robust print and electronic press and a growing advertising base in one of Europe's better economies. Among newspapers, it has nine nationwide dailies, 46 regional dailies, 120 national weeklies and many hundreds of general and specialized periodicals. All newspapers are in private hands with one or two exceptions, and the local press listed more than 1,200 titles in 1996. By 1997, the National Broadcasting Council had issued 208 radio broadcast licenses, 21 TV licenses to commercial ventures and two for satellite broadcasting. About 3.3 million households, or 25 percent, take cable or satellite services. Polsat, a private nationwide TV network, competes head to head with Polish Public TV, with Polsat garnering 26 percent of the audience and PTV 35 percent.

Gazeta Wyborcza, with former underground links to Solidarity, emerged as an election gazette in 1989 and never stopped. It is now one of the country's most popular serious content papers with a daily circulation of more than 500,000, weekends 700,000. With 17 regional editions and computerized delivery of copy to regional printing plants it has nationwide reach and is fat with advertising and magazine inserts. Elsewhere, *Twoj Styl (Your Style)*, a women's magazine, has a circulation of 450,000. El żbieta Oyrzanowska, media and publishing coordinator at the Stefan Batory Foundation in Warsaw, says its count of women's interest magazines shows 192 titles, with 72 of them distributed nationally.

Today in Poland, Hungary and the Czech Republic, we see a rapidly maturing democratic press and an infrastructure in place for advertising that supports independent media. All of these nations, however, still confront an overcrowded media field that must be thinned out, problems of insufficient distance between some news media and ruling politicians, and the uncertainty of rapidly changing audiences and reader habits.

The media in the former Yugoslavia confront all of these problems and more. This is both tragic and ironic: for many years, while the media of Warsaw Pact countries such as Poland were suppressed, the Yugoslav press benefited from a more relaxed government attitude toward the press. Yugoslav journalists, though restricted, were freer to travel and cover controversial issues. In the '90s, however, the situation has reversed. While the media have improved in countries such as Poland, Hungary and the Czech Republic, the media in the former Yugoslavia have deteriorated.

Before the NATO bombing in spring 1999, major efforts were under way to assist the independent media in Serbia and Montenegro. Mark Whitehouse, a senior program officer in Washington who oversaw the IREX ProMedia efforts there and in Bosnia and Herzegovina, said resources supported a network of independent broadcasters and a planned radio training center in Belgrade. With the print press, the focus was on helping newspapers, like *Danas (Today)*, in Belgrade restructure themselves and operate with more business management efficiency. Sensationalist tabloids throughout the region constantly siphon readership from serious newspapers, so ProMedia planned a Serbian readership survey to pinpoint reader interests and find ways to nurture "family" newspapers. All of this halted abruptly when NATO began bombing, and ProMedia staff, like their many foreign counterparts, had to leave the country hastily.

Though not as devastated, Serbia now faces a major rebuilding of its infrastructure and, in Kosovo, occupation by an international force of peacekeepers. Its independent media are in tatters, but there are lessons to be learned from its neighbor and former fellow republic, Bosnia and Herzegovina, in the quest for independent media.

Weighing strategies to assist independent media in Serbia once there is an opportunity to return, Whitehouse believes a Bosnian syndrome must be avoided—"too much money going after too few media . . . a tendency to overbuild media beyond what can be sustained when assistance ends." The media must also avoid dependency on foreign donors, operate with more business efficiency and stop fragmenting an already saturated media market.

With 4 million people, Bosnia and Herzegovina counts more than 300 print and electronic media, an oversaturated market in a weak economy, without sufficient advertising revenue to support an independent media. In its semiannual report of July-December 1998, ProMedia describes this along with a media environment riddled with political meddling; government printing houses enforcing pricing monopolies and advertising governed by ethnic and political affiliations.

Professor Jelenka Voćkić-Avdagić, former head of the journalism department at University of Sarajevo, with whom I direct a joint USIA grant program to help modernize its curriculum, reports that in Bosnia there are 122 radio and 48 TV stations in the Muslim-Croat Federation and 84 radio and 28 TV stations in Republika Srpska, including two state networks representing each ethnic entity, and the Open Broadcasting Network. There are approximately 138 print titles in the country and nearly a dozen news agencies. Bosnia-Herzegovina has little outside foreign investment for media, but much international media aid from government and foundation sources.

The ethnic fissures through which hatreds caustically seep to the surface are very much influenced by the news media's actions. ProMedia, with the goal of encouraging responsible voices, assisted seven publications in the Muslim-Croat Federation—including daily newspapers and magazines in Sarajevo and several publications in Banja Luka in Republika Srpska. It also provided legal regulatory guidance for the media, advising an Independent Media Council set up by international oversight groups as part of the Dayton Agreement following the 1992-95 Bosnian war. Besides issuing broadcast licenses, the council rides herd on all the news media to discourage blatant ethnic bias and to promote ethics guidelines among journalists. International peacekeepers could even shut down egregious violators of its mandates for ethnic harmony.

To nurture a nongovernmental news agency that wanted to report across ethnic enclaves that now divided Muslim, Croat and Serb sectors of Bosnia, ProMedia provided special assistance. In the winter of 1999, I conducted a VOA International Media Training Center program in New York and Washington for the directors of four of the major news agencies in Bosnia and found a real willingness to cooperate across ethnic lines and to build business ties.

As for effective training, some like Whitehouse believe that "workshop fatigue" has set in within the region. ProMedia focused instead on placing resident advisors in its target countries, encouraging them to build trust with editors, long-term relationships with the media and a deeper sense of the culture in which they work.

ANOTHER HALLMARK OF THE WORK in Bosnia and Herzegovina that can carry over to Serbia or Kosovo is the need to introduce practical training and business practices in the media. Internews, a California nonprofit group, has provided media assistance in more than 25 countries and since 1992 trained 7,000 professionals worldwide. It subcontracted with ProMedia in Bosnia and reports that it gave practical, hands-on training to broadcasters in 25 Bosnian cities. Internews says that at stations it assisted local news production increased 50 percent, ad revenue grew 100 percent and multiple news sourcing (essential for less ethnically biased reporting) rose 90 percent, and indigenous groups produced more than 96 hours of special programming.

IN OTHER FORMER ENTITIES OF Yugoslavia, now independent, there are similar problems. Macedonia, a former Yugoslav republic that won independence for its 2 million people without violence, struggles with a dismal economy and shock waves from the war in Kosovo. Professor Dona Kolar-Panov, chair of communication studies at St. Cyril and Methodius University in Skopje, is doing a major media audience analysis with European Commission support. Her media plan will assess the highly deregulated environment in which 210 radio, television or combined RTV stations registered and scrambled to find a market. Macedonia must make order of the chaos that ensued with its earlier *laissez-faire* broadcast environment and tolerance for program piracy, and must serve both general and segmented ethnic audiences in an oversaturated media environment—classic media problems in all of the region.

Meanwhile, Croatia continues to see independent media harassed with a flood of intimidating libel suits. Cases must be heard within eight days when a public official files suit, and crushing fines must be paid instantly even though the conviction may be under appeal. Economically strapped papers have difficulty collecting distribution sales revenue from the party-controlled distributor, according to ProMedia. A fiber optic network for independent Croatian broadcasting was planned but hampered by government opposition to any network that would threaten its state television dominance.

Where once the totalitarian governments of the communist era arbitrarily muzzled the press by fiat, we see in the Central and Eastern European region today intimidation by legal suits. Journalists are increasingly threatened with criminal libel and slander. Monitors report serious cases in Bulgaria and Romania, but there is some improvement in Slovakia and Albania where less restrictive governments were elected recently. Jane Kirtley, former executive director of the Reporters Committee for Freedom of the Press in Washington, speaks in the region often and is concerned with the spread of draconian criminal libel laws and the promotion of press laws that ostensibly guarantee press freedom but allow governments to meddle in content. She hopes journalists associations will set aside rivalries and adopt ethical standards that are self-enforced without any outside tribunal or government body involved.

Nowhere in the entire Balkan region do you confront as complex and potentially lethal a challenge to restoring independent media as you do in Serbia and Montenegro, all that remains of the former Yugoslavia. In the immediate aftermath of Kosovo, a defeated, heavily bombed population in Serbia, harangued by extreme nationalists looking for revenge, may have little tolerance for an independent press or broadcasting.

The excitement, the precariousness and the hope of future independent media in the country are exemplified by B92, the maverick radio station in Belgrade and the Association of Independent Electronic Media (ANEM) it helped found with six other stations in 1993. ANEM had 33 local radio stations and 18 television stations, covered nearly 70 percent of the country of 11 million and was the second most listened to source of radio news when it was shut down by the Milošević government in spring 1999, shortly after the NATO bombings began. A ProMedia national survey found the radio network attracting 1.65 million listeners in Serbia and Montenegro, compared to 2.5 million state radio listeners. B92, the network's keystone station that provided a daily feed to member stations, along with ANEM, had the inspired leadership of Veran Matić, who as editor in chief of the station and head of ANEM, became internationally recognized.

In 1996, Serbs demonstrated to protest democratic local elections nullified by the Milošević regime. B92 became their key news source and itself a rallying point when the station was shut down. Off the air, B92 used its "OpenNet" Internet network to send audio reports globally via the Web, which were then fed back into Serbia by international broadcasters. Its bulletins in a Web newsletter format on the computer screen were easily reproduced. The bulletins were read aloud in town squares and posted on walls and billboards. Towns without Internet service received reports by fax. They were copied, put on local radio or passed hand to hand, Matić reports.

Under this information blitz, the Milošević regime relented and B92 was back on the air toward the end of 1996. The station was again closed in spring of 1999 when NATO bombings began. Matić was briefly arrested and released, and B92's independent status ended. B92 was reconstituted as a government-controlled station. But its original staff in exile launched an opposition underground Internet site with Web allies in the Netherlands, and within a few days registered millions of visitors according to reports on its "Help B92" Web site (www.helpB92.xs4all.nl).

IN THE FALL OF 1998, I HAD A VIVID LOOK at the extraordinary spirit behind all of this when I led a team of American broadcasters that included Stephani Shelton, formerly of CBS News, and Michael Fairhurst, former news director of the New Jersey Public Broadcasting Network. We held broadcast journalism workshops in Belgrade and four other Serbian cities including Čačak and Niš for about 100 staffers. The workshops were organized by ANEM for its member stations and supported by the U.S. Information Service and the American Embassy in Belgrade. On the day of our last workshop in October, word came that NATO might bomb Serbia. Our workshop focus with ANEM station managers meeting in Belgrade shifted to how to confront war censorship or closure.

Throughout Serbia, we heard firsthand how local radio and television stations struggled to maintain independence. Radio staffers in Čačak in 1996 took to the road and broadcast from a mobile van to elude police. Elsewhere, villagers blocked the road when officials tried to seize a local TV transmitter. When another local TV station was shut, staffers beamed the news on a building wall.

Our host in Niš, Nikola Djurić, was a television anchor who founded an ANEM affiliate, City Radio, with his wife, Svetlana, only to see it shut months later. He was convicted in January 1999 for "illegally" operating a station (his main crime being independent news reporting) and given a suspended sentence. On a U.S. study tour in March when the bombing began, he decided it was unsafe to return. His wife and small child joined him, and in the fall of 1999 he was to begin a Nieman Fellowship at Harvard University.

Less fortunate was Slavko Čuruvija, founder of the daily newspaper *Dnevni Telegraf (Daily Telegraph)* and the weekly *Evropljanin (European)* in Belgrade. Čuruvija's publications were closed in late fall of 1998 after Serbia passed a draconian Public Information Law that forbade any reports that could be interpreted as anti-government slander or supportive of Serbia's enemies. He attempted to later reconstitute the publications in more liberal Montenegro but this was short-lived. Exorbitant fines, imposed immediately in rapid-fire trials with little chance to prepare a defense, closed several publications and broadcast stations.

It was a foretaste of the spring of 1999, when all independent media were stifled. Worse, Čuruvija was gunned down with 15 bullets to the back outside his apartment shortly after the bombing began. State television reported his death with a sour commentary that "traitors" should be similarly dealt with, according to the Institute of War and Peace Reporting.

THE SAFETY OF JOURNALISTS throughout the region is a continuing concern. The Committee to Protect Journalists (CPJ) in New York estimates that from 1989 to 1998 there were 131 journalists killed in all of Europe and the former Soviet republics, according to Chrystyna Lapychak, CPJ's program coordinator for Eastern Europe. In the Russian Federation alone, 31 were among the dead. Ann K. Cooper, CPJ executive director and a former National Public Radio correspondent in Moscow, remembers after the euphoric free press renaissance in Russia came a surge in organized crime, with law and order unable to cope. Assassinations of journalists with bombs and guns produced a "chilling effect" on investigative reporting, a danger growing throughout the region. In Bosnia, CPJ saw increasing incidents of independent journalists beaten or harassed in the Republika Srpska after the start of NATO bombings. German journalists were shot to death covering Kosovo and the Serb withdrawal. In Serbia, the atmosphere was even more poisonous.

In this difficult climate, B92 and ANEM have received help from a variety of international sources, including the Soros Fund for an Open Society-Yugoslavia. Velimir Curgus Kazimir, its public relations officer, reports in the spring 1999 issue of the Soros *Open Society News* that from 1992 to 1998 the Fund helped create six independent dailies in Serbia, including Kosovo and Montenegro, several weeklies and independent news agencies, more than 50 independent radio and television stations, a press center, and several independent journalist associations. With the flood of Kosovo refugees into Albania and Macedonia, Soros was gathering refugees' testimony to be published in Albanian newspapers, supporting radio programs for refugees and purchasing newspapers for free distribution in the refugee camps.

Soros and other organizations also wanted to help independent media like the newspapers *Koha Ditore (Daily Times)* and *Rilindja (Rebirth)* and Radio-TV 21, whose facilities were destroyed by Serbs in Kosovo, to provide the refugee camps with news and information. *Koha Ditore* was Priština's largest paper until Serb police ransacked its facilities and killed its night watchman. Editors hid, emerging in Macedonia with borrowed computers, an Internet connection at a local cafe and a daily run of papers eagerly snapped up by Kosovo refugees in camps along the Albanian and Macedonian borders, according to MSNBC.

Long-range Western commitment to independent media in the Balkans, particularly the former Yugoslavia, requires restoring media facilities destroyed or seized in Kosovo and elsewhere in Serbia. The ANEM network in Serbia will need support, both economical and political, to succeed.

When I interviewed Matić, the head of B92 and ANEM, last October after the Serb government passed the repressive public information law and launched its media crackdown, he saw these actions as those of a panicked regime fearful of the future. He anticipated prophetically the time that might, and did, come with the total shutdown of independent media.

"We may be forced like Solidarity in Poland to wait underground for the dictatorship to exhaust itself. It has no future for sure," Matić wrote to me by e-mail then. "Even after they've punished, closed and banned us all—energy and creativeness that was visible during the demonstrations of 1996–97 will definitively revive again and again

Looking back on the last decade of emerging democracies in Central and Eastern Europe, efforts to help these nations craft independent media provide insights into how we might act elsewhere.

Avoid unprepared, short-term speakers parachuted in with insufficient knowledge of the country or media environment who may alienate journalists with free-press platitudes rather than substance.

Expect resistance from media born in a command economy of government subsidy and control and accustomed to job padding, when you introduce better business practices. ("We pretend to work and you pretend to pay us," was an old communist adage.)

Double check applicants for media assistance. Ownership is not always transparent, and shadow owners may be the politically connected who damaged the free press in the first place.

Assign permanent resident advisors with media experience and knowledge of the language and culture. Pair them with indigenous staff trained to take over the centers and resources when it is time to leave. Have an exit plan with a sunset date agreed upon for your departure.

Give equal attention to the needs of local and regional media, and avoid over-concentration of funding and training in major media capital cities to the detriment of the regional press.

Target local universities for special assistance, but get their commitment to modernize curriculum, invigorate faculties and connect with media professionals as advisors, adjunct teachers, guest speakers and internship mentors.

Anticipate long-range needs of journalists who will want new ideas and specialized reporting and editing skills as they progress in their careers.

Work closely with editors to overcome a frequent complaint of journalists who return from training with new skills and find their editors hostile to change. Pairing editors and reporters in joint training helps offset this.

Instill in those fledgling independent media who are first given help the importance of "payback." Foreign assistance will inevitably end. As newspapers, magazines, radio, television and on-line media prosper over the years, they should provide scholarships, training grants and foundation assistance to their fellow countrymen and women who are still climbing the precarious ladder in pursuit of the independent media.

and turn into a general rebellion against dictatorship. I hope that the result of that protest will be the beginning of the democratization of the country."

Jerome Aumente, professor and director of the Journalism Resources Institute in the School of Communication, Information and Library Studies at Rutgers University, has led media assistance programs in Central and Eastern Europe since 1989.

21

B92 of Belgrade

Free voices on the airwaves and the Internet

Dražen Pantić

THE YEAR 1989 HAD A VERY different meaning in Yugoslavia than in the rest of Central and Eastern Europe. While citizens across the rest of the Soviet bloc were breaking down walls through velvet and steel revolutions, Slobodan Milošević was consolidating power in Yugoslavia. Quickly gaining control over Serbian and federal state media, Milošević made sure that growing social conflicts among Yugoslav national groups and the transition toward capitalism were broadcast to society only in the form of brutal, one-sided propaganda that favored Milošević. The explosive fragmentation of the country was virtually inevitable.

In this desolate environment, a group of Belgrade media activists launched a bold experiment in democratic media, the first and for years the only independent radio station in Serbia, Radio B92. In May 1989, a group of young Belgrade journalists, including Veran Matić, who had been working with student and alternative newspapers, asked for permission to open a radio station for experimental programs. The government, anticipating nothing more than an apolitical but funky student radio show, granted them a 15-day permit on an FM frequency and a small room in downtown Belgrade, crowded with minutes from forgotten Communist Party Central Committee meetings. They threw out the old material and started a radio station that would put Belgrade on the global media map. The start-up broadcast was a severe critique of the official celebration of the late president Tito's birthday on the grounds that the event perpetuated the aura of a dictator who was eight years dead. By the end of the 15 days, the broadcasters were having so much fun that they decided to keep on going under the motto "Radio B92: the radio you listen to, watch, read, touch . . . the radio that lives." The authorities, trapped in their own inertia, were incapable or unwilling to stop something they had allowed to start.

Almost simultaneously, government-appointed rectors and high-ranking technical executives from all the Yugoslav universities gathered in Belgrade to decide which communications path Yugoslavia would take. Would the country become open to the Internet or closed to the world inside the virtual walls of centralized control? University moguls, thinking in lockstep as hardcore Communists, decided that the Internet was an imperialistic conspiracy and a tool of propaganda. To maintain the ideological purity of the universities, they decided to keep the Internet at arm's length. Serbia and all the Yugoslav republics would become members of the European Academic and Research Network. EARN was organized around the BITNET network, which offered e-mail exchanges between academic institutions and avoided direct interactive communication.

The BITNET model was obviously inferior to the Internet. It seemed attractive, though, to Communist loyalists: it opened a basic communication channel, but only for a closed group around the universities. Even more attractive for future possible censorship was the fact that EARN was organized through central national hubs—and Yugoslavia's hub was the Institute for Statistics of Serbia, which was utterly loyal to the Milošević regime.

The die was cast. While others in the region moved to open their countries, totalitarian forces in Yugoslavia wanted to go back to the future. War in Slovenia and Croatia loomed in the near future. New, progressive media were either demonized or forced to operate within strict, predefined limits.

IN THIS CONTEXT, B92 BEGAN AS A local radio station emphasizing urban music and brief but objective news flashes. Its very limited audience was confined to the urban young to middle aged, but its influence grew quickly. With irreverence and imagination, B92 opposed war and promoted ideas of democracy, economic reform and respect for ethnic minorities. The station sponsored anti-war demonstrations, which drew tens of thousands of people, as well as peace concerts and candlelit processions. During anti-government riots in March 1991, sparked by police attacks on opponents of the regime, authorities shut down B92 for the first time, accusing it of fomenting trouble. The station's answer came through music: the entire next day the radio played songs like the rap tune "Fight the Power" by Public Enemy.

From the earliest days at B92, station managers involved leading intellectuals in special projects, including book and CD publishing as well as video and film production, that promoted an urban spirit of tolerance and humor. Within B92's publishing palette were the only Roma children's magazine in the world, the internationally successful feature film *Marble Ass* about the local gay community and a cartoon book by the Belgrade author Corax that brutally satirized Milošević and sold more than 200,000 copies in 1997—a number equivalent to roughly 15 percent of Belgrade's population. B92 became an alternative media center, a force for openness in music, arts and culture, and, most important, a force for reliable news and information in a society smothering in propaganda.

With its commitment to using all media to spread its message, it was natural for B92 to establish an Internet site under its own umbrella. The obstacles were great, including misunderstanding and mistrust in Serbia's official agencies and departments and difficulties in locating foreign partners who were willing to work in a country under international sanctions for waging war in Bosnia. A major breakthrough came in September 1994 when the Amsterdam Internet center XS4ALL agreed to become an Internet provider for B92. It took another year for B92 to clear all of the paperwork, locate space, arrange for just one leased telephone line to Amsterdam and obtain funding for this new adventure.

OpenNet.org, Belgrade Radio B92's Internet center, opened in November 1995 and initiated a new era for Serbian electronic media. OpenNet set up a Web site for B92 itself and became Serbia's first Internet service provider, offering Internet access to an abundance of independent media, human rights groups and academics. OpenNet and B92 broke through the global information embargo that Milošević had placed over most of what remained of Yugoslavia—basically Serbia and Montenegro—after three years of warfare and ethnic cleansing.

Milošević could have cut the line to Amsterdam, but he underestimated the political significance of the Internet and, in any case, would have been causing himself telecommunications problems.

THE INTERNET HIT CENTER STAGE in the Serbian struggle for media freedom in December 1996. After huge and brutal election fraud during local elections in Serbia, massive anti-Milošević demonstrations sprang up across major cities. The weak and disoriented opposition parties were united against the regime's manipulation. They relayed messages across Serbia urging opponents of the government to go into the streets. B92 informed people about the election fraud and covered demonstrations in virtually round-the-clock, live broadcasts from the streets. The Milošević regime, recognizing that B92 was the most powerful prodemocratic voice in Serbia, responded with intensive jamming. A few days later, the government banned the station.

Through OpenNet, B92 immediately redirected its program and began live broadcasts over the Internet. People then downloaded news clips from the Internet and relayed them across the country in all possible ways, from e-mail to telephone. The memorable opening jingle, "Radio B92—Serbia Calling," could be heard all around Serbia and all around the world. The action sent a strong message of resistance to censorship and triggered powerful international political support for B92. After 51 hours, the Milošević regime could not resist any longer and allowed B92 to continue its programming. The symbolism was strong. For the first time, Milošević had lost a battle of politics and media on his own ground in Serbia. His advisers vowed, however, that such a defeat would not be repeated.

The success of the distribution of radio programs by the Internet gave impetus to an old idea of extending the B92 program to cover all Serbia. In the political context, B92 never would have been granted a license to broadcast over all Serbia. By the middle of 1997, B92 initiated a network of radio stations, the Association of Independent Electronic Media (ANEM), consisting of more than 30 local radio stations from all parts of Serbia and Montenegro. With the help of the British Broadcasting Corp. a unique rebroadcasting scheme was established: every day four hours of B92 and ANEM news programs were sent via the Internet to Amsterdam and then to London. The BBC then uplinked the B92 and ANEM broadcasts to its satellite, from which ANEM local radio stations would download them and then rebroadcast them across Yugoslav airways. Serbs and Montenegrins could now speak to each other in uncensored radio programs.

When NATO launched its air war in March 1999, the Serbian government used the opportunity to silence B92 and all other independent media. B92 transmitters were closed down on the first day of the war, and all independent print media put under strict editorial control. Despite the shutdown, B92 journalists continued broadcasting through Internet and satellite retransmission. The creative use of technology and the worldwide solidarity of media activists again worked around the censorship.

But this time the regime was determined to silence independent voices completely. On April 2, 1999, with the help of special police and on the basis of an illegal decree, Radio B92 was taken over by regime loyalists who installed new management. All departments of B92 were closed down, including OpenNet. The staff of Radio B92 was denied access to the premises, but the government initiated its own broadcasts using B92's frequency and station identification. The audience was not informed in any way about the change—except that they now found on B92 dramatically different, propagandistic content.

Even that did not silence democratic voices from Serbia. B92 staff and supporters launched a FreeB92 Internet site in Amsterdam immediately, with B92 announcements, all available independent news and e-mail reports, and testimonies from Serbia. The motto of the site— "Trust no one not even us . . . but keep the faith!"—reflected the spirit and humor of B92. Numerous OpenNet users migrated to other Internet providers in Serbia and used encrypted e-mail and anonymizers to secretly send short reports and diaries from Serbia. E-mail reports were not always up to the highest journalistic standards, but they were the only source of independent news from Serbian sources during the war.

THE STORY OF B92 AND OPENNET demonstrates that media activists can use new technologies in creative ways, gain widespread national and international support, and overcome even the most hostile actions of a repressive regime. The only way for such a regime to stop independent media is to dispense with any pretense of legality or national security and initiate direct brutal aggression, threats and murders— such as the killing of the journalist Slavko Ćuruvija, head of the Belgrade independent newspaper *Dnevni Telegraf (Daily Telegraph)*, who was attacked and murdered on the street a few days after publishing a bitter editorial about Milošević's policies. That was a strong and clear message to independent media. But even then, the democratic nature of the Internet enables the army of anonymous users to sustain the fight for freedom of expression and democracy.

Ten years after 1989, at the end of the Kosovo war, Serbia found itself stuck where it was a decade ago, with no functioning independent media outlets. But the experiences of B92 and OpenNet provide critical lessons to help rebuild Serbian media and, indeed, to support independent media in many other harsh political environments. The collective intelligence of international media activists, expressed in the creative use of technology, is an unbeatable force for promoting free speech over the Internet and on electronic media.

Dražen Pantić, director of the Technology, Media and Democracy Program at New York University's Center for War, Peace, and the News Media, founded OpenNet, Radio B92's Internet service provider.

22

Seeing Past the Wall

Network coverage of Central and Eastern Europe since 1989

Andrew Tyndall

THE FALL OF THE BERLIN WALL IN November 1989 was a news event that was uniquely suited for coverage by television—a world historical event illustrated by vivid human emotions in an iconic setting. The sight of the jubilant youth of Berlin swinging away with pickaxes at that hated concrete has survived—in documentaries and advertising, in art and fashion—as the defining symbol of the endgame of the Cold War. Being the first American TV news anchor on the scene is the crowning achievement in Tom Brokaw's résumé at NBC News: "Non-stop and peaceful like Woodstock, this is the Fourth of July and Armistice Day all wrapped into one," he rejoiced at the time.

It crowned a year of exceptional news images: the pageantry of superpower summits, the carnage of the pro-democracy protests in Tiananmen Square and the destruction from the World Series earthquake in the San Francisco Bay area. This is how I explained why the Fall of the Wall was a news story for the ages in *The Tyndall Report:* "Coverage combined aspects of a superpower summit and an earthquake. A Summit is the quintessential example of a set-piece news event. The actual events—photo opportunities, signing ceremonies, walkabouts—are orchestrated and symbolic, but are reported as news developments because of the importance of the things they symbolize. A Quake is the opposite: a single, radical, unpredictable transforming event. The power of the opening of the Wall as a news story was that it was the two things simultaneously: a symbol and a transformation."

There was no chance that the countries of Eastern Europe that left the Soviet bloc could sustain the giddy interest they received from the American news media in that exultant autumn 10 years ago. The fall of the Berlin Wall was its climax—but the other members of the Warsaw Pact also received levels of news coverage in 1989 that have not been repeated since: Poland's election of a Solidarity government, Hungary's opening of its borders to permit an East German brain drain, Czechoslovakia's Velvet Revolution and Romania's Genius of the Carpathians, as Nicolae Ceauşescu and his wife Elena met their grisly end.

This rush of events was not only astonishing, it was also, from the partisan perspective of the American news media, triumphant: NATO's patient policy of defensive containment had been vindicated; the Cold War had ended without ever turning hot; communist governments had surrendered power peacefully instead of resorting to the police-state tactics of Budapest 1956, Prague 1968 or, most obviously, Beijing just five months earlier.

THE FALL OF 1989 SAW THE ULTIMATE happy ending. As far as an American general news viewer is concerned, the ensuing events in Eastern Europe were reported as merely procedural and hardly controversial. In orderly fashion over the ensuing decade the Warsaw Pact has disbanded, Germany has been unified, Czechoslovakia has been divided, East Germany has been reconstructed and formerly central-planned economies have been liberalized. Apart from the unification of Germany in 1990, none of these developments was presented on the networks' nightly newscasts as especially newsworthy. (See Table 1.)

Told this way, Eastern Europe has slipped peacefully off the world stage: the countries of the former Warsaw Pact no longer seem worth the attention of the mass of Americans. The region now seems to be treated as one that can be safely left to the foreign policy elites, who do not need to get their news of the world from generalist mainstream journalists. Consider NATO's decision to expand eastward to include Poland, Hungary and the Czech Republic: in the last decade of coverage of the alliance's European military planning, expansion received

TABLE 1
Annual coverage (in minutes) of the political and economic changes in five
selected former Warsaw Pact countries on the networks' weekday nightly
newscast (*1999 data are partial through the end of May.)

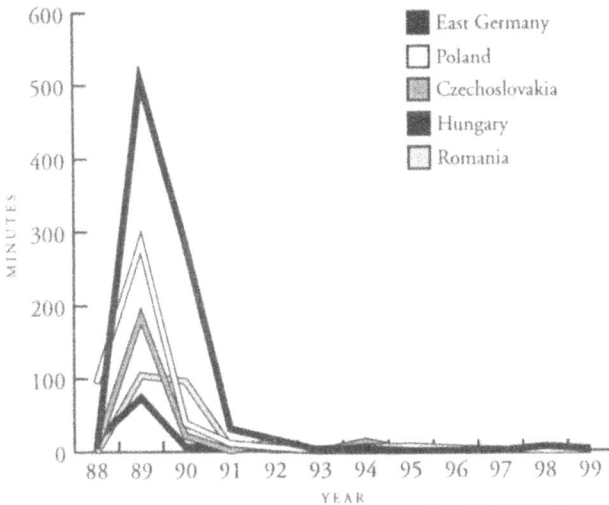

Notes: Coverage of East Germany includes German unification; George Bush's 1989
trip to both Poland and Hungary is classified under "Poland" so the Hungary totals
are understated; Czechoslovakia includes both its successor nations, the Czech Republic and Slovakia

much less fanfare than the arms control debates with the Warsaw Pact
of the late '80s and early '90s. (See Table 2.)

However, such a narrative, which has Eastern Europe peacefully
slipping off center stage is too narrow. It misconstrues events back in
1989 since it describes the fall of the Berlin Wall purely as a Central
European event. True, the Wall marked the dividing line between East
and West Germany—but it also was the dividing line between the two
nuclear superpowers so it was a Cold War story too.

For viewers of the network news each night, coverage of the Cold
War did not end in the fall of 1989. Its reverberations did not even
finish with the disintegration of the Soviet Union two years later. The
unraveling of the post-World War II European order over the past 10
years has not been miraculously peaceful. And the networks have not
turned their backs on the murderous conflicts that ensued.

Back in 1989, the political changes in the Soviet bloc nations of

TABLE 2
Annual coverage (in minutes) of arms control and military planning
between the United States, the former Soviet Union, the Warsaw Pact
and NATO on the networks' weekday nightly newscast
(*1999 data are partial through the end of May).

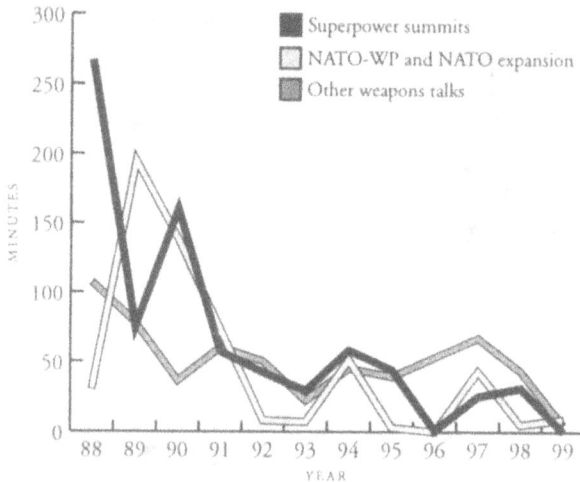

Eastern Europe represented but one strand of a larger complex of news stories. The pivotal figure of the entire complex was Mikhail Gorbachev, at that time the General Secretary of the Soviet Communist Party. He had a tangential role in the collapse of the Berlin Wall, having refused to dispatch Red Army troops to support the discredited regime of Erich Honecker when he attended the 40th anniversary celebrations of the GDR. But he had such a central role in so many other stories that he was *Time* magazine's Man of the Decade.

In the late '80s, Gorbachev's superpower summits in Reykjavik (before our database began), Washington (190 minutes), Moscow (123 minutes) and Malta (56 minutes) with Ronald Reagan and George Bush always attracted saturation coverage. In turn, the summits became the news hooks for swarms of reporters to cover the changes over which Gorbachev was presiding inside the Soviet Union: his policies of *glasnost* and *perestroika* became household words. Gorbachev's loosening of censorship laws allowed the Western news media to report on the dysfunctional domestic Soviet infrastructure in depth for the first time when they covered the December 1988 earthquake in Armenia (131 minutes). Gorbachev's initiatives in arms control made the alphabet soup of START, INF, SNF and CFE part of the nightly diet on the network news. Network anchors followed him to Havana (36 minutes) and the Vatican (51 minutes): Gorbachev's visit to Beijing for talks with China's Deng Xiaoping (33 minutes) was the reason the mainstream American news media was on hand in force to cover the Tiananmen Square story, which began during his trip there.

Warsaw, Budapest, Berlin, Prague and Bucharest were mere chapters in an overarching story: how completely would the power of the Kremlin be rolled back? Losing control over the Soviet bloc nations of Eastern Europe was but one facet. Disarming the Soviet military was another. Loosening the Communist Party's monopoly on political power was one more, as was reform of the centrally planned economy and the state-run news media. Anti-communism was the organizing ideology that bound all these strands together: while NATO, the military alliance, was designed for defensive containment, on the political, economic and ideological fronts, Cold War capitalism was militant.

In 1990, the spotlight shifted to the Soviet Union proper, with coverage that was every bit as intense as Eastern Europe received during the previous year. Ironically, however, the headlines in early 1990, although inspired by the events of the fall of the previous year, were about national independence, not anti-communism per se. Even as the political and economic reforms that Gorbachev had put in motion started to accelerate out of his control, the most newsworthy opposition to the Kremlin inside the USSR came from the non-Russian republics. At the time this was called the Nationalities Issue: following their co-religionist Catholics in nearby Poland, the Communists of independence-minded Lithuania broke with the Kremlin, and Gorbachev threatened blockade and military rule to keep his Union together. At the same time Soviet tanks rolled into Baku to suppress secessionists in Azerbaijan. (See Table 3.)

The exhilaration of 1989 inspired two sets of progeny. In the short run anti-communist fervor was still the headline grabber, culminating in the attempted coup against Gorbachev in the summer of 1991 when Boris Yeltsin, defiantly standing on a Moscow tank, established himself as Russia's leader. During the decade as a whole, however, the dominant image of the postcommunist world that the American mainstream news media have provided for their viewers has been darker.

The non-Russian republics of the Soviet Union managed to secede

TABLE 3
Annual coverage (in minutes) of domestic reforms inside the former Soviet
Union on the networks' weekday nightly newscast (*1999 data are partial
through the end of May). The second peak of nationalities coverage after the
Soviet Union broke up in 1995 represents the war in Chechnya

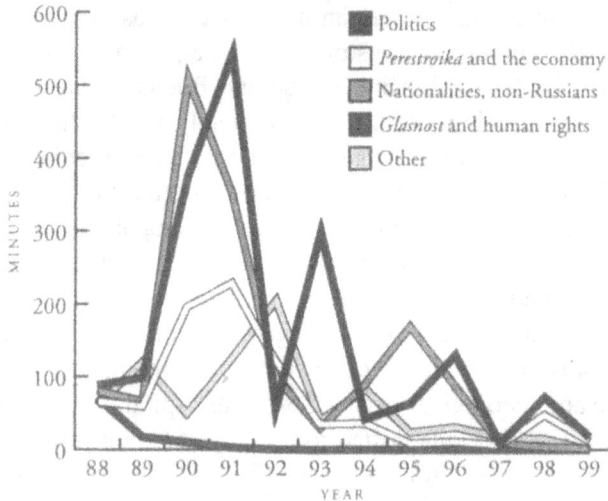

from Kremlin control without much mayhem until the war in Chechnya.
The component republics of Yugoslavia had less luck. Turmoil makes
more news than harmony. It is the duty of journalists to spend more
time delving into atrocities than into amity. While Poland and Hungary and the Czech Republic were slowly but surely joining the Western alliance of pluralist democrats, they did so with little media scrutiny. While their neighbors to the south were tearing Yugoslavia apart
in an orgy of atrocities, war crimes and ethnic cleansing, they occupied the media spotlight. The four-year civil war in Bosnia attracted
three times as much coverage as Eastern Europe's peaceful rollback of
Soviet influence in 1989. The mid-90s was a period when, overall, the
networks cut back their international coverage precipitously—except
for Yugoslavia, whose intractable ethnic hatred was constantly at the
top of the networks' overseas reporting. Measured in minutes of air-
time, Yugoslavia attracted as much attention in the mid-90s as the
Warsaw Pact did in 1989: as a proportion of the networks' overseas
coverage, Yugoslavia's share was even higher. (See Table 4.)

For a diplomatic historian, lumping Yugoslavia into an account of
the coverage of post-Cold War Europe may seem a stretch, since it

TABLE 4
Annual coverage (in minutes) of the former Yugoslavia, the rest of
Eastern Europe and Chechnya on the networks' weekday nightly nescasts
(*1999 data are partial through the end of May). compared with all other
overseas coverage.

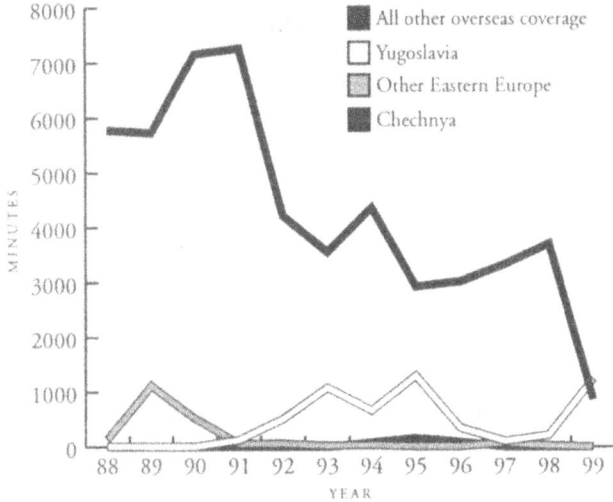

managed to remain communist but nonaligned for the duration of the superpower conflict. For an observer of the journalism of the period, however, Yugoslavia is a crucial part of the story: the narrative strand starting with Gorbachev, spreading through Eastern Europe to the non-Russian republics and to Chechnya illustrates that the triumph of ethnic nationalism and the failure of internationalism was as integral as anti-communism to the collapse of the Soviet Union and its sphere of influence.

The nationalism that NATO's leaders in Washington championed in the Baltics because it was so destabilizing to the USSR became a threat to regional instability in the Balkans. The war in Bosnia dominated regional news as the United States and its allies sought to use diplomacy to find a way to persuade Serbs, Croats and Muslims to live together in a multiethnic state. This year, NATO resorted to military force to try to oblige ethnic Serbs and Albanians to live together in harmony in Kosovo.

THUS THE TWO NARRATIVE STRANDS that were set in motion in the fall of 1989, ethnic nationalism and the triumph of NATO, met again in the spring of 1999. In the absence of public debate or media scrutiny, Poland, Hungary and the Czech Republic joined NATO. No sooner had they done so than the alliance, whose watchwords had always been defensive containment, took the offensive over Kosovo. The little debate about NATO that had reached the airwaves concerned how eastward expansion might threaten Moscow. The idea that a larger, aggressive alliance might commit itself to a Balkan adventure, with all the complications that entailed for member states Hungary, Greece, Turkey and Italy, went practically unmentioned. Suddenly, NATO started bombing. With its war against Yugoslavia, Eastern Europe once again dominated the networks' news agenda, becoming the biggest foreign policy story of Bill Clinton's presidency.

The mainstream news media showed little enthusiasm for covering the procedural debates that led to this change in the alliance's borders and its military philosophy but great appetite for covering its results. The degradation of the ethnically cleansed refugees from Kosovo was every bit as vivid as the jubilation of the youth of Berlin at their Wall 10 years earlier. Back then ethnic nationalism was an ally in an epic struggle for the heart of Europe; now it seems like its very sickness.

Andrew Tyndall is publisher of The Tyndall Report, *a weekly analysis of network broadcast news.*

Review Essay

Media and Eastern Europe since 1989

23

Power from the People

News media in and about East Central Europe

Owen V. Johnson

COMMUNISM DID NOT COLLAPSE in East Central Europe because of the actions of heroic dissidents or the fiery broadcasts of foreign radios. The Western military buildup under Ronald Reagan may have hastened the process along, but it wasn't decisive. Instead, the citizens in these countries lost whatever faith they may have once had in the system because they could see that reality didn't correspond with what they were told about reality. In Poland, millions joined the Solidarity trade union. In Hungary, hundreds of thousands pursued the profits (and losses) of small business in the 1970s and '80s. In Czechoslovakia, the regime promised not a chicken in every pot, but a cabin in the countryside and relatively plenty to eat in return for citizens' not opposing the regime. But the Communist Party increasingly couldn't keep its end of the bargain. When Czechs and Slovaks had the chance in 1989, they came out and shouted down the regime. Václav Havel may have been the darling of the Western media, a sometime politician who masterfully crafted his own speeches, but the real story was the people who said collectively that they wouldn't take it anymore.

Cornell political scientist Valerie Bunce, in her book *Subversive Institutions: The Design and the Destruction of Socialism and the State*, says the design of communist systems "functioned over time to divide and weaken the powerful, homogenize and strengthen the weak, and undercut economic performance." Instead of the powerful strongman wielding power (there were no women with real influence) these systems were gradually deregulating and decentralizing themselves. The peoples began to bargain with their states. To try to maintain themselves in power, states became "nationalist to the core." When communism fell, the nationalism was unleashed. Western journalists failed to see it coming.

SINCE 1989, CITIZENS of these countries have discovered that capitalism and democracy are not easy, that crime, inequality and commercialism are part of capitalism. They face problems that are variations on West European themes. No longer part of the evil empire, these countries are no more important than Spain, Sweden or Austria, except among some Western analysts who believe these countries should still belong to the Russian sphere of influence. The story of social, cultural and economic change is not one that Western journalists tell very often. In addition, distracted by or ordered by their editors to focus their attention on the brutal ethnic cleansing in the former Yugoslavia, foreign correspondents are missing the re-Europeanization story in East Central Europe.

Most U.S. reporters who studied journalism in college learned the four theories of the press. One of the theories, which were elaborated by Wilbur Schramm, was the "Soviet-Communist" theory of the press, admittedly an ideal drawn from scattered ideological treatises, according to which all media activity in communist countries was harnessed by the Party to help it carry out its goals. With such power in the leaders' hands, it was hard to imagine how the communist systems could ever collapse.

When despite this power they did collapse, the usual explanation was that foreign broadcasting must have had something to do with it. Foreign correspondents, based mostly in Moscow and Warsaw, reported how various of their sources listened to and discussed and debated the information they heard. Lech Wałęsa, Havel and even Mikhail Gorbachev praised the broadcasts from Radio Free Europe/ Radio Liberty, Voice of America and the BBC. Dissidents and regime opponents were encouraged when they heard reports on the radios about their activities, renewing their faith that they were engaged in successful and meaningful activities.

Despite such testimony, however, the foreign radios reached a small percentage of listeners in any country. They changed few minds, since most listeners (except for many of those working for the KGB and police forces in other communist-ruled countries) had already lost faith in their rulers. These listeners were simply interested in a wider range of information about what was happening in their countries. In 1985, then Polish government spokesman Jerzy Urban told me that all the members of the Polish government received a summary each morning of the most important points of the previous night's RFE Polish-language broadcasts. Apparently, these high officials found the RFE information useful in filling information gaps.

If regime media systems were failing in their mission to inspire their listeners, and if foreign radios reached only a small listenership, how could the communist systems collapse so quickly? The answer to this question suggests some of the challenges facing both foreign correspondents in Eastern Europe and journalists in the postcommunist states themselves. Media in the Czech Republic, Hungary, Poland and Slovakia are further along towards solving these problems than are the foreign correspondents.

The late Polish historian Oskar Halecki referred to these countries as "the lands between," sandwiched between Russia's and Germany's empires. The geographical borders were vague and variable. The four countries discussed here were almost always treated as a group, primarily because all of them had at least partly belonged to the Hapsburg Empire before its demise in 1918. The Baltic countries of Estonia, Latvia and Lithuania should probably be included, too, because of the close connections they had for many years with German or Polish overlords to the west. In contrast to Russia, the defining modern experience of the seven countries has not been communism, but their periods of independence and the road to that independence. Furthermore, as Irena Maryniak notes in the introduction to *The Fall of Communism*, "The European cultural emphasis on individual dignity and worth had [also] not been fully erased by communism."

The seven countries mentioned above incorporate a melange of languages and historical experiences. Only a polyglot could move fluently among them. Foreign correspondents, in contrast, are fluent in— at best—one of the languages. These nations' histories are little known to most Americans. I am fascinated by how many people confuse Yugoslavia with Czechoslovakia, neither of which really exists anymore, or interchange the terms Baltic and Balkan. European history courses in high school rarely include any material apart from the 19th-century great powers of Great Britain, France, Germany and Russia. A decade ago, I spent some time looking at how U.S. newspapers and magazines portrayed Czechs and the Czech lands in their columns from 1848 to 1914. Czechs were generally seen as dirty, lazy folk who spoke an unintelligible jawbreaking language, in contrast to the clean, efficient and intelligent Germans. Nineteenth-century reporters who happened through Prague on the train trip from Berlin or Dresden to Vienna would smell "the scent of Asia" in the air.

THE COUNTRIES OF EAST CENTRAL Europe received much more coverage during the period of their communist rule precisely because they were communist. They were on the front lines of the Cold War. Anytime they sneezed—as Hungary did in 1956, Czechoslovakia in 1968 and Poland in 1956, 1970 and 1980–81—the Soviet Union was seen as possibly catching cold, which could always turn into pneumonia, and perhaps dying. Most Western news organizations interested in Eastern Europe set up bureaus, either in Vienna or, as time went on, more often in Warsaw. Already in 1956, Western reporters in Poland could gain relatively easy access not only to opponents of the communist regimes but to regime representatives as well. When Gen. Wojciech Jaruzelski declared martial law in Poland in 1981—he said it would prevent a Soviet invasion—the feisty, big-eared journalist Jerzy Urban became the government's spokesman and prided himself on always being accessible to journalists. His weekly press conferences provided journalists the opportunity to ask any kind of question they wanted. The press conferences were usually televised, and the only minimally edited transcripts were published in a general-circulation Polish newspaper. With an actively involved church, a workers' movement and articulate dissident leaders who interacted with the workers, Poland constituted a lively story for more than three decades.

Reporters based in Poland usually were responsible for covering all of the countries of Eastern Europe. But with so much happening in Poland, their travels to the other countries were infrequent, their sources there underdeveloped. Few reporters recognized the rapidly growing use of the nationalist card in Yugoslavia, despite unrest that broke out in Kosovo in 1981 after the death of Marshal Josip Broz Tito in 1980. In Czechoslovakia, they failed to see the rapid decline of public toleration for the regime because their only sources were the dissidents who continued to paint political pictures in black and white terms.

Three challenges presented themselves when communism collapsed in East Central Europe in 1989. The first was the generally centralized political systems that had ruled in each country, governed by Party presidia in each country, under strong observation by the Soviet Union. In many ways, that was the easiest task. The four countries all had some experience in public memory of democratic systems. More important was the Hapsburg heritage. Three of these nations and part of the fourth (the Poles) had first developed their modern political culture while under the rule of Franz Josef and his ancestors. In varying degree, they learned the ideas of a free press, civic activism, checks on official power, an independent judiciary and increasingly assertive legislative bodies. The rule of law was widely recognized. Citizens engaged in political activity, although under the recognized direction of party leaders and intellectuals.

The second challenge was the economy, which had been based on central planning, reflecting an idealistic solution to the problems of 19th-century industrialization, and clearly dated in the information-based world of the late 20th century. It had to be transferred to private ownership in an increasingly globalized world.

The third problem was nationalism. Further east, the Soviet Union collapsed, replaced by 15 countries. Further South, Yugoslavia exploded into ethnic violence and tragedy. Czechoslovakia quietly divided at the end of 1992.

Western reporters found themselves drawn most to only one aspect of the first challenge: would the Communists come back to power, or how well was life being de-communized? Even Pope John Paul II's trip home at the end of the millennium was most often framed around his role in helping bring about the end of communism, not on his function as the spiritual leader of the overwhelming majority of Poles in an increasingly secular world.

TIMOTHY GARTON ASH, AN OXFORD public intellectual, has been fascinated for two decades by the conversation and activities of public intellectuals in East Central Europe. His books recall the long conversations Hapsburg intellectuals had a century ago in the cafes and tiny apartments of Vienna, Prague, Budapest and Cracow, where they addressed the political, international and literary questions of the day.

His books draw on his conversations with intellectuals and dissidents who became the first postcommunist leaders of their countries. He somehow managed to be on the scene whenever intellectuals swung into action in 1989. But as his book *History of the Present: Essays, Sketches and Despatches from Europe in the 1990s* demonstrates, he sees intellectuals as the heart and soul of Central Europe and moving forces of history. How undemocratic! "[The intellectuals] will probably never recover the social status and influence they once had," writes Richard Davy in *Freedom for Publishing—Publishing for Freedom*, who thinks that as the intellectuals' reading tastes diverge from that of the general public, "an element of social cohesion" is being lost. The intellectuals seem to have been all for people power until it threatened their own influence.

Garton Ash's intellectual orientation is evident in his description of the project to support Central and East European publishing and translation in area languages, a nearly decade-long, $3.3 million undertaking that bridged the end of communist rule. The project began by supporting dissident publications with actual cash handouts and ended by helping publications that could not survive in the marketplace. The result, says Garton Ash, was "freedom." That's all?

But Garton Ash and the rest of the reporters who covered East Central Europe missed the real story, that this was a peoples' revolution. In Poland, 10 million Poles joined Solidarity in 1980. They turned out by the millions to welcome the Polish Pope on his first visit back to his homeland. In Czechoslovakia, hundreds of thousands of people in Prague and Bratislava and other cities came out into the streets in November 1989 to show the Communist leadership that its time was up. In Hungary, people consumed media that had only a few limitations on what they could publish. If reporters had spent more time talking and interacting with ordinary people, they would have seen much sooner that the regimes were doomed. Hardly anyone in these countries seriously believed in communism anymore. People only joined the Party because it was the ticket to the best jobs, housing, university admission and foreign travel. In Czechoslovakia (and East Germany), it is true that correspondents were watched by the secret police, so that reporters making contact with ordinary East Germans, Czechs and Slovaks could seriously complicate the lives of these ordinary people. But that was far less often the case in Poland or Hungary.

Journalists could have used alternative sources, such as published survey research, census data and sociological studies, to describe the rapid social and cultural changes that were transforming these societies, which were rapidly growing more urban and more secular. People became more independent, almost out of reach of the Party's propaganda efforts. They read newspapers to extract needed facts, not to make regime goals their own. They loved the entertainment programs. When I visited Poland in 1985, I was surprised one day to find a spontaneous crowd had gathered in front of a hotel to wait for the appearance of the two stars of a Brazilian soap opera, whose showing on TV each night brought any other activity to a stop. This was not the way communist media and politics were supposed to be.

Even though Poland had one of the most open media systems in the Communist bloc, readers and viewers no longer trusted the news. They said it lied. The people had become the driving force in the Polish People's Republic. In 1956, the people had been with the Party in staring down the threats of Nikita Khrushchev. Then they had split. The people and the party led different lives. When shortages developed and prices rose in the 1970s, the people made their presence felt in the streets, the mines and the shipyards. From then on, the party was on the defensive. In the 1980s, it withered away.

TINA ROSENBERG'S prize-winning book, *The Haunted Land*, begins to show how the pressures of life under communism affected not only leaders, such as Polish Gen. Wojciech Jaruzelski, but also ordinary people, some of whom would later come into prominence. She tells the story of these countries' attempts to come to terms with their communist pasts. In Czechoslovakia, the published list of thousands of alleged communist collaborators turned out sometimes to be incomplete and inaccurate. It could not distinguish between major and minor infractions. It got caught up in politics and took on a life of its own. The most fascinating story Rosenberg tells is about ordinary East Germans. Some became informers because they were ambitious, or they wanted better lives. Some had their lives virtually destroyed by people who informed on them. Some heroically held out against state pressure, but often at enormous cost to their families. Some led dual identities, one private and one public. How easy it is for us to sit in judgment. What decision would we have made if we were told our children would not be admitted to college unless we informed on our neighbors? "We are all guilty," Havel said.

A MacArthur "genius" award gave Rosenberg the wherewithal and the time to investigate this story. It would be much harder for a full-time correspondent working on deadline. Rosenberg is a marvelous storyteller, but she admits she's not an area specialist and her only relevant language skill is rudimentary German, so she doesn't always get the picture completely right, particularly the historical details.

Journalists were fascinated by the dissidents and intellectuals whom they met. Not only were these people articulate, but their strong moral perspective offered alternatives to the communist monopoly of power. These dissidents and intellectuals, it turns out, were not always heroes, and they very often failed as politicians. So many of the first members of postcommunist cabinets were intellectuals, but they were not in touch with ordinary people, and they didn't know how to engage in that crucial element of democracy—compromise. Idealism and purity can be a powerful alternative in a communist totalitarian system, but it is disruptive in a democracy.

Václav Havel's book *The Art of the Impossible* is a collection of 35 speeches, eight of them given in the United States, which often sound like a teacher lecturing to students. It's not clear he's a democrat. He wants people—the ordinary and the statesmen—to act morally, but he wants to be their guide. His literature is modern, but his sometimes paternalistic ideas hark back to the interwar era, or even earlier. Like Walter Lippmann, he doesn't fully trust the people. While Western journalists marveled at his rhetoric and his ideas, his Czechs increasingly found him impossibly out of touch. They wanted real politicians.

Adam Michnik was only 15 when he first attracted the attention of the Polish authorities as a free thinker. Seven years later he was arrested for the first time. Today, he's more of a partisan than a full-time politician. In 1976, he helped found the Workers' Defense Committee, which linked Polish intellectuals and workers. He remains an individual who wants to engage people morally in the civic and moral process. The newspaper *Gazeta Wyborcza* is the ticket. "*Gazeta* is not just a newspaper," he writes, "it's an institution of civil society, an institution of Polish democracy." This is public journalism par excellence.

The Fall of Communism and the Rise of Nationalism, a book of readings from the magazine *Index on Censorship*, which celebrated its 25th anniversary in 1997, is evidence of the positive role intellectuals played under communism as symbols of opposition or as actual leaders of reform efforts. Maryniak, the Eastern Europe editor of *Index*, thinks they will continue to do so. She is wrong. But the 31 articles in the book show intellectuals as symbols during the communist period and the more intolerant attitudes that followed the end of communism in some countries. Perhaps individually these intellectuals convinced few people to change their minds. More importantly, their presence in the marketplace of ideas showed that alternatives to the authoritarian systems existed. That's why intellectuals were so important.

WHEN COMMUNISM COLLAPSED in 1989, First Amendment prophets in the United States and like-minded Europeans quickly mobilized to teach Poles, Czechs, Slovaks and Hungarians how to practice journalism. "You must be objective," they said. "You must serve as a watchdog." The prophets rarely had much knowledge or experience in the area. Less often did they even speak the local language. They were blissfully unaware that very talented journalists, committed more to their readers and viewers than to their Party directors, had been pushing the possibilities of journalism in Eastern Europe for years. Jane Leftwich Curry, in *Poland's Journalists: Professionalism and Politics*, published a decade ago, observed how they had followed professional models that committed them to serving the public. But for some of the postcommunist political leaders, freedom of the press did not necessarily mean objectivity. Sometimes, their view of freedom of speech meant freedom of speech for themselves, not for their opponents. At best, under the influence of the European journalism tradition, they believed in the old Miltonian concept of a battle of ideas in the marketplace.

Meanwhile, the prophets traipsed through the towns and cities teaching how to do journalism the American way. As Davy puts it, these aid projects were characterized by shallow thinking, self-interested promotion of national interests and generous funding of consultants of mixed ability in glossy hotels. A decade later, it's hard to see that they made a difference in journalistic products. Almost all of the newspapers that survive today in Central and Eastern Europe began their lives under communism, or even predated communism. The special exception is *Gazeta Wyborcza*, the Polish newspaper that is both the most widely circulated and the most influential in the country. Its purpose, writes Ken Jowitt in the introduction to *Letters from Freedom*, "is to overcome the weakness and formlessness that characterize so much of

Polish life." Michnik is its editor and its intellectual force. It was Michnik, for instance, who first publicly proposed sharing power with the Communist Party in 1989, in an editorial, "Your President, Our Prime Minister." At least as influential in the paper's success is Helena Łuczywo, whose business savvy was first developed when she ran the underground *Tygodnik Mazowsze (Weekly of Mazowia)* in the 1980s. She has developed the paper's advertising and its regional editions. She has nourished a combination of fact and opinion and marketing that has made the paper the envy of every other Central and Eastern European publisher.

In the Czech Republic, *Mladá fronta dnes (Youth Front Today)* has established itself as the most broadbased newspaper with multiple sections daily, along with regional editions. *Právo (Truth)*, the left-leaning continuation of the old communist *Rudé právo (Red Truth)*, has carved out a place for itself as a combative but solidly journalistic newspaper. Some older papers have not always adjusted easily to competitive commercial markets. But in general, the press, following the trend elsewhere in Europe, is evolving toward a stratified system, serving different audiences in different social niches.

Postcommunist Central and Eastern European broadcasting has varied enormously from country to country. But certain experiences are common. The old state communist stations generally have become state or public systems, according to the differing broadcast laws. These overstaffed organizations were saddled with ancient facilities and equipment. Still, the newly installed governments sought, in most cases, to maintain state control of broadcasting so that they could address the public directly about their politics and their plans. The governments have tried to pack broadcasting commissions with their own people to try to make sure broadcast license awards would go to their supporters, and that their opponents would have some difficulty gaining access to the airwaves. In both Poland and Hungary, passage of new broadcasting laws was hung up on political matters.

But while these battles went on, commercial TV, beginning with TV Nova in Prague in 1994, has changed the face of broadcasting in the area. Using a Fox network-like mix of popular U.S. programs and entertaining Czech material, TV Nova quickly claimed more than half of the Czech audience for its Central European Media owners. The same company set up broadcasting operations in Ukraine, Slovakia, Poland, Slovenia, Romania and elsewhere, using proceeds from the

Nova cash cow. But over-the-air commercial operations had to battle with the inflow of cable and satellite operations.

By the end of the century, the television operations increasingly looked like their West European counterparts, divided between public and private operations, and uncertain how the mix of over-the-air, satellite and cable systems would be affected by the possibilities of media convergence and the growth of the Internet. The often woefully ancient analog wires will limit the digital possibilities for a while.

NO SCHOLAR CAN HOPE TO SYNTHESIZE the story of media change in the East Central European countries. The pace of change, the increasing difficulty of finding information about private businesses and the lack of language facility make this an impossible task.

Liana Giorgi's book *The Post-Socialist Media*, part of a series of studies by The Interdisciplinary Center for Comparative Research in the Social Sciences, investigates the transformation of the media systems of Poland, Czechoslovakia and Hungary from 1989-93. "It is about the effects of the transition to market economy and political pluralism on media structures and media legislation and, by extent, communication politics," she writes. She is particularly interested in regulation and control. She claims that public opinion and identities are formed and mobilized by the media, but she doesn't show us how, although she does worry at the end about commercialization and the "proliferation of an entertainment and infotainment culture." Nevertheless, drawing on the assistance of five East Central European researchers, the book provides a well-organized description of the institutional changes of the first five postcommunist years.

Post-Communism and the Media in Eastern Europe, edited by Patrick O'Neil, which first appeared as a special issue of *The Journal of Communist Studies and Transition Politics*, is a collection of seven country studies by East European journalism researchers and U.S. political scientists. They tell seven different stories because, as O'Neil writes, "the role of the media in fact was distinctive in each case, reflecting the particular contours of each nation-state." There's no there in East European media studies anymore, just a collection of countries whose media systems, or at least those in East Central Europe, now face problems little different from those in other European countries.

Peter Gross' detailed study of changes in the Romanian news media, *Mass Media in Revolution and National Development*, is designed to serve as a model for studies of other countries in the region. But he ends up admitting that Romania is, like the other countries, a special case. Its media, Gross regrets, are both politicized and sensationalist, forgetting that perhaps politics and sensationalism will draw readers and viewers into the circle of political participation.

In *Communism, Capitalism and the Mass Media*, Colin Sparks discusses the changes in the broadcasting landscape. Sparks, who calls himself a "contemporary Marxist," argues—as did many non-Marxist reform-minded East Central European scholars in the 1970s and 1980s—in favor of reining in the profit-oriented owners of the media. Influenced by the interesting but artificial concept of "civil society," they dream of some kind of third way, of media systems committed to the public good but controlled by neither government nor corporations. At considerable length, Sparks asserts that the old communist systems were actually "not alternatives to capitalism but one especially horrible variant of it." Therefore, these humanist Marxists continue to believe that their dream of the state acting as agent for the liberation of the people is still valid. But they remain rather vague as to how this dream can be realized. What misleads Sparks is his belief "in the very limited extent to which the fall of communism was accomplished by the active self-mobilization of the mass of the population." As this essay has made clear, gradually over four decades the "mass of the population" had withdrawn its support for the communist system. Without that support, communism eventually had to collapse.

"[T]he central political question in postcommunist countries," Rosenberg writes, is whether democracy is "a process or an outcome." If democracy is "a process," the news media in East Central Europe clearly have a role to play, providing political, economic and social information and opinions so that citizens have the possibility of making informed choices in and for their societies. If democracy is an outcome, it would seem the news media should be helping to sustain, consolidate and institutionalize the democratic process. But the greatest risk is that the news media will be consumer and entertainment media, designed to sell audiences to advertisers, or "people with the politics left out." Given the highly politicized media of the communist years, that would be both ironic and tragic. But the people will decide.

Owen V. Johnson, a member of the journalism and history faculties at Indiana University, is co-author of Eastern European Journalism Before, During and After Communism.

For Further Reading

After the Fall

Aumente, Jerome, Peter Gross, Ray Hiebert, Owen V. Johnson and Dean Mills. *Eastern European Journalism Before, During and After Communism.* Cresskill, N.J.: Hampton Press, 1999.

Bucloh, Stephan, and Stephan Russ-Mohl. *Securing Quality: European and American Perspectives of Continuing Education in Journalism.* Berlin: Freie Universität Berlin, 1993.

Bunce, Valerie. *Subversive Institutions: The Design and the Destruction of Socialism and the State.* New York: Cambridge University Press, 1999.

Burg, Steven L. *War or Peace? Nationalism, Democracy, and American Foreign Policy in Post-Communist Europe.* New York: New York University Press, 1996.

Carothers, Thomas. *Assessing Democracy Assistance: The Case of Romania.* Washington: Carnegie Endowment, 1996.

Curry, Jane Leftwich, and Luba Fajfer. *Poland's Permanent Revolution: People vs. Elites, 1956 to the Present.* Washington: American University Press, 1996.

Dahlgren, Peter, and Colin Sparks. *Communication and Citizenship: Journalism and the Public Sphere.* London: Routledge, 1991.

Darnton, Robert. *Berlin Journal: 1989-1990.* New York: Norton, 1991.

Dawisha, Karen, and Bruce Parrott, eds. *The Consolidation of Democracy in East-Central Europe.* New York: Cambridge University Press, 1997.

Drakulić, Slavenka. *Café Europa: Life After Communism.* London: Abacus, 1996.

_____. *Balkan Express: Fragments from the Other Side of War.* Translated by Maja Soljan. London: Hutchinson, 1993.

Garton Ash, Timothy. *The File: A Personal History.* New York: Random House, 1997.

_____. *The Magic Lantern: The Revolution of '89 Witnessed in Warsaw, Budapest, Berlin and Prague.* New York: Vintage, 1993.

Garton Ash, Timothy, Ralf Dahrendorf, Richard Davy, and Elizabeth Winter, eds. *Freedom for Publishing—Publishing for Freedom: The Central and East European Publishing Project*. Budapest, Hungary: Central European University Press, 1995.

Giorgi, Liana. *The Post-Socialist Media: What Power the West? The Changing Media Landscape in Poland, Hungary, and the Czech Republic*. Brookfield, Vt.: Avebury, 1995.

Gjelten, Tom. *Sarajevo Daily: A City and Its Newspaper Under Siege*. New York: Harper Collins Publishers, 1995.

Glenny, Misha. *The Rebirth of History: Eastern Europe in the Age of Democracy*. New York: Penguin Books, 1990.

Goban-Klas, Tomasz. *The Orchestration of the Media: The Politics of Mass Communications in Communist Poland and the Aftermath*. Boulder, Colo.: Westview Press, 1994.

Gow, James, Richard Paterson, and Alison Preston, eds. *Bosnia by Television*. London: British Film Institute, 1996.

Gross, Peter. *Mass Media in Revolution and National Development: The Romanian Laboratory*. Ames, Iowa: Iowa State University Press, 1996.

Gruber, Ruth Ellen. *Upon the Doorposts of Thy House: Jewish Life in East-Central Europe, Yesterday and Today*. New York: J. Wiley, 1994.

Haraszti, Miklós. *The Velvet Prison: Artists Under State Socialism*. Translated by Katalin and Stephen Landesmann. New York: Basic Books, 1987.

Havel, Václav. *The Art of the Impossible: Politics as Morality in Practice*. Speeches and Writings, 1990-1996. Translated by Paul Wilson, et al. New York: Alfred A. Knopf, 1997.

Hester, Al. *Revolutions for Freedom: The Mass Media in Eastern and Central Europe*. Athens, Ga.: James M. Cox, Jr. Center, 1991.

Hoffman, Eva. *Exit into History: A Journey Through the New Eastern Europe*. New York: Viking, 1993.

Ignatieff, Michael. *The Warrior's Honor: Ethnic War and the Modern Conscience*. London: Chatto & Windus, 1998.

_____. *Blood and Belonging: Journeys into the New Nationalism*. New York: Farrar Straus, and Giroux, 1994.

Jakubowicz, Karol. *Conquest or Partnership? East-West European Integration in the Media Field*. Dusseldorf, Germany: European Institute for the Media, 1996.

Jakubowicz, Karol, David Paletz, and Pavao Novosel, eds. *Glasnost and After: Media and Change in Central and Eastern Europe*. Cresskill, N.J.: Hampton Press, 1995.

Kurspahic, Kemal. *As Long As Sarajevo Exists*. Stony Creek, Conn.: Pamphleteer's Press, 1997.

Leff, Carol Skalnik. *The Czech and Slovak Republics: Nation Versus State*. Boulder, Colo.: Westview Press, 1997.

Lendvai, Paul. *Blacklisted: A Journalist's Life in Central Europe*. London: I.B. Tauris, 1998.

Mayhew, Alan. *Recreating Europe: The European Union's Policy Towards Central & Eastern Europe*. New York: Cambridge University Press, 1998.

Michnik, Adam. *Letters from Freedom: Post-Cold War Realities and Perspectives.* (Societies and Culture in East-Central Europe, No 10). Edited by Irena Grudzi'nska Gross. Berkeley, Calif.: University of California Press, 1998.

_____. *Letters from Prison and Other Essays.* Translated by Maya Latynski. Berkeley, Calif.: University of California Press, 1985.

Miller, William L., Stephen White and Paul Heywood. *Values and Political Change in Post-Communist Europe.* New York: St. Martin's Press, 1998.

Moeller, Susan D. *Compassion Fatigue: How the Media Sell Disease, Famine, War and Death.* New York: Routledge, 1999.

Mowlana, Hamid, and Nanette S. Levinson. *Telecommunications and International Relations: An East-West Perspective.* Washington: American University Press, 1991.

Nelson, Michael. *War of the Black Heavens: The Battles of Western Broadcasting in the Cold War.* Syracuse, N.Y.: Syracuse University Press, 1997.

Noam, Eli. *Telecommunications in Europe.* New York: Oxford University Press, 1992.

O'Neil, Patrick H., ed. *Post-Communism and the Media in Eastern Europe.* Portland, Ore: Frank Cass, 1997.

Petrie, Ruth, ed. *The Fall of Communism and the Rise of Nationalism: The Index Reader.* Washington: Cassell, 1997.

Popkin, Jeremy D., ed. *Media and Revolution: Comparative Perspectives.* Lexington, Ky.: University Press of Kentucky, 1995.

Price, Monroe E. *Comparing Broadcast Structures: Transnational Perspectives and Post-Communist Examples.* New York: Benjamin N. Cardozo School of Law, 1993.

Raboy, Marc, and Bernard Dagenais. *Media, Crisis, and Democracy: Mass Communication and the Disruption of Socialist Order.* London: Sage, 1992.

Ramet, Sabrina P. Nihil Obstat: *Religion, Politics, and Social Change in East-Central Europe and Russia.* Durham, N.C.: Duke University Press, 1998.

Rosenberg, Tina. *The Haunted Land: Facing Europe's Ghosts After Communism.* New York: Random House, 1995.

Semetko, Holli A., and Klaus Schoenbach. *Germany's Unity Election: Voters and the Media.* Cresskill, N.J.: Hampton Press, 1994.

Shriver, Donald W., Jr. *An Ethic for Enemies: Forgiveness in Politics.* New York: Oxford University Press, 1995.

Sparks, Colin, with Anna Reading. *Communism, Capitalism, and the Mass Media.* Thousand Oaks, Calif: Sage Publications, 1998.

Steinlauf, Michael C. *Bondage to the Dead: Poland and the Memory of the Holocaust.* Syracuse, N.Y.: Syracuse University Press, 1997.

Taras, Raymond. Consolidating Democracy in Poland. Boulder, Colo.: Westview, 1995.

Tusa, Ann, and John Tusa. *The Berlin Airlift.* New York: Atheneum, 1988.

Tusa, John. *A World in Your Ear: Reflections on Changes.* London: Broadside Books, 1992.

Urban, George R. *Radio Free Europe and the Pursuit of Democracy: My War Within the Cold War.* New Haven, Conn.: Yale University Press, 1997.

Urban, Jan. *Democracy and Nationalism in Central and Eastern Europe.* London: The David Davies Memorial Institute of International Studies, 1991.

Verdery, Katherine. *What Was Socialism and What Comes Next?* Princeton, N.J.: Princeton University Press, 1996.

von Beyme, Klaus. *Transition to Democracy in Eastern Europe.* New York: St. Martin's Press, 1996.

Weschler, Lawrence. *The Passion of Poland: From Solidarity Through the State of War.* New York: Pantheon Books, 1984.

Subject Index

Poland, 75–76
Romania, 76–77
Slovakia, 78–79
Warsaw Stock Exchange, 172
Warszawski, Dawid, 180
Washington Post, 52, 113
Welle, Deutsche, 14
Westdeutsche Allgemeine Zeitung, 71, 177
Whitehouse, Mark, 193
Wieseltier, Leon, 48
Wolff, Jochen, 131
Women
  Communist system and, 218
  literacy importance, 112
  Polish underground and, 5
  See also Anna Husarska; Slaven ka Drakulić
Worker Defense Committee (KOR), 4
World Bank, 119
World Economic Weekly, 146

Y
Yavlinsky, Grigory, 67

Yayovlev, Alexander, 34
Yeltsin, Boris, 43, 211
Yugoslavia
  B92 radio and, 202–203, 205
  independent journalism problems, 193
  independent radio origins, 201–202
  Internet access and, 202
  media activist impact, 205–206
  media rebuilding in, 206
  Milosevic power consolidating, 201
  NATO air wars, 205
  Serbian media freedom, 204–205
Yumashev, Valentin, 42

Z
Zakowski, journalist "civic attitude," 65
Železný, General Director, 83–84
  criticisms of, 88
  influence of, 89
Zhirinovsky, Vladimir, 95
Ziarul Financiar (Financial Daily), 177
Zolotov, Andrei, 65
Zyuganov, Gennady, 95

For Product Safety Concerns and Information please contact our EU
representative GPSR@taylorandfrancis.com
Taylor & Francis Verlag GmbH, Kaufingerstraße 24, 80331 München, Germany

www.ingramcontent.com/pod-product-compliance
Lightning Source LLC
Chambersburg PA
CBHW050416280326
41932CB00013BA/1880

9 780765 807380